CANADIAN STUDIES IN CRIMINOLOGY

D1277715

The Ordering of Justice: A Study of Accused Persons as Dependants in the Criminal Process

Richard V. Ericson
Patricia M. Baranek

Published in association with
the Centre of Criminology,
University of Toronto, by
UNIVERSITY OF TORONTO PRESS
Toronto   Buffalo   London

© University of Toronto Press 1982
Toronto   Buffalo   London
Printed in Canada

ISBN 0-8020-2451-3 (cloth)
    0-8020-6463-9 (paper)

Canadian Cataloguing in Publication Data

Ericson, Richard V., 1948-
  The ordering of justice

  (Canadian studies in criminology; 6)
  Bibliography: p.
  Includes index.
  ISBN 0-8020-2451-3 (bound). – ISBN 0-8020-6463-9 (pbk.)
  1. Criminal procedure – Canada.
  2. Criminal justice, Administration of – Canada.
  3. Crime and criminals – Canada.
  I. Baranek, Patricia, 1946-
  II. University of Toronto. Centre of Criminology.
  III. Title. IV. Series.
  KE9260.E74   345.71'05   C81-095095-2

To Mathew and Joshua,
who have ensured that we shall
remain students of dependency
for years to come

Contents

Tables

Acknowledgments

A number of people have provided us with comments on part or all of earlier versions of this book. We are grateful for the comments of John Baldwin, Pat Carlen, Leonard Doob, Malcolm Feeley, Edgar Friedenberg, Marc Galanter, James Giffen, Milton Heumann, Birthe Jorgensen, Doreen McBarnet, Michael McConville, Dianne Macfarlane, Andrew Scull, and Simon Verdun-Jones. We have considered very seriously each comment made, and through that process each of these persons has contributed to this book.

We reserve a special gratitude for Anthony Doob, director of the Centre of Criminology at the University of Toronto. He has been extremely supportive in responding to our ideas over the past several years and in seeing this book through to completion. His intellectual and administrative strengths have greatly enhanced our work.

We are grateful to Dianne Macfarlane for allowing us access to her interview materials concerning lawyers representing the accused persons we studied, and to James Wilkins for allowing us access to tape recordings of conversations in the crown attorney's office and to the court documents he collected. We also thank Alison de Pelham for research assistance.

In the initial drafting of this book, we both benefitted from the academic environments at the Centre of Criminology, University of Toronto, and the Institute of Criminology, University of Cambridge. Richard Ericson also acknowledges the fellowship at Churchill College, Cambridge, which provided a haven for him during the initial drafting period.

We offer thanks to Senga Nicholson, Lynn Bailey, Marie Pearce, Marbeth Greer, and Dina Migoel who have typed parts of successive drafts of this book. We also thank Dianna Ericson for assistance in preparing the index.

We are grateful for the support of Virgil Duff in seeing this manuscript through to publication, and for the editing skills of John Parry.

The research upon which this book is based was generously funded by the University of Toronto, the Donner foundation, and especially the Social Sciences and Humanities Research Council of Canada. This book has been published with the help of grants from the Social Science Federation of Canada, using funds provided by the Social Sciences and Humanities Research Council of Canada, and from the Publications Fund of University of Toronto Press.

This book is our means of paying back the many persons and organizations who have contributed to it. Most of all we are indebted to the accused in our sample who generously gave of their time to further our understanding of their position. Of course, we assume full responsibility for the research and the way we have carried it out. It was a tall order; the reader must judge whether we have done it justice.

RVE
PB

Foreword

Critics of the functionalist approach to research in sociology usually consider its most serious defect to be its normative, and hence apologetic, character. Guided by their commitment as scientists to what they conceive to be ethical neutrality, and dealing only with empirical aspects of reality, many sociologists write as if it was their duty, as well as their pleasure, to allow the claims of established social institutions to set their working agenda, determining what an appropriate research problem might be. Having accepted such a problem, the sociologist then proceeds to define it as concerned with institutional *means*, not with ends; for science, it is held, cannot contribute to the assessment of ends, which is a matter for value judgments. Once the political processes that direct a society have determined what is to be done, the scientist can help to determine how best to do it. But he cannot, in his professional capacity, raise questions about whether it should be done. That is for reformers, terrorists, and other kinds of troublemakers to do. The sociologist can, of course, study *them*, as examples of social deviance, and help develop programs for controlling them.

This, somewhat simplified but not greatly distorted, is the conventional view of what science should do held by a plurality of those who trouble to formulate their assumptions about it. The informal view is worse: scientists, especially social scientists, should help get the world's work done and not 'butt in' on those who have been authorized, by whatever means, to say what that work is. I live with this fact, in angry frustration, continually because nearly everyone I deal with as a professor of education thinks I ought to be trying to find out something that would make the public schools more effective and be helpful to their administrators in their appointed tasks. In fact, I find schools interesting but generally pernicious in both intent and effect and am grateful that they are no more effective than they are.

Criminologists, I should imagine, encounter even more of this sort of thing than professors of education. Everybody knows that none of the methods of 'corrections' works; and there is even fairly widespread public understanding that, in principle, they cannot work because their ends conflict: humiliation and deliberately inflicted protracted suffering do not rehabilitate. (The reasons why schools do not educate in any profound humanistic sense are far more imperfectly understood; many people still expect them to do so.) Nevertheless, the impossibility, both practical and theoretical, of making the criminal justice system work so as to make life in society safer and less impoverished – let alone more satisfying or more just – even for law-abiding citizens seems to have had no effect whatever on the legitimacy of the system, which remains legitimacy incarnate; and it has not led many scientists to enquire what – if it doesn't do what it's supposed to do – it *does* do. In terms of public policy, debate, often highly acrimonious, tends to pit hardliners such as James Q. Wilson against advocates of 'decarceration' in one form or another who get accused of coddling criminals. But none of the protagonists has solid evidence that their program would improve the environment; and hardly anybody bothers to ask what the hell, in that case, is going on. And *that*, after all, is a thoroughly empirical question, though potentially very embarrassing. The answer comes in the form of evidence and cannot be dismissed as mere serum exudate from bleeding hearts.

Richard V. Ericson is a notable exception. 'What the hell is going on?' is exactly what he does ask about successive aspects of the criminal justice system. In his 1981 study, *Making Crime*, Ericson reports on a thoroughgoing investigation of the functioning of detectives in generating the phenomena which they subsequently control and in determining who, by sometimes devious processes, will be stigmatized and punished as a criminal. In 1981 also, in the monograph *Decarceration and the Economy of Penal Reform*, Ericson and Janet B.L. Chan examine critically the thesis that decarceration results in lowered costs by reducing prison populations, substituting less oppressive as well as less expensive forms of social control for confinement. In fact, the thesis does not hold; the prisons remain as crowded as ever while the newly established forms of surveillance and control justify their existence and their budgets by defining more and more marginal individuals as clients requiring judicious, if not judicial, control. Neither of these works, however, approaches *The Ordering of Justice* in theoretical breadth.

Like *Making Crime, The Ordering of Justice* provides an account of the criminal justice system at work based on close and systematic observation. It is more concerned, however, with the articulation among the various processes and roles which operate to turn people into criminals. (In Canada, criminals are not quite regarded as people; *vide* a recent CBC news report in which a highly and properly indignant spokeswoman, deploring the wretched and degraded conditions of the elderly in a number of British Columbia nursing homes, demanded rhetorically 'Are we going to treat these people like human beings, or like prisoners?' Apparently neither she nor her intervening editors noticed the meaning of what she had said.) One hundred and one individuals who had been charged with criminal offences were included in the study – 30 others approached either refused to co-operate or became unavailable – and each participated in two comprehensive interviews. Meanwhile, observers from the research team recorded as much as possible of the dealings among police officers, crown officials, defence attorneys, and judges that determined their fate. Only rarely and marginally were the accused also involved in such dealings except to give formal assent to the arrangements made to dispose of them. Unfamiliar, in varying degrees, with their roles, most of them literally did not know what was going on. Victims of a strange and wasting social disease, they were not really consulted by the professionals who decided what to do to them. The charges against 11 were withdrawn; those against 4 others were dismissed. Two were even acquitted. The process, then, was 84 per cent efficient.

But efficient at what? Canada has long enjoyed an enviable position, among North American anglophone democratic states, for its relative generosity in government support for the arts. *The Ordering of Justice*, however, astonishes by making it very clear how much that support has been underestimated by most of us, distracted as we may have been by the recurrent problems at Stratford or the triumph of the Shaw Festival. The Canadian system of criminal justice is truly one of the dramaturgical wonders of the modern world – a kind of traditional morality play with modern stage techniques and a cast of thousands. It is much concerned with guilt and innocence, and with assigning those who become involved with it to the role of the innocent or the guilty; but its procedures seem better designed to ensure full houses than to make valid, open, and clearly comprehensible distinctions between them. In any case, the roles portrayed and the lines spoken are carefully scripted. Yet, though it provides employment for some truly gifted artists, including prestidigitators who can make people disappear for years and *never* return in recognizable form, the system of criminal justice is not exactly art either. It is more like the cinema, designed to generate social consensus among a mass audience and provide its practitioners with a handsome and prestigious living; but not, as the arts surely must, to increase our insight into what our lives and our society are really like. Its spectacles move us to terror but rarely to pity and, except in the occasional utterly terrified victim, they induce no catharsis.

A book such as *The Ordering of Justice*, which operates wholly within the canons of social-scientific inquiry, has, for readers like ourselves who have so largely been taught that only science has access to truth, far more impact than any exhortation on behalf of persons caught in the toils of the legal system could. Ericson and Baranek are not reformers; indeed, I doubt that they believe that really significant reform would be tolerated by the Canadian social system; try to transplant a better heart into it and the organ would be rejected. Social systems have a remarkable tendency toward homeostasis and quickly restore themselves to their previous condition. Still, there are limits to the evil most of us can go on doing as we become more and more aware of it; we may not repent, but the extra effort required to justify ourselves to ourselves and others takes its toll in energy, and leaves less for sinning. The criminal justice system is sinful rather than criminal; and to understand it more fully, as any reader of this book must, is at least to increase and deepen one's sense of responsibility for its character and its consequences. *Tout comprendre, c'est tout pardonner?* Not in the case of *the wretched of Canada* v *Regina*, if it should ever be brought to bar. On the basis of the evidence in this book, the best *Regina* could hope for would be a highly conditional discharge. Except that, on that same evidence, evidence doesn't have that much to do with what happens in court.

EDGAR Z. FRIEDENBERG

THE ORDERING OF JUSTICE

1

The Ordering of Justice

Today there's law and order in everything. You can't beat anybody for nothing.
If you do beat anyone, it's got to be for the sake of order.
  Maxim Gorky, *The Lower Depths* (1903)

Everywhere there is one principle of justice, which is the interest of the stronger.
  Plato, *Republic* (4th century BC)

The Ordering of Justice

The accused in the criminal process is caught up in an organizational machinery not of his own making. Furthermore, as a 'one-shot' or occasional actor in the process, rather than a full-time organizational member (Galanter, 1974), he is not in a position to make decisions about most aspects of what is happening to him. Instead, he is subject to the orders or commands of criminal control agents and to the order (systematic patterns of relationships) these agents reproduce in their routine work with the accused and their cases. The options open to the accused are defined by the structure of the criminal process and how that structure is interpreted by the agents who man it, so that the accused's freedom to make choices that might potentially serve his own interests is clearly circumscribed, and often foreclosed.

As a 'one-shot' player, the accused lacks the 'recipe' knowledge (pragmatic, organizational knowledge – see Berger and Luckmann, 1966) and access to other power resources that would allow him to 'fight back' and 'resist the pull' even at a minimal level comparable to inmates of total institutions (Goffman, 1961). The accused must accept the order of rules made and used by others, even if he sees these rules as arbitrary rather than as arbiters.

The agents of criminal control, as regular organizational participants, can selectively use, abuse, or ignore a range of rules to legitimate the actions they take. They take over the conflicts of private citizens and make them state property (Christie, 1977), serving the ideological interests of state-subject authority relations and the organizational interests of the controlling bureaucracies along with, and sometimes instead of, the interests of the individual citizens.

A large part of the agents' discretion – defined as power or autonomy in decision-making – comes from the structure of enabling legal rules that have evolved to order their working environment (see generally McBarnet, 1981). The enabling structures give the police (e.g. Chevigny, 1969; Ericson, 1981, 1982), lawyers (e.g. Blumberg, 1967; Baldwin and McConville, 1977; Macfarlane, 1982), and other court agents (e.g. Carlen, 1976) discretion to frame the accused's actions to the point where the accused's 'decisions' are no more than the agents' commands. Indeed, the power imbalance is typically so great that it is a distortion to characterize any discussion between accused and agent and subsequent decision as negotiated, and more accurate to conceive it as manipulated and/or coerced (Strauss, 1978). Whether it be, for example, a decision to act as an informant to the police, or a decision to plead guilty on a lawyer-arranged plea settlement, the offer is likely to be framed as one that cannot be refused.

The accused is best seen as a dependant rather than as a defendant. This conception is consistent with research literature portraying the accused as passive (e.g. Dell, 1971; Bottoms and McClean, 1976; Carlen, 1976).

It would be a mistake, however, to view the accused's passivity as resulting from his or her lack of perception or inability to calculate rationally a suitable course of action. The accused is acutely aware that he is subject to an ordering process which makes it wise for him to be passive, because there is little scope to act otherwise without being subjected to further negative consequences. If he sits back and accepts the majesty, justice, and mercy of the law (Hay, 1975), he indicates a deference to the wider order of things that may reap for him the immediate reward of leniency. By remaining passive the accused makes a small testimony to that order and allows himself to be used on behalf of the state's need to reproduce order. In return, he is reaccepted as part of that order.

Generally, the accused realizes that above all else he must appear co-operative in his relations with police, his lawyer, and in court. The rules of order which some researchers (e.g. Carlen, 1976) have depicted as intimidating the accused and foreclosing his options in the courtroom are not without counterparts in the police interrogation room, the lawyer's office, and remand facilities. Just as he learns the rules of decorum in the courtroom, and that defiance can result in further charges, such as contempt of court, or can affect negatively judicial decisions, he knows that the other agents also have their orders backed by powerful sanctions. Refusal to co-operate with the police can bring further charges (obstructing police, causing a disturbance, resisting arrest, etc) or more summary forms of punishment. Refusal to co-operate with one's lawyer can bring cessation of the relationship, or a less strident defence. Refusal to co-operate in clinical assessments on remand can produce negative reports which will be reflected in his sentence. Indeed, by the time he reaches court the accused has been so bombarded with the principles of deference to other peoples' orders that he is most unlikely to violate the rules of decorum in the courtroom.

A View from the Accused

The socio-legal literature, reflecting the emphasis in the criminal process itself, has focused overwhelmingly on the perspectives and actions of criminal control agents and includes very little on the perspective of the accused. Although we shall consider this literature in the next section, and draw upon it in our analysis, it is best here to introduce our analysis and the thesis it supports by offering a detailed case illustration from our research sample.[1] This particular case is selected because it includes a full range of steps in the criminal process and illuminates key issues examined later. We use this case to introduce our thesis in an *illustrative* manner and not as representative of some defined universe of accused persons.

The accused whose case we use was an 18-year-old man with no previous convictions. He was charged with attempt rape, and prior to this charge he had also been charged for possession of marijuana and failure to appear in court. In the accused's account of the events leading to the attempt rape charge – an account provided in interview after he was convicted and sentenced to a 4-year penitentiary term, 2½ months after the offence took place – he felt it was necessary to provide some background information.

According to the accused, on the day before the incident he had slipped and banged his head while washing his father's car at a commercial car wash. He returned home and later passed out for a period, and when he awoke he started taking valium pills. During the next day he took six more valium pills. That evening he went for a walk, 'And somehow or other I ended up about a mile from the house on a path. I walked up behind [the victim]. Ah, I guess I pulled a knife out of my pocket or something, and I held it up to her neck, I threw her in the snow, and I attempted to rape her. Luckily enough, I didn't actually do it. Uh, I started walking home, and uh, lost the knife. I don't know if the police have found it or not. I started walking home. I was about three quarters of the way home from where it happened, and the police picked me up, and they asked me to go over to the car, and I did.'

In recounting the events in interview, the accused claimed that he was very uncertain as to what part of this account was from his own memory and what part he was simply repeating from what he had heard in court and what appeared in a written statement of confession presented in evidence by the police. At several points in the interview he answered questions from the interviewer by saying he did not know what happened, and then referred to what the police statement said about the matter. For example, when asked about how the encounter with the victim terminated, he replied: 'I personally don't know how it ended. Um, on the statement – the confession that I gave – I told them that I had led her up and helped her put her pants back on, and told her to go. And then I remained to look for my knife. And then I supposedly – I did – walk to the other end of the path, where I reversed my coat and jacket – or my shirt and jacket – for a difference in colours. And then I attempted to walk along—road towards my house. And then they picked me up.'

During the course of the interview, he repeatedly referred to the event factually as an attempt rape, but kept stating that he had little memory of it and that what recall he did have was confused by the accounts of officials he had heard in court and in a psychiatric remand facility. In interview, he could not recall if he had penetrated the victim, and said he thought it was called an attempt rape and not a rape because there were no signs of semen. In any case, the accused stated that he believed he had committed the offence only because he had been convinced by the accounts of others:

> I thought, like, up until [sentencing date in court] I couldn't believe that I had done it. And the only reason I believe it now is because of the signed confession and because of the fact I drove them [police] back to where it happened without them showing me. Um, up until [sentencing date], I had believed that I had just been out walking. And because of the valium, I was in a sense too stoned to remember what I had done. So when they pulled me over, I had no clue as to what I had done. Um, because it's something, I heard it in [the psychiatric remand facility] called, uh, repression, I think it is. Something that you forget, because it's so bad, or if you try to forget it's called suppression. Um, in my case, it could be either. I don't remember doing anything to try and forget it because I don't remember remembering it. Um, like the crown, in [the psychiatric remand facility] and the judge called me a liar, but that doesn't make any sense. Because what would I gain by not remembering it?

Regardless of the accused's accounts of his activities, the police had something very definite to act upon as a result of complaints from the victim. The agenda for the police included not only this particular incident, but also a series of unsolved indecent assaults against women in the same area which were causing considerable concern among members of the community and the police administration.[2]

During the course of multiple interrogations – which the accused described as 'just like TV, there'd be one good cop and one bad cop' – the accused said he was repeatedly denied his requests for a telephone call to a third party. He said he believed at the time that he was entitled to a telephone call before he said anything to the police because 'I'm a big TV enthusiast and I guess I was following what I seen on TV... I can't distinguish between the Canadian and American rights.' The accused did recall being given the 'right to remain silent' cautions prior to giving the written statement regarding the attempt rape, but he said he paid no attention to it because 'I was too upset to really be listening.'

According to the accused's accounts in interview the various interrogating detectives tried a wide variety of tactics to induce a confession. An underlying tone throughout was that non-co-operation might yield more aggressive detective action: 'They never once attempted to hit me, or punish me, or hurt me, in any way. But they kept bringing up the point that it has happened, to other people ... [later] Like you can threaten to kill somebody, or you can threaten that you're going to threaten to kill them. And that's mostly what they were doing all night ... [later] Right out of the blue, they'd bring up – 'Did you ever hear about so and so getting beat up in another division?' ... They always kept me thinking about the possibility that it could happen to me.'

He said he eventually confessed to the attempt rape charge in the belief that he would then be allowed to telephone his father. He said his main concern at this stage was to have other family members out of the house by the time the detectives arrived to conduct a search, because he did not want anyone else to know about the matter. However, after writing the statement, the detectives proceeded to interrogate the accused on the indecent assault (female) occurrences without allowing him to speak with any third party:

A: The one officer'd say something to the other, and the other would type it down. And they'd ask me if that was right. And they did that through the whole thing, writing it down – typing it down, I should say – and then asking me at the end of that sentence if that was right or wrong.

Q: But you never provided them with the words?

A: No, I don't believe I did.

Q: Have you any idea why you signed that statement?

A: I was scared.

Q: OK, now then –

A: I was upset.

Q: When they asked you whether that was right or wrong, eh?

A: I said 'right' hoping I would be able to phone my father.

Q: But –

A: They had led me to believe I would be able to.

Q: Uh huh, now at that point, when you said 'right,' did you remember that you had done that or were you just saying?

A: I don't think I was even listening. When he looked at me I said 'right' and I looked down at the floor again.

Q: So you can't really be sure that you remembered it, even at that point?

A: I don't think I had, because all of that night, they had questioned me for a
lengthy amount of time – even as to the one I had committed. And that night
I had forgotten immediately after it had happened, as far as I know, until I was
picked up by the police. Well, until sort of three or four o'clock, when I was
being questioned. And then I started to remember points of it, which was probably my –

A: I think it was after I signed the confession. And then he, and then they started
questioning me about the other ones. Uh, Detective —— 's, almost his exact
words were, 'Well, we've had to pry it out of you for five hours, or seven hours,
to get you to admit to this one. So, we'll just sit here and do it until you admit to
all of them.' And, in that state of mind I believe if he had questioned me any
further, I probably would have even though I don't believe I did them.

Concerning the interrogations on the indecent assault (female) occurrences, the accused claimed that he was promised several concessions in
exchange for confessions, including the likelihood of bail, a lenient sentence
(concurrent sentencing on all counts, probably a short jail term or even
probation), and a favourable representation in court by the crown attorney
who would stress his 'co-operation.' He added that at a later stage in the
interrogation he was asked to act as an informant on property crimes, and to
confess to property crimes, in exchange for 'saying that I was co-operative
and reducing the amount of time [sentence].'

In his discussion of this interrogation, the accused continually raised
issues indicating that the experience had taught him many things about the
disadvantaged position he was placed in. He did not see the statement as
voluntary. He questioned why a psychiatrist or other outsider was not
immediately brought in to assess his mental condition: 'Like, I always
believed that you were innocent until proven guilty. And that's not true. I've
seen – I've seen a lot of people here, and in [the psychiatric remand facility],
and it's certainly not true, in any sense. I don't think anybody goes into court
thinking, "OK, now they have to prove me guilty." They go into court and
they, by all means, have to prove their innocence, which is the exact opposite
of what I thought it really, logically, should be.'

The accused was kept in custody for a bail hearing. In the mean time, his
father hired a lawyer to represent him. In the 'five or ten minutes' the accused
had in conversation with the lawyer prior to the bail hearing, he learned
enough to assess the nature of their relationship: 'Q: What did he advise you to
do at your bail hearing? A: Nothing. He just said, "When I tell you to stand up,
stand up, and if they ask you a question, I'll answer it for you."'

During the bail hearing, he also learned about the order in the court. He
said that he did not understand the proceedings, mainly because the language
used by the officials was foreign and no one took the time to ensure that he

understood it in his own terms: 'I couldn't answer the questions properly 'cause I didn't understand them; and, I believed at that time that I was rushed through it without having the proper assistance I needed to answer such questions, even though my lawyer did answer them for me. Like, he asked me, like uh, if I wanted to do this, this or this. And I said, "Well I don't understand." He goes, "Well, OK, we'll say this, you know, so if they ask you, say this." But if they had asked me a question directly, I don't think I would have been able to answer.'

The lack of understanding made it difficult for him to assess his lawyer's performance. He had a sense of things not working out according to his own interests, but felt helpless to assert an alternative:

Q: Are you pleased with the way [your lawyer] handled the bail hearing?

A: I can't answer that because I don't understand his actions. ...

Q: Do you feel you had enough opportunity to explain yourself at the bail hearing, either by yourself or through [your lawyer]?

A: No I don't.

Q: Why?

A: I've never had the opportunity to explain anything.

Q: Do you feel [your lawyer] explained things on your behalf sufficiently?

A: No I don't. But I know why he didn't ... At the bail hearing ... they called me a dangerous criminal person, and at that time I believed that I was not guilty and that I was not a dangerous person. And I don't believe [my lawyer] tried to defend that.

Q: Do you see any reason why he didn't?

A: Because of the signed confession.

After bail was denied, the lawyer immediately arranged for the accused to be remanded to the psychiatric remand facility for an assessment of fitness to stand trial. The accused said he collaborated in this decision because he still thought he had not committed the alleged offence and that there must be something wrong with him to be defying the assertions of everyone else. He did not know the nature of the régime at the facility or the jeopardy he could be placed in by refusing to accept it. Both he and his lawyer in interview stated that his refusal to co-operate with the authorities at the facility resulted in a four-year penitentiary term as opposed to an anticipated term in a provincial reformatory (under two years' imprisonment). The lawyer claimed that if the accused had been granted bail he could have been seen by private psychiatrists in a non-custodial setting, and this would have provided the necessary appearances for a favourable assessment report.[3]

For the accused, the experience at the psychiatric remand facility was a further excursion into the oppressive ordering of the criminal control process. Although the transactions with the police, the lawyer, and at the bail hearing were almost entirely beyond his control, he was at least willing to concede to them some legitimacy. This was not the case with the ordering at the psychiatric remand facility, which pervaded every area of the accused's life.

As described by the accused, the régime at the psychiatric remand facility had remarkable similarities to the extreme forms of carceral power exhibited in mid-nineteenth century prisons modelled on the Auburn system (see e.g. Beattie, 1977; Foucault, 1977; Ignatieff, 1978). The fact that the accused was still awaiting the possibility of a trial rather than serving as a convicted prisoner made it all the more remarkable. It is worthwhile to consider the accused's account in detail, for more than any other experience in the process it taught him the extreme lengths to which the criminal control apparatus would go to keep him in order. It also *finally* taught him that any form of resistance would be met with disproportionate counter-measures, so that ultimately outward compliance to the power of the 'authorities' was the only 'sane' approach:

> They go on the assumption that the person did commit the crime. And they try to find the breaking point. But once they do find your breaking point, once you do finally turn around and say, 'I'm not going to take any more of this, leave me alone, go to hell,' whatever, they certify you from one to two months, which means that you stay there for that amount of time. They have the authority to do that. If you blow up, and you turn around and tell them to do it again, after that two months, they certify you for a further six months. And if you do it within that time, they certify you for another year, and then, it's a year every time after that. Every time you so much as say boo ...
>
> If you do not participate in groups you get thrown in [solitary] confinement for four days. Every time you do something wrong, you get thrown in confinement for four days, no less ...
>
> You're not allowed to communicate in any way with anyone, unless you are told to. You're not allowed to cry, you're not allowed to laugh, you're not allowed to get mad, you're not allowed to be in a good mood.[4]

This knowledge was apparently gained not only through the accounts of other inmates or observation of their experiences. He related that he had attempted to assert his own version of reality from time to time and was met with immediate suppression. Similar to his experiences in police interrogation, he learned that his efforts would not result in a negotiated version of reality, but rather renewed efforts by the authorities to have him accept their version:

> I seriously believe that if I had been sarcastic or argued with anything one more time, that I would still be there, certified. Ah, while we were reading one of the papers, I put up my hand and I said I disagree with this. I said this is not true. This may be true in – like, they were trying to relate the papers as to how we should be on the streets, how people react on the streets. And there was one

question, or one statement, that I disagreed with. And I said, OK, this may be true in a situation such as this when you have stress surrounding you 24 hours a day, but it's not true on the street. And, I got very – they took me up front, to talk to the guards, who we were not allowed to call guards, we have to call them staff. And they condemned me for being verbally aggressive and disagreeing with something that I very honestly disagreed with. I thought I was just being myself, in stating something I thought, you know, should have been stated for the benefit of the other people there, and myself. And they said that I was very domineering for thinking that way, and for thinking at all ...

I stopped [reading] once without the teacher telling me to. And he asked me why I had stopped. And I said, 'Well, —— has his hand up.' I said, 'He wanted a question.' He goes, 'Well, you're thinking for yourself.' And I says, 'Yes, well, I was trying to be considerate.' And he says, 'Well don't.' He says, 'You're not allowed to think for yourself here. That's what we're trying to get you away from.' And there again, I got myself in trouble. I said, 'I'm not here to make friends, I'm not here to make enemies, I'm not here to get help, I'm here to be assessed.' And he says, 'No you're not, you are here to receive help.' I says, 'The court sent me here for assessment.' And because of my arguing back, defending what I thought was right, I was then again taken up front, which, after one more time I had disagreed with something, I had been thrown into confinement for eight days and stripped of all privileges ...

The accused stated in interview that he became thoroughly confused as to what strategy he should adopt to ensure his best interests. He did not want to accept the authorities' definition of his illness for fear that he would be permanently committed to a psychiatric institution without being allowed to stand trial. To this end, he said he frantically memorized and rehearsed what he thought were relevant sections of the law, so that he could show that 'I was sane enough to understand the court proceedings.' He also objected to what they were trying to make him out to be. He believed that this resistance led to the label of 'aggressive' and 'anti-social,' a 'fact' which both the accused and his lawyer subsequently perceived as the paramount reason for a doubling of the sentence the lawyer had been predicting.

The accused's dilemma is revealed in an interview statement which followed reference to a fellow inmate who had been 'certified' for reacting against controls being placed upon him. 'And you know, it's because of that – like on the report they sent back [to the court from the psychiatric remand facility] on me, they said I was unco-operative and very aggressive-... that I could have been violent in the near future if I didn't receive help. And like, the only reason that I would not accept the fact and admit that I needed treatment up there is because I was afraid to get there ... And you get to a point up there where you don't trust anybody, you don't trust the other inmates, you don't trust even the psychiatrists. And now more than ever, I distrust [names psychiatrist]. I think he saw me once in the sixty days I was up there. And yet he sent back a two page report on me.'

While a suitable definition of the accused was being made at the facility his lawyer undertook various out-of-court inquiries in preparation for court hearings. An account of the lawyer's work was obtained from an interview conducted with him one week after his client had been sentenced.

The lawyer said his initial strategy was to obtain a remand to the psychiatric facility for the accused, after predicting that the accused would be denied bail because of the nature of the alleged offence. He stated in interview that he wanted to have the accused sent to a different psychiatric remand facility for the assessment, but there was a waiting period of six weeks. He believed that there was a chance for a much more favourable assessment at this facility, but he did not want to have his client wait because his client said if he was returned to the local jail he would either be killed by other inmates or commit suicide. The less preferable facility thus became a means for moving the accused out of jail and for obtaining a psychiatric assessment.

The lawyer said he made several contacts with one of the investigating detectives in order to obtain disclosure, to assess the police practices in the case, and to attempt a plea settlement. At various points in the interview, he stated that he most frequently contacts and negotiates with the police rather than the crown attorneys because, 1) he has an ongoing relationship with police officers whom he can trust, 2) the crown attorneys on any one case change, so that an arrangement made with one is not necessarily adhered to by another, and 3) the crown attorneys in this jurisdiction are very sensitive to police wishes and will not usually make an arrangement without police input.

The lawyer's major discovery was that the police had obtained a statement which was 'so full ... that it ... left the options open very narrow indeed.' In the lawyer's eyes, the fact that the accused was not given legal counsel while in police custody led him to give a statement which was greatly to his disadvantage in mounting a defence: 'He was arrested and held by the police without being able to talk even with his father. Uh, for hours and hours. And, of course, all, whatever damages there was done to his case from a defence point of view was already done by the time he got out of the police station.'

The lawyer stated that when the accused returned from the psychiatric remand facility, 'I had ... a bad feeling in the pit of my stomach that I didn't want to participate in shipping him off for something he hadn't really done.' He therefore attempted to explore with the police 'a possibility that they, in their zeal, had simply dictated a statement to him, and he'd signed it, for whatever mental reasons he had.' During the course of the interview, the lawyer indicated that there had been, and still were, considerable doubts about the voluntariness of the statement, as well as questionable police practices throughout the extensive interrogations. Referring to the police, the lawyer stated: 'I don't think they were desperately unfair. Uh, they were certainly aggressive in their investigation of it ... I think it was an encounter that didn't really take into account the obvious mental distress the boy was under. They weren't very solicitous of him. But, uh, as I say, I keep saying it, I'm used to the idea that their minds talk about the ends justifying the means ... I think that he was under a great deal of mental stress, and it probably had quite a cathartic effect for him.'

Based upon his discussion with the detectives, the lawyer came to the conclusion that there was other evidence to indicate the accused had committed the alleged offence: 'For instance, he led them to the place where the knife was without any prompting. And, uh, he went and he found the knife for them in the snow. And, uh, he was that co-operative. And he was directing them around the different streets to the spot, you see.' Given the law of confessions in Canada, which allows the admission of other evidence obtained via a statement legally or illegally obtained, and the admission of that part of a statement confirmed by the discovery of other evidence (cf Kaufman, 1974), the lawyer presumably felt that an open challenge to the statement might prove fruitless or even detrimental.

The lawyer also indicated that a key reason for not pursuing the propriety of police practices in obtaining the statement was the relationship of trust he had established with the detective. He had a long-standing rapport with the detective, which had been useful in the past and which would prove useful in the future. This relationship was apparently the reason for accepting the detective's account and for not offering a competing version which would upset their future dealings.

L: With one of the officers, I've dealt with him probably on 150 different cases.

Q: So you have a reasonably, uh, a good rapport?

L: Yeah, that's right. He, uh, to use an indelicate phrase, he knows not to bullshit me ... uh, that to bullshit me would ruin, you know, a trust relationship ... Uh, curiously enough, even though you, you know a number of unfair things that they do, the whole defence counsel set up does in a way work best on the basis of being able to look the detective in the eye, and be fairly clear that he's going to be honest –

Q: Yes.

L: – with you.

Q: Exactly.

L: Uh, if you can't do that, well, you don't trust the guy, and you don't give him anything either.

Q: Uh-huh, uh-huh.

L: You deal with him at arms's length. But, people that you do know, that you can trust, and it's sort of a thing you can't really define. You know, whether you can trust him by looking into his eyes. After fifteen years, you get pretty good at knowing whether a man's lying to you.

In the lawyer's view, his ongoing relations with the police enabled him to accept their accounts and take for granted the practices they engaged in. Moreover, in his eyes there was no doubt that in this case, and in general, police practices and versions of the truth[5] could regularly be open to question but rarely are:

> I've defended policemen on charges, in which they've eventually told me that they lied in court ... The courtroom is a place of fear ... symbolically a place of death. As I was saying, I think, the other day. But, ah, people really, you know, winning becomes very important. And, ah, the end justifies the means for a lot of policemen. But, uh, they do have feet of clay. I mean, I think you have to have a healthy skepticism of a lot of what they say. A lot of judges don't. And I think Judge — [judge in this case] has a hard time believing that they would shade it, but I think, I believe they shade it, but I don't so much blame them ... If he's [police officer] just an ordinary guy, he's going to have a certain bias in his evidence ... And internally, the whole system – that is, law enforcement – is geared towards that.

Holzner (1972: 167) defines trust as 'the acceptance of a social relation or state of affairs as unproblematic and therefore a reliable context for action. Trust consists in the naive and unreflected acceptance of states of affairs as straight forward and valid on the terms on which they present themselves, excluding noxious consequences ... Trust ... reduces social complexity.' The ongoing relationship of 'trust' among lawyers and other criminal control agents can be contrasted with transactions between the lawyer and the accused. The accused does not typically have a relationship with his lawyer that would allow trust to be built up and used on either side to accept evidence at face value; furthermore, the accused and lawyer do not have the same stake in a future relationship that must be kept in mind in conducting transactions. The accused's trust in his lawyer is, thus, of another order: a forced faith that his lawyer will act in his best interests. The faith is forced because the accused has neither the knowledge nor the history of a relationship to rely upon, but only the lawyer's professional status. In some instances, lawyers make trust a precondition for a relationship with a client and this relationship of trust goes only one way. If the client does not accept unquestioningly the lawyer's actions and advice, the lawyer terminates the relationship.

In particular, the accused has little choice but to accept matters on blind faith when his lawyer attempts out-of-court settlements with the police and crown attorney. He is nearly always excluded from these transactions and therefore must rely on his lawyer's account of what happened and what it is possible to achieve.

In the present case, there were a number of factors which led the lawyer to decide that a guilty plea was in order. First, as previously mentioned, he did not see fit to challenge in open court the voluntariness of the accused's statement, but instead accepted the detective's viewpoint. Second, the lawyer said in interview that a full trial in which the victim would have to appear to give testimony would have had very negative consequences for his client; he believed that a judge would have been very sympathetic with the victim's testimony and might have sentenced more severely as a result. Third, the accused continued to be concerned for his health and safety in jail after his return from the psychiatric remand facility; a remand for a higher-court trial would have delayed matters for several more weeks. The most expedient way around this problem was to elect a hearing at the provincial court level, enter a guilty plea, and seek a sentencing hearing as soon as possible.

The lawyer related that the accused continued to have reservations about entering a guilty plea for something he could still not remember doing. However, for the above-stated reasons the lawyer did not have similar reservations. The lawyer said he 'motivated' the accused into believing that he needed treatment. Part of this 'motivation' was based on getting the matter over with quickly so that the accused could get out of the jail setting, while another part was based on the prediction that the accused would receive a provincial reformatory sentence in a treatment-oriented facility. According to the lawyer, the accused ultimately 'left it in my hands.' While the accused continued to have personal reservations about his guilt, he did, in his lawyer's words, '*accept* that he's guilty.'

With the matter firmly in his hands, the lawyer asked the detective for a charge reduction to indecent assault (female) in exchange for a guilty plea. The detective would not entertain this suggestion, and the lawyer said that he did not approach the crown attorney with the same proposal because if the police would not accept it neither would the crown attorney. The lawyer related that he did discuss with the crown attorney a sentence recommendation for reformatory time as part of a 'package' for a guilty plea to attempt rape, but a different crown attorney appeared at the sentencing hearing and did not follow through with the previous discussions of his colleague.

The accused could only rely upon what his lawyer told him: the prosecution would not change the charge, but there was *hope* for a reformatory sentence. The 'trial' had been conducted outside court, where it had been deemed 'in order' to plead guilty to 'attempt rape.' It remained for the accused to confront the order of the court in sentencing, a process he was at least in a position to observe.

For the accused, the ritual in court was a culmination of the ordering he had been subjected to since his initial contact with the police. It was simply the public confirmation of his place in the order of things, foreclosed by others long before this apparent judgment day.

The accused recognized that any effort he made to influence the course of events would have no impact. His one act to influence the outcome of his appearance in court was to wear his glasses, which he usually only wore while driving. He believed they would make him 'look half intelligent,' which he equated with looking respectable.

The accused claimed to have little understanding of what was said or done in court. He felt that his lawyer might have enlightened him more about the proceedings, but it was of little consequence: 'It wouldn't make any difference if I understood what was going on; I wouldn't be able to defend myself any better than I am.' He realized that the matter had been taken out of his hands and remained silent in court against his own wishes because others had so ordered it.

Q: Now did you ever take the stand at all throughout any of this?
A: Never.
Q: So you never spoke?
A: I was never able to voice my opinion at all.
Q: Now why didn't you take the stand?
A: I was never asked to.
Q: Did [names lawyer] ever talk to you about that question, about whether you should?
A: I had asked him if I could take the stand but he gave reasons why I shouldn't. He said I might possibly incriminate myself but I still don't understand that because I've already pleaded to the offence and I've been co-operative in any way. I don't see how I could hurt myself any more

There were several occasions during the sentencing hearing when he wanted to object to what was being said by the crown attorney, especially as it related to the psychiatric report. However, he knew that it was not in order to do so.

A: There was quite a few times that I wanted to jump out of my chair and, you know, say, 'Hey, that's not true, I'm not like that.'
Q: Why didn't you?
A: Because that would be contempt of court.
Q: Do you feel you have the right to speak in court?
A: If I've elected to take the stand I do, but I can only answer the questions that are asked.
Q: But otherwise you feel you don't have the right to speak?
A: Not at all, no.

He also felt prohibited from speaking with his lawyer, even on an informal level. This was mainly due to the physical distance created by his place in the prisoner's box. For example, at one point he wanted to speak with his lawyer about the unfairness of the psychiatric report and the fact that he was being called 'violent' and 'aggressive' by the crown attorney. The accused wanted his lawyer to challenge these labels by arguing that although he was reportedly beaten, spit at, and had cigarettes thrown in his food by other inmates in jail, he did not retaliate: what better evidence could there be that he was not inherently 'violent'?:

A: When the accusations were made on the psychiatric report, I had glanced at him [lawyer] with a very troubled look on my face and more or less motioned him to come over. And I had asked one of the guards to ask, you know, to wave him over, but he [lawyer] just sort of sat there and winked with one eye sort of thing and, you know, raised his hand, sort of motioned it up and down as to get me to calm down a bit. Um, showing me that he had things in what he thought was control.

Q: I see, do you think he should have come over and talked to you when you wanted him to?

A: Um, at the time I would have liked him to. I thought I was being fairly run around at the time ... and I didn't think any of my views were being stated correctly.

The lawyer strongly affirmed the accused's views on the unfair nature of the psychiatric report:

I don't approve of [the psychiatric remand facility] at all. I've had occasion to cross-examine the doctor who gave the report, Dr —. And whatever else he may be, I don't think that he has a very good attitude. I think that he has a custodial institution attitude. He is more of a civil servant than I would want him to be ...

The sort of thing which upsets me is that the letter that they sent back [from the psychiatric remand facility] with the accused I could, if I pulled the files out, if I could remember the names, could pull you the files out, and each of the letters say exactly the same thing with the arrangement of the paragraphs identical. I feel that it's just a *pro forma* letter which is typed up to appear to be ... an in-depth thing, but it really isn't ... When [the accused] went up there he was under a lot of stress. He had the perception that if he acted out, or that if he co-operated too much, or sort of didn't keep his cards too close to the vest, that he would be certified. [He] was terrified of the sort of dissociated guys that he saw up there. So, this was taken for a lack of co-operation. The lack of co-operation translated itself into the judge's mind as lack of desire for rehabilitation. And, that's where the tragedy of the case lay. I would say that lack of co-operation is regarded by – in the civil service professional, as perhaps the most churlish sort of thing that a person can do. And it's my perception in this case that in a way, poor [accused] was punished by the doctors who gave him a bad report because he wouldn't co-operate. He didn't want to take the sodium amytal treatment. So, they said, in effect, screw you.

In spite of these views, the lawyer did not concur with the client's view that the credibility of the psychiatric report should be challenged in court.

Just as he had decided not to challenge police credibility by obtaining a voir dire hearing on the accused's written statement of confession, he decided not to challenge directly the psychiatric report for fear of raising the ire of the judge and possibly creating more serious consequences. The lawyer, too, deferred to the ordering of the criminal process.

The lawyer said that he saw the psychiatric assessment only a few minutes before the beginning of the sentencing hearing. He said that he had hurriedly decided to call the accused's father as a character witness to 'counteract [the psychiatrist's] hypothesis that this was a dangerous fellow, and violently acting out.' However, he did not have much opportunity to coach his witness, so that in his opinion the witness 'went a little overboard ... and lost credibility' by condemning the psychiatric remand facility and what it had allegedly done to his son. When the four-year penitentiary sentence was handed down, both the lawyer and the accused had confirmed their view that a critical challenge in court to any part of the criminal process and the agents who represent it might only serve to aggravate rather than mitigate.

The lawyer attributed the severity of the sentence received to the psychiatrist's report, believing that the report had an effect 'probably to a greater extent than in any other case I've ever had ... [It] was absolutely pivotal in the judge's decision.' In interview, the lawyer was self-critical concerning matters of omission and commission. He felt that he should have obtained a remand after receiving the report so that he could get another psychiatrist to produce a counter-interpretation, adding that he did not do so because his client did not want to remain in jail any longer. He had considered judge-shopping but did not do so because this particular judge was by reputation sensitive to a belief that he was being regularly avoided for being too 'hard nosed,' and because he believed the judge would accept the argument that the accused needed treatment in a reformatory setting.

The sentence placed the accused in the very position he thought he could avoid by pleading guilty and appearing contrite. He did not wish to go to penitentiary for fear that he would be continually harassed by other inmates because of the nature of his offence. He therefore supported his lawyer's wish to launch an appeal against sentence based on the strategy of obtaining a further psychiatric assessment from another source. However, in the interim the accused remained lodged in the local jail setting that he had been trying to avoid through the original plea and election strategy. In terms of delay, serving time in a setting he wanted out of, and sentence, the accused realized he was no better off than if he had pleaded not guilty. In terms of legal fees required for hiring a new lawyer on appeal, he was undoubtedly worse off. What else could he have done once caught up in a process that was not of his own making?

A View from the Literature

The detailed accounting of this case provides us with a point of departure for considering wider issues in the ordering of justice. We shall refer to features of this case as well as to the sociological and socio-legal literature.

Packer (1968: 5) states that 'the criminal sanction is the paradigm case of the controlled use of power within a society.' Our study raises many questions, and answers some, about how the criminal process is ordered according to the relative power of the various participants. Which actors in the process have the power to effect compliance that serves particular interests over and against other interests? What are the resources which 'enable' this power? How is this power used, and in what ways is it controlled? What are the implications of this for the accused person? What are the implications of this for reform of the criminal process?

The primary power of criminal control agents emanates from the institution of law itself, including the various formal organizations which comprise that institution. Agents are also very adaptive in developing secondary power resources when the institutional ones prove less than adequate. The combination of these primary and secondary powers usually means that once the agents of criminal control have an accused in their web, they can tailor a patterned outcome to suit their interests.

This accomplishment is typically very easy because the forces of power are there even when they are not exercised. As we can readily observe from our case example, most of the accused's actions and many of his lawyer's actions were based on the perception that the police, the crown attorney, the psychiatrist, and the judge had overpowering resources to counter any contrary effort the accused and his lawyer might have made. In some areas the accused and/or his lawyer tested these powers, but in the main they decided not to pursue particular actions because of the *potential* for using power resources (rather than actual use of them) by the various criminal control agents.

The power resources available to agents within the criminal process include physical coercion, organization, control over rule-production and enforcement, control of information, and knowledge (specialist and 'recipe'). In combination, these resources structurally produce the commanding position of law enforcement personnel and the subservient position of the accused within the criminal process. The only access the accused has to these power resources is through his lawyer, who typically only has partial access. Moreover, the fuller the lawyer's access, the greater the potential for being 'co-opted' as part of the law-enforcement machinery rather than for functioning as its adversary (cf Blumberg, 1967).

Organizations serve to facilitate the collective action of people with related interests (cf Silverman, 1970; Eisenstein and Jacob, 1977; Ranson et al, 1980). They provide a hierarchy of authority, procedures for accomplishing collective tasks, and appropriate modes and channels of communication. Organizations provide the forum for common work activity, allowing the work to proceed on an unproblematic, taken-for-granted, 'trustful' basis.

Access to organization provides access to other power resources – specialist (expert) and 'recipe' (pragmatic) knowledge, rules, and information- – which are necessary to secure control over areas of interest to organizational members. Without this access, a person remains powerless to influence organizational activity. This is precisely the position of the accused person acting on his own. He is legally incompetent because he is not a regular organizational participant: his role is defined unilaterally by others; he is brought into a foreign setting with its alien forms of practice and discourse; and he is given only partial glimpses into some of the workings which ultimately make up what others do to him (see especially Carlen, 1976; McBarnet, 1981).

An accused person is no more competent in the criminal process than a judge would be in using the language and obeying other rules of social organization that pertain among youths who regularly congregate in the parking lot of a hamburger stand. The difference is, of course, that the judge can leave rather than pay lip service to thoughts and actions he might find foreign or even repulsive; he would only suffer embarrassment. The accused is moved from setting to setting (police station, remand facility, courts) where he must perpetually pay respect to persons talking in foreign tongues about matters not of his own making; apart from suffering embarrassment, he must also endure physical constraints and other long-term punishments determined in part by the degree to which he has offended the orders of these others.

A major power resource of organizational participants is rules which legitimate taking control of others. The organization of criminal justice is replete with formal legal rules as well as organizational rules, which legitimate a hierarchy of who can do what to whom, how it can be done, and how it can be undone if need be. It has become commonplace to recognize that criminal control agents are empowered with an enormous array of enabling rules which can be selected and employed to legitimate the course of action they choose to take (cf McBarnet, 1981).

This power resource is in turn tied in with the power to 'produce reality' (cf Berger and Luckmann, 1966: especially 134, 137) by selecting what will be regarded as 'fact.' This is especially a resource of the police and is as much a matter of omitting certain information as it is of committing selected features of events to official documents and thus lending them the character of 'fact' (Ericson, 1981, 1982; McBarnet, 1981). As many writers have recognized (e.g. Feeley, 1973; Carlen, 1976; Morris, 1978), police accounts come to stand for *the* truth at subsequent stages of the criminal process and are not routinely challenged.

As we learned from the case example, the statement of confession came to stand for 'what happened' after the lawyer accepted on trust the 'fact' that the police version of what happened was *'the* truth.' This document then became at once the lawyer's reason and his excuse for not entertaining other possible defences. Similarly, the lawyer and the accused believed that the psychiatric report came to stand for the 'facts' of the accused's basic nature in the eyes of the judge, and it was deemed potentially injurious to challenge these 'facts' in court even though the lawyer and the accused saw them as a fabrication. To have challenged the legitimacy of these 'facts' would itself have been tantamount to deviance: better to bow out to powerful versions of the truth than to discover even more forcefully just how powerful they can be.

In the criminal process as in other social organizations and social settings, different parties construct and mediate versions of the truth to serve their own interests. Of course, the accused is as likely to do this as is his lawyer, the police, the crown attorney, the psychiatrist, the probation officer, and so on. However, the accused is not as likely to have his version accepted because of his position at the bottom of the power structure, on the bottom rung of the 'hierarchy of credibility' (Becker, 1967).

The highly adhesive quality of the material used by criminal control agents to make their case stick comes from the power of rules at their disposal. These allow them to isolate the accused on their own terms and thereby to produce what they know is necessary to secure the result they want. In this view, both the rules and the facts are instrumental tools for justifying official action. Justice becomes a matter of justification, i.e. of supplying legitimated rationales for action. Feeley (1973: 420–1) makes this point succinctly:

> The process of selecting which 'facts' to consider and which 'rule' to apply to define the activity is in itself a discretionary matter of considerable importance. The variety of available 'legal' alternatives allows the actor a wide latitude for discretion, and of course a very valuable commodity to bargain with in the system of exchange. In this view the interpretation and use of the rules themselves are viewed as instruments of rationalization, not application. That is, the rules are selected and used as weapons or supports at the whim of, and in the particular interests of, the various actors in the system. This ambiguity and discretion are inherent in the very nature of all elaborate systems of rules, and 'force' enforcement and administrative officials – the so-called rule 'appliers' – into a position of making 'lawless' decisions.

See generally Kadish and Kadish, 1973; Feeley, 1979; Rothman, 1980.

The array of rules and versions of the truth available make it highly contingent as to what rules and versions will be selected and used in any given case. This unpredictability also serves as part of the overall control strategy, for it enables the agents of law enforcement to resist dependencies that would grow out of readily predictable actions (cf Silverman, 1970: 208). This is not to say that the actions of criminal control agents are not predictable and therefore not orderly. Rather, similar to organized gambling, there is a cultivation of unpredictability in a predictable manner which guarantees that the game is played only by the rules of the house and that while there may be the odd lucky winner among the one-shot players, in the long run only the house wins. The perceptive accused learns that the odds are heavily stacked against him, and that the best bet is to minimize repeated playing.

One major problem for the accused as a 'one-shot' player is that he is excluded from access to 'recipe' knowledge that would enable him to judge the realities that he is presented with, and to act accordingly. The accused cannot possibly learn the organizational rules and attendant practices by which the police, crown attorney, and lawyer construct his case for court appearance. Moreover, even if he learned these rules in abstract they would be of very limited value. The great advantage possessed by law enforcement 'regulars' is that they not only know the rules in abstract, but they also know the contexts of rule application so that the rules can be used to enable and justify particular actions in particular circumstances. Indeed, this is the first lesson of the lawyer stepping out of law school and into criminal law practice: his competence as a professional lawyer depends far more upon his ability to acquire 'recipe' knowledge than it does on the abilities he displayed in law school (Heumann, 1978). One of the few astute choices an accused can make is to hire a lawyer who has this 'recipe' knowledge at his disposal; one of the worst choices he can make is to hire a lawyer who has developed too many 'trusting' relationships within this community, or who is not an accepted member of the community at all.

The accused can play little or no part in constructing the reality about his case. He is at the bottom of the 'hierarchy of credibility' and the very fact that he has allegedly committed a crime makes what he has to say discreditable, and sometimes incredible.[6] Moreover, he does not have the resources to assess independently the realities being presented to him by other agents, including his lawyer. For example, if his lawyer tells him that he was unable to arrange a charge reduction or a lenient sentence recommendation, how is the accused to know if this is the case or if his lawyer has tried every reasonable means at his disposal (Baldwin and McConville, 1977)?

Reality is 'a quality appertaining to phenomena that we recognize as having a being independent of our own volition (we cannot "wish them away")' (Berger and Luckmann, 1966: 13). By the time he reaches the court-room, the accused confronts a reality constructed by criminal control agents which he cannot effectively counter, or indeed, 'wish away.' As we learned from the accused in the case example, he remained uncertain about the police version of reality and explicitly denied the psychiatrist's version of reality; however, he ultimately remained silent on orders from his lawyer, who believed that any attempt to discredit these realities would bring the accused further discredit. Documents presented by officials in courtroom settings take on the character of fact, rather than merely official descriptions and interpretations of events. As Carlen (1976: 114) observes, even if there is no written statement of confession, the police can use their notebook material as if it represents objective and independent fact:

> What 'everybody knows' has to be continuously related to some operant sym-
> bol in which 'everybody trusts', such as law, knowledge, or religion. The diffi-
> culty of repudiating 'everyday knowledge' once it has become explicitly
> legitimated through successful linkage to legal action was recognized by W.G.
> Sumner at the beginning of this century. He cogently made the point that,
> 'Everybody knows that there were witches. If not, who were the people who
> were burnt?' In the case of the forgetful defendant, [police] notes made at *the*
> time are interpreted in such a way as to establish the nature of the event for *all*
> time. The policeman's notebook is not only a strategic prop in establishing the
> certain meaning of disputed past events; it implies that such certain meaning is
> *external* to the people involved.

Of course, the accused is not likely to be more 'forgetful' than anyone else who tries to describe and interpret events that happened months before his being called into account. However, he might appear to be forgetful, incon-sistent, or even a liar because he does not have recourse to similar legitimated representations of fact.

The opportunities for the accused appear greater when it comes to challenging other representations of reality, such as pre-sentence, probation, and psychiatric reports. Counter-reports can be obtained and character witnesses paraded, but, as we have seen in the case example, these opportuni-ties are not always pursued. Moreover, when such challenges are made, they are typically constructed according to the lawyer's designs.

In most cases, the reality of the dispute and of the accused's character has been constructed by others and established as truth long before the matter reaches court. The court partly functions to legitimate the reality constructed by these agents of criminal control. In court, the prior work-oriented con-structions of reality by the police, crown attorney, lawyer, probation officer, and/or psychiatrist are given authority; they are thereby transformed into ideological tools to justify all that the agents did in the particular case and all that they do generally (cf Holzer, 1972: especially 144–7).

Bottoms and McClean (1976: 226–7), in dealing with the accused's exclusion from participation, challenge Packer's (1968) view that accused people fight every inch of the way once they are caught up in the criminal process. Bottoms and McClean argue that the accused's options are usually foreclosed from the beginning and that the crucial point of closure occurs during transactions between police officers and the suspect.

Our argument has been that this is the case because the accused is a dependant rather than a defendant in the criminal process. He is forcefully brought into a web of organizations not of his own making and subjected to rules structured to control him and be enabling for law enforcement agents. This control is even more powerful than that experienced by persons at the bottom end of 'total institutions' (Goffman, 1968). In total institutions, even those at the bottom end are participants in the organization, and this allows them some access to resources for 'fighting back' against the oppressive features. The difference for the accused is that without participatory membership he does not have a similar 'fighting chance,' except through hiring an agent who may be beneficial.

The accused has his role defined for him, and that role becomes reified so that he sees it as inevitable (cf Berger and Luckmann, 1966: 108). As a 'reified client' he is treated as an object who is acted upon rather than as a subject who acts: 'His own wishes and purposes are not considered except as symptoms' (Friedenberg, 1975: 19).

For the accused, there are such gross disparities of power that it is appropriate to view transactions with him as characterized by manipulation and coercion, not negotiation (cf Strauss, 1978; Klein, 1976). The position of his lawyer is somewhat different. The lawyer does participate somewhat in the organizations of criminal control and is thus able to negotiate with other agents in a way his client cannot. Let us now consider the nature of these negotiations, and the complications that arise for the interests of accused persons.

It is generally regarded as advantageous for an accused person to hire a lawyer because a lawyer is structurally more able to change the character of transactions to make them at least partially negotiation. The lawyer has ties within the organizational network of criminal control agents, which among other benefits gives him more power than the accused possesses to influence these agents. The lawyer also has more experience, which potentially enables him to see more options and to make more informed guesses as to the likely outcome of choosing a particular option. However, his position also carries potential liabilities for the accused, the greatest of which is that relationships with other agents will lead him to make concessions that favour these relationships rather than the accused.

These assets and liabilities are both manifested when the lawyer enters the one arena from which the accused is usually excluded, namely out-of-court discussions concerning recommendations about evidence, plea, and sentence. The bulk of research and writing on this topic (e.g. Newman, 1966; Blumberg, 1967, in the United States; Baldwin and McConville, 1977, in England) suggests that the accused is greatly disadvantaged by these dealings because lawyers tend to compromise too much, and in conditions of 'low visibility' which make review impossible. Others argue that these transactions are still adversarial in nature, with a number of power resources available to both sides (Utz, 1978). Whether or not these transactions are adversarial is an empirical question, and one that we consider in detail in chapter 4.

We can gain some understanding of out-of-court transactions by describing and analysing them according to Strauss's model of 'negotiation contexts.' Strauss (1978: 99 – 100) instructs us to consider these in terms of the following properties:

1) The *number* of negotiators, their relative *experience* in negotiating, and whom they *represent*.
2) Whether the negotiations are *one-shot*, *repeated*, *sequential*, *serial*, *multiple*, or *linked*.
3) The relative *balance of power* exhibited by the respective parties *in* the negotiation itself.
4) The nature of their respective *stakes* in the negotiation.
5) The visibility of the transactions to others; that is, their overt or covert characters.
6) The *number* and *complexity* of the *issues* negotiated.
7) The *clarity of legitimacy* boundaries of the *issues* negotiated.
8) The *options* to avoiding or discontinuing negotiation; that is, the alternative modes of action perceived as available.

We shall consider the lawyer's involvements in our case example according to these properties. This allows us to raise many of the typical features of relationships among accused, lawyer, and law enforcement agents that we expand upon in subsequent chapters.

The experience of lawyers in the criminal process is almost invariably greater than that of the accused, but they frequently do not have the same degree and variety of experience in criminal law work as the other agents they deal with. The vast majority of lawyers in our sample only did criminal law work on a part-time basis, and the majority of their practice related to other types of law. The lawyer is ostensibly there to represent the accused and his own personal and professional interests. The law-enforcement personnel are ostensibly there to represent the victim, the state, and their own organizational interests. As happened in the case example, a lawyer who has considerable experience in criminal law work within a particular criminal control community develops relationships of trust with other agents, which he uses to make intuitive judgments about strategy.

Negotiations in any one case are normally 'one-shot' in nature, although there may be several telephone calls or brief meetings with the police and/or crown attorney. In this case, the lawyer said he engaged in 'two or three' telephone conversations with the police detective in charge of the case, and talked with two different crown attorneys prior to two different court hearings.

The balance of power in out-of-court negotiations typically resides with the police and crown attorney. The reasons are complex, but relate to the fact that up until the point the lawyer starts working on the case, the police have 'managed' the 'reality' construction of the case. They have usually constructed evidence and laid charges in a way that allows them to command conviction and sentencing (cf Ericson, 1981, 1982; Helder, 1979). The accused very often gives up potential defence resources by co-operating with the police, especially in giving a signed statement of confession.

The research literature has focused upon 'successful' negotiations, i.e. those in which some concessions have been made. However, lawyers can make unsuccessful efforts at obtaining concessions. These efforts are unsuccessful because the police and/or crown attorney choose not to negotiate and they have the power to back up their choice. This occurred in our case example. As stated earlier, the lawyer said he attempted to secure a reduction from attempt rape to indecent assault (female), but the detective refused to consider it. The lawyer said that he also attempted to have the crown attorney collaborate in not objecting to a reformatory sentence recommendation; initially one crown attorney tentatively agreed, but at the next court hearing a different crown attorney took over the case and refused to consider the matter. The lawyer apparently had nothing to offer to further his efforts, and the police and crown attorney remained in the commanding position the police had established from the outset.

The various actors involved and represented obviously have different stakes in any negotiation. The accused's stakes are 'one-shot' rather than ongoing. The accused judges the entire process by the end results – his conviction, and especially his sentence (since he usually sees the conviction as foreclosed) – rather than by the means used by his lawyer and the law enforcers to arrive at those results (cf Morris, White, and Lewis, 1973).

The law enforcers have reasons to do with organizational and occupational success for also concentrating on the end results, although they may want different results than the accused. The law enforcers also have some stake in relationships with other 'regulars,' including the judge and the lawyer for the accused.

The lawyer has a particularly complex set of stakes. These involve a balance between doing a job which appears competent to his client and maintaining the professional respect and collaboration of criminal control officials. In this case, the lawyer made special mention of his relationship with the police detective in charge of the case, and he used that to justify not opposing the police methods which produced the damaging confession. He also implied that he did not challenge the psychiatric report because it is not 'in order' to discredit publicly colleagues. The only challenge deemed appropriate was in terms of their own professional framework, i.e. to obtain the opinion of other professional psychiatrists who are also professionally controlled.

The lawyer's out-of-court efforts to secure leniency regarding evidence, charges, and sentence recommendations are almost always invisible to the accused. The accused either remains ignorant that transactions took place at all, or is left with accepting his lawyer's account of why a particular settlement was arrived at. Without a sense of the possible, the accused is forced to accept the reality of what his lawyer says is. This was the situation of the accused in this case: he had to accept his lawyer's judgment that there should be no challenge in court to the police or psychiatric statements even though both the accused and his lawyer questioned them privately. The accused's only *possible* option was to fire his lawyer and to hire another lawyer. However, this was an unlikely move because he would be in no better position to judge the second lawyer's efforts. Therefore, the only *real* option was to have faith or to give up.

As we learn further in chapter 4, in many cases there are several complex issues at stake, while in others there is little scope for debate. In a case such as this one, the lawyer saw the potential for debate about evidence (e.g. the police statement), charge (e.g. possible reduction), and sentence (e.g. reformatory recommendation) and said that he made some efforts in these areas. As he mentioned in interview, he might also have opened a number of other issues, e.g. by going to trial and challenging the victim's account or by obtaining an independent psychiatric assessment.

The legitimacy boundaries of what is possible vary according to legal constraints (e.g. the evidence required to support a particular charge) as well as organizational constraints (e.g. the bounds of what it is acceptable to request from the police and crown attorney based upon what they have 'bought' in the past). While these constraints provide a general framework for transactions, the legitimacy boundaries themselves can be tested. This boundary negotiation is of course greatly facilitated by the 'low visibility' under which lawyers, police, and crown attorneys test each other out, and by the trust they have in each other that what they have tried to make legitimate out of court will not be subject to a legitimacy test once in court.

In this case, the lawyer deemed that it was 'in order' to raise with the detectives, out of court, questions about the legitimacy of the confession as well as the charge of attempt rape and, with the crown attorneys, about sentence recommendations. He did not achieve any concessions and was effectively bound into accepting the boundaries of legitimacy constructed by the police and crown attorneys.

There are two basic options open if out-of-court negotiations fail or have not been attempted. The first is to concede entirely what the law enforcers have constructed (e.g. not challenge evidence; plead guilty as charged; leave sentencing up to the judge without any particular recommendation). The second is to fight any one or more of the issues according to the order in the court (e.g. plead not guilty and challenge the crown attorney's evidence; make sentencing submissions believed to be favourable to the accused's interests).

In this case, the lawyer did not see a full trial as a viable option after failing to gain concessions from the police and crown attorney. He said he wished to avoid a trial because he predicted that the victim's testimony in court might be very damaging to the accused. Instead, he chose a guilty plea for his client and made some effort at influencing sentence by calling the accused's father as a character witness. He said he did not obtain another psychiatric assessment because of the accused's wish to have the matter settled and to get out of the jail remand facility.

As Strauss (1978: 102) emphasizes, 'The important property of the structural context bearing on any given set of negotiations is the respective actors' *theories* (usually implicit) of negotiation.' As we can see from the lawyer's account, he made a number of intuitive predictions which led to his decisions on how the case could best be dealt with. Some of these decisions were apparently based upon 'situated' features, such as the accused's desire to get out of jail. Others were based upon 'experience,' such as guessing that the victim's testimony would damage the accused's interests and that the provincial court judge would be favourable to reformatory 'treatment.' The fact that the lawyer retrospectively questioned some of his own judgments indicates that at least part of his decision-making was guess work, and that some of his practical theorizing was in need of revision.

As a practical social theorist who ostensibly tries to arrange the outcome in the accused's favour, the lawyer has the organizational advantages of access from which the accused is excluded and the experience built up from his career in making use of this access. The lawyer thus has the *potential* to win greater advantage than the accused could gain for himself, but he can go wrong. Inevitably, hiring a lawyer, like all other aspects of the criminal justice lottery, carries a degree of unpredictability and attendant risks.

In concluding this section, we wish to stress that our purpose is not to question the legitimacy of why someone was brought to police attention in the first place. We are not out to demonstrate that masses of accused people are innocently cast into the criminal process, although some are. Rather, we wish to analyse the form this casting takes, and to show that, contrary to popular belief, once the mould is set by law enforcement agents there are few resources available to the accused to shape his destiny within the criminal process.

We selected for discussion and interpretation in this opening chapter a case involving very serious allegations of violence. Most people would agree that forceful state intervention is required when someone alleges that he or she has been threatened with a knife and assaulted. Among other things, the use of this particular example allows us to raise problems other than those of concern to critical criminologists (e.g. Taylor, Walton, and Young, 1973, 1975) who view criminal law enforcement against property offenders and 'victimless crime' offenders as a tool of the powerful to maintain and enhance their privileged position within the political economic order.

Unless one views a 14-year-old girl walking in a public park as public property which can be legitimately taken by force, there is no argument about the legitimacy of the initial police intervention. Our argument in this case begins once the state legitimately intervened. Our purpose in considering this case was to point out that once intervention occurred and an accusation was made, the accused was effectively foreclosed from taking action other than faithfully and fatefully to put matters completely in the hands of others. It is this ordering of accused people that we are interested in analysing and ultimately questioning, although we do consider in chapter 2 the views of the accused and the lawyer on the legitimacy of the charging practices of the police.

A Research Strategy

There has been little effort by criminologists to take the perspective of the accused as a focus of inquiry in studying the criminal process up to the point of sentencing. Studies of offenders' views of their situation have been concerned with post-disposition stages of the criminal process (e.g. Glaser, 1964; Irwin, 1970; Waller, 1974; Ericson, 1975). Studies of accused people have typically examined the differential selection of offenders from the administrative viewpoint (e.g. Goldman, 1963; Skolnick, 1966; Reiss, 1971; Hogarth, 1971; Doob and Chan, 1977). The importance of the accused's perspective has only recently been stressed through the vehicle of interview studies. These have been conducted in the United States by Casper (1972, 1978), in Britain by Bottoms and McClean (1976) and Baldwin and McConville (1977), and in Canada by Klein (1976).

Researchers who have considered the accused's perspective have stressed that the accused is in a unique position because he is the only actor who experiences the process from beginning to end. Moreover, they have ably demonstrated that ordering is very much weighted against the accused, and in at least one study (Baldwin and McConville, 1977) have raised important questions about the very negative consequences of this ordering for the accused (e.g. technically innocent people pleading guilty).

Our study is informed by the issues raised in these previous efforts, but it is also designed to go beyond them by providing more than just the accused's accounts. As Klein (1974) stated in concluding his thesis, 'Further research ... should have as its scope the study of the offender's career from first contact with officials to the final disposition of the case. Obviously, there is no *official* record which will completely reflect the dynamics of this process.'

A research design which took these considerations into account was developed in the form of a research program at the Centre of Criminology, University of Toronto. This program, entitled A Longitudinal Study of the Cumulative Effects of Discretionary Decisions in the Criminal Process, includes a series of sub-studies dealing with the involvements of accused persons, victims, uniformed patrol officers, detectives, lawyers, and crown attorneys, within the criminal process. Each of these sub-studies has its own agenda, but they all have in common a small number of cases that were generated from the studies of the patrol officer and the detective.

Our sample of accused persons whose careers were followed from arrest to final disposition came from cases observed by researchers studying uniformed officers and detectives in a Canadian municipal police force. All cases in which an accused was charged with at least one offence under the Criminal Code or Narcotics Control Act became part of the follow-up sample.[7]

The patrol study involved five fieldworkers who engaged in systematic observation of patrol officers over 348 shifts from May to September 1976. These shifts were selected on a simple random basis for all patrol areas, all days of the week, and all shift periods. Research fieldworkers were instructed to record details about shift activity and encounters with citizens on schedules developed for this purpose, and to keep detailed fieldnotes. In situations where suspects were charged with offences under the Criminal Code and/or Narcotics Control Act, the fieldworkers recorded on the schedules, details about the transactions and submitted the name of the accused to the other researchers so that they could follow the case through court.

The detective study involved two fieldworkers observing the activities of six different two-person detective teams over 179 shifts from May 1976 to March 1977. All cases taken on by each detective team while they were being observed were included in the study sample, producing a total of 295 cases. This was not a random selection, although it is arguable that these cases were typical of those dealt with by general investigation detectives (Ericson, 1981: chapter 2). Cases which resulted in charges under the Criminal Code and/or Narcotics Control Act being laid against one or more accused were fed into the follow-up sample according to the same procedures employed in the patrol study.

In total, the police studies generated 131 accused people in 100 cases to be followed by the personnel from the study of the accused as well as by those studying other actors in the process. Obviously the nature of this sample was affected by the way it was produced through the police studies. We shall discuss issues in sampling and characteristics of the sample shortly, including the fact that 30 of the 131 accused were not interviewed.

The appreciative focus of the study of accused persons led us to choose an open-focused interview technique.[8] An interview schedule was drawn up to provide questions that would be asked of all accused persons, thus ensuring that key topics would be systematically covered. The open-focused format allowed the respondents to interpret questions, discuss meanings with the interviewer, and eventually supply an account in their own words.

We were committed to taking the accused's accounts as seriously as accounts offered by other participants in the criminal process. While there have been many studies of the defence side in criminal cases, these have most often been from the lawyer's perspective and usually ignore the fact that the accused's interests and position differ from those of the lawyer. There is a need to understand the defence position as the accused has constructed it and is obstructed by it. If the scales of justice are supposed to be evenly balanced, or even tipped in favour of the accused, then it is essential to treat the accused's version of reality as seriously as any other versions.[9] In light of this, it is indeed remarkable that there has not been greater effort by criminologists to obtain accounts from accused persons.[10]

An advantage of taking our sample from the wider research program is that we can see the other versions of reality produced by the different actors in the process. We can thence learn how these varying versions are reduced to one, official, legitimated reality. While the perspective of the criminal control agents is the topic of other books from the research program, and not a central concern of this book, we do incorporate findings of the other studies as they become relevant to an understanding of the accused's position.[11]

A further important advantage of this approach is that verbalized 'inaccuracies' about procedures and decisions, far from discrediting the accused's account, reflect the state of affairs as the accused experiences and interprets them. It is his version that is important in appreciating his ordered position within the criminal process and in understanding how this position relates to the decisions taken in his defence. For example, although police activities in a particular case may have been observed to have been conducted with procedural regularity, it is important to know whether a suspect felt that there was no option to giving a signed statement of confession which confirmed his status as an accused person. If he felt no option, it is an indication that the law as written and/or practised does not safeguard the few resources suspects and accused have at their disposal.

The interviewing began in May 1976 and continued until April 1978. Since the time from charging to final disposition of a case could (and did) stretch to a year or more, it was decided that each accused would be interviewed twice in order to reduce problems with recall.

The first interview took place as soon as possible after the first court appearance, which was the first public access to the accused and to the public knowledge concerning the nature of the offence. This interview included six sections: demographic background of the accused; his account of the alleged offence; his previous criminal history, including contacts with the police; his description of the initial contact with the police; his description of contact with the police at the station, if any; and his description of a bail hearing, if any.

The second interview was conducted as soon as possible after the final disposition of the case and covered events after the first court appearance.

The first section covered the accused's decisions on whether or not to obtain counsel; the type of representation he chose; his opinion of each type; the nature of his relations with his lawyer; his knowledge of, and involvement in, decision-making surrounding key issues; and his evaluation of his counsel. Subsequent sections included questions on the accused's knowledge of, and involvement in, decisions regarding elections, preliminary hearings, plea, the trial process, sentencing, and appeals. The accused's perceptions of the role of the police, crown attorney, defence, judge, and victim in producing the outcome of his case were explored, as well as his perceptions of the general role of these persons within the criminal process. Finally, we included a section which allowed the accused to speculate on how he would handle the decisions made at each stage if he could do it all again.

Our hope of conducting two separate interviews with each accused was only partially met because of events during the course of the fieldwork. For 43 of 101 accused persons interviewed, the first and second interviews took place at the same time: when he pleaded guilty and was sentenced on his first court appearance day, or when he consented to an interview only after the disposition of the case. For the latter group, this created problems of memory because considerable time (6 to 12 months) had elapsed from the time of the offence to the time of the interview. These accused tended to be those with more serious charges against them. Among the remaining 58 accused, 55 were interviewed on 2 separate occasions, while 3 participated in the first interview only and could not be traced for the second interview.

The time lapse between the day of the alleged offence and the first interview ranged from less than one month to over a year. The longer time lapses usually involved persons who refused to be interviewed until the disposition of their case. Among the 101 interviewed, 37 were interviewed within a month of the offence, 67 within three months, 82 within six months, and 94 within a year. The time lapse between the disposition of the case and the second interview ranged from less than two weeks to just over six months.

The vast majority of the interviews were conducted by Pat Baranek. Two part-time assistants occasionally did observations and interviews when it was impossible for Pat Baranek to conduct them (e.g. when more than one accused's case came up on the same day in different courtrooms). With few exceptions, the fieldworkers were present at each court appearance for each accused, and they kept fieldnotes on courtroom interactions involving each accused. The notes on the courtroom interaction are as close to verbatim accounts as is possible when transcribing by hand under poor acoustical conditions. As other researchers have noted (e.g. Bottoms and McClean, 1976, who in turn cite Martin and Webster, 1971), the presence of the researcher in court helped to establish rapport with the accused which subsequently eased the relationship. Some accused made explicit mention of this fact.

When the accused had been dealt with by the court on his first appearance (e.g. the next appearance date had been set, or the accused had indicated he would be pleading guilty and was therefore transferred to another court), he was approached by the researcher. The researcher identified herself, explained the purpose of the study, assured the accused of the confidentiality of all information given, and then asked the accused if he wished to participate.

The interviews varied in duration from one to four hours. It was decided to tape-record interviews to ensure that accurate accounts in the accused's own words would be available and to allow for a more natural flow of conversation unbroken by the distraction of writing down responses. Only three accused refused to allow their interviews to be recorded. Under such circumstances, the researcher made written notes as the respondents answered her questions.

The interviews were conducted in a variety of settings. Many took place in lawyer-client interview rooms within the courthouse. In other cases, an appointment was made to meet the accused elsewhere: the alternative meeting place was most often the accused's residence, but interviews were also conducted at a residence belonging to a friend of the accused, in a restaurant, in the University of Toronto Centre of Criminology, and in an accused's car. Permission was obtained from the superintendents of the local jails, the Ontario Ministry of Corrections, and the Federal Penitentiary Service to interview members of our sample who were in custody. These interviews took place in different locations within the institutions, including a lawyer-client interview room, a medical office, and a superintendent's office.

When the first and second interviews were not combined into one, the accused was asked at the completion of the first interview if he was agreeable to a second interview after the disposition of the case. Consent to the second interview was invariably given, although three persons could not be traced for the second interview.

Among the 131 persons initially in the sample, 20 refused to be interviewed, including all 4 accused in one case. Another four persons never appeared in court throughout the duration of the study. Bench warrants were issued for three of them, while the fourth person had his lawyer arrange with the crown attorney to withdraw the one charge of possession of marijuana against him. Another three accused were impossible to trace. Among the remaining three accused who were never interviewed, one person (in custody) was deported before an interview could be arranged, one had his charges transferred to another jurisdiction, and one had his charges dropped by the police before the scheduled date for the first court appearance.

When an accused failed to appear in court, it was difficult to trace him. Sometimes tracing was possible through the researchers in the police studies, who would inform us if and when the accused was again apprehended by the police. Often it was a matter of chance that we would discover the accused on the docket again.

Among the 101 who consented to an interview, there was a considerable difference in the degree of co-operation. On the one hand, a few accused persisted in giving short replies in the hope of a quick conclusion to the matter, including one person who was already standing with his hand on the doorknob ready to make a hasty departure while still being asked the final questions. On the other hand, some respondents raised additional issues in extended interviews, and a few made voluntary contacts with the interviewer on occasions subsequent to the interviewing sessions.

Given the fact that the interview was an even more novel experience for most accused than what they faced in their interactions with criminal control agents, it was not surprising to find initial reticence in some accused. For example, an accused who pleaded not guilty and was eventually acquitted while his three co-accused were convicted seemed particularly sensitive when he was later asked in interview to describe what had happened in the alleged offences leading to his arrest. As he began to describe the events, he smiled. When asked why he was smiling, he replied, 'I don't know what's going on here. There's no cameras around here is there?'

It is difficult to assess why the accused volunteered for the interviews. We cannot rule out the possibility that some volunteered because they believed the researcher was but one more agent in the process to be co-operative with for strategic purposes. The fact that some accused fully confided in the researcher, even to the point of revealing offences unknown to the police, makes this possibility doubtful in their cases. However, in other cases the accused gave indirect indications that they may have perceived the situation as somewhat coerced. For example, a handful of respondents made disquieting comparisons between the interview room in the courthouse and the interrogation room in the police station, after they were asked to describe the nature and context of the police interrogation.

We hasten to point out that the interviewer did make every effort to stress the voluntary nature of participation in the study, and to dissociate herself from the criminal control agents. The fact that 20 accused blatantly refused to co-operate and thus were not interviewed at least demonstrates that participation in our enterprise was taken as much more voluntary than participation with the police and other criminal control agents, who only 'lost' three persons from their 'sample' (i.e. three persons failed to appear for court and remained subject to outstanding warrants).

Some accused may have had strategic reasons for volunteering to participate in the research interview. In one case a senior official in the prison where the respondent was serving his sentence stated that we could not even enter the prison to talk with the respondent because the respondent adamantly refused to co-operate. However, we persisted through repeated telephone calls to the official, and he eventually stated that the respondent had changed his mind and that we could enter the prison to conduct the interview. Upon completion of the interview, the respondent informed the interviewer that he had agreed to the interview in exchange for a promise of a transfer within the prison system. Among other things, this example shows that on the rare occasions when an accused was able to muster a strategic resource to use in negotiation, he was very capable of implementing it to his advantage. As discussed in the previous sections, the problem for the accused is not a personal lack of ability to deal with the world, only a basic lack of power resources similar to those available to other actors in the process.

In order to examine aspects of a case which the accused was unaware of or otherwise had no control over, especially concerning plea settlements worked out by others (chapter 4), we decided to make use of data from other sub-studies within the research program. Qualitative data from the defence lawyer, crown attorney, and police sub-studies were indexed to supplement and add to data available from the interviews with the accused. For each accused, we also made summaries containing a description of the original charges, changes in charges by the time of the trial date, numbers and types of court appearances and notes on the interaction that took place in each, and information about known discussions among any of the actors which pertained to the production of case outcomes. In relation to each accused interviewed, a file was created to include: 1) transcripts of the interview(s) with the accused, 2) transcripts of interviews with lawyers, 3) transcripts of conversations in the crown attorney's office, 4) summaries of observations made during study of the police, and 5) observational notes (not verbatim transcripts) on courtroom transactions, all of which were summarized on 6) index cards for the purpose of preparing the research report.

Extended methodological discussions for each of the sub-studies are contained in the respective reports on them. Ericson (1982) also includes a brief description of the municipality and the court system within which the research was conducted. We have previously sketched outlines of the methods for collection of data for the police studies, and we will here add outlines of the methods employed for the studies of the defence lawyer and the crown attorney.

The study of defence lawyers (Macfarlane, 1982) included one post-disposition interview with each lawyer who represented an accused in the sample, excluding two lawyers who refused to be interviewed. Except in two cases, duty counsel were excluded from the study because their involvement in any given case is minimal. The interview had an open-focused format, with an interview schedule to cover areas of questioning in a systematic manner. The interviews averaged three-quarters of an hour in length and covered background information about each lawyer, opinions regarding the legitimacy of the charges against their clients and police investigation of the case, and any discussions and negotiations, attempted and effected, among the lawyer, police, crown attorney, judge, and accused concerning issues related to bail hearings, elections, preliminary hearings, plea, sentence, and appeal. The total sample consisted of 75 interviews with 53 different lawyers representing 64 of 101 accused we interviewed and 19 of 30 accused we were unable to interview. Gaining co-operation from the lawyers was partly facilitated by the fact that each accused signed waivers giving his or her lawyer permission to divulge what would otherwise have been privileged information.

The primary data collected for the study of crown attorneys (Wilkins, 1982) were tape-recorded transcripts of discussions which took place in the crown attorney's office, particularly between 9 and 10 am, before court first convened for the day. Upon arriving in court, the researchers obtained all the courtroom dockets. They ascertained the courtroom in which an accused in the sample was appearing, and then the crown attorney handling the cases in that particular court was the subject of observation for the day. In addition, observations were made in the courtroom, and 'court packages' (the documents assembled by the police for the crown attorney, giving details about the alleged offence and the accused) were collected.

Data from the other sub-studies was used to determine what took place in transactions among the police, the lawyer, and the crown attorney, which the accused did not participate in, but which had a decided impact upon the outcome of his case. In some instances, the data from these other studies also proved to be a useful comparison with the accounts given by the accused.

There are obvious problems in trying to use material from a variety of studies with different theoretical agendas and different methodological approaches. One obvious problem is that there may well be different and even conflicting accounts available among the sources of data. Our sources include fieldnotes by observers, transcripts of conversations held in crown attorneys' offices, retrospective discussions with accused people, retrospective discussions with lawyers, and the official documents assembled by the various agents. In developing case analyses, one must piece together a wide range of viewpoints and discontinuous accounts of actions which do not always indicate clearly how decisions were made.

Some problems have been indicated through the material we presented in our case example. The accused gave an account of what happened during his interrogations, but we were not first-hand witnesses, because our police researcher was excluded from the interrogations. The lawyer's account indicates his belief that the accused was subject to unfair practices which may have led to an involuntary statement. Of course, he too was forced to rely upon accounts, first of the accused and then of the investigating detective, in making his assessment. Unless we make judgments democratically by deciding something did happen in a particular way because more than one of the actors said so, we are unable to say anything about whether it actually did.

We learned from the lawyer that he talked 'two or three times' by telephone with the detective about charge reduction and evidence. It was obviously impossible for us to 'tap' this information by any other means. The lawyer also said he talked about sentence recommendations with the crown attorney, but we have no conversation transcripts from the crown attorney sub-study to verify this. In this case at least, our knowledge of any transactions had to depend on the lawyer's account alone.

In each case we missed obtaining observations which might have confirmed or not particular accounts. We were only able to 'jump in' and take a snapshot of particular pieces of the process, rather than to shoot motion pictures of it from beginning to end. The problem manifests itself particularly when the snapshots are spliced together: the moving picture comes out disjointed and difficult to comprehend.

The disadvantages of restricted access for observational work were at least partially overcome in the studies of accused people and of lawyers by asking for accounts of all parts of the process. Restricted access did not mean completely ignoring certain issues, as with the police studies and the crown attorney study. The interview method allowed us to obtain data not otherwise available.

For example, if we consider aspects of transactions between police and accused, the interview with the accused gives us data on 1) processes we were excluded from observing (e.g. many interrogations), 2) processes we were unaware of through observation (e.g. whether the accused felt intimidated/ psychologically coerced into giving a statement), and 3) aspects we would not know the meaning of solely by observing them (e.g. while an accused may be given right-to-silence cautions, they may be irrelevant because the accused is unable to understand them or is too distressed to be paying attention – as the accused in our case example stated, he was 'too upset to be listening' when the cautions were given).

The interview method and the commitment to obtain accounts on all parts of the process were common to both the accused and lawyer studies. We thus rely on the lawyer material in particular, and in some instances we systematically link quantitative data from the two studies; we also rely on related qualitative material from them. Moreover, as we mentioned previously, our main interest in this study is to consider the ordering of the process as the accused perceives it, and his accounts are therefore given a central place. It is only in chapter 4 that we give detailed and sustained attention to the materials from the other sub-studies.

Another obvious methodological issue to raise is the problem of the subject's recall of events which sometimes took place weeks and even months prior to the interview. In the case example, the accused appeared to have particular difficulty in remembering events. His difficulty may have been more acute than most accused people we interviewed. However, many other accused claimed to have been high on drugs at the time of the offence and during their dealings with the police. The accused in the case example stated that he could not recall if he actually committed the act, or if he was giving an account which was a repetition of what was said by others about the act during the court hearings. In discussing his inability to recall the event clearly, he referred to the problem of 'suppression' or 'repression' which he might be experiencing, a 'fact' which he learned at the psychiatric remand facility. In talking about his dealings with the police, he refers to what was written on the police statement as what probably happened, but he said he could not otherwise recall. He also made frequent reference to television shows. All of these things indicate that for the accused who has been worked on by a number of agents and agencies, it is difficult to sort out what are *his* memories and interpretations as opposed to those supplied by someone else. This is not a problem peculiar to the situation of the accused.[12] Rather, we argue that the ordering the accused is subject to in the criminal process makes this a particular problem when asking him to reconstruct and reinterpret what has happened to him.

The discussion of these limitations is to be taken by the reader as an important cautionary note in assessing the following chapters. We wish to stress that we are sensitive to these limitations and have taken them into account in preparing this report. Such awareness is valuable in understanding both the situation of the accused and of the researcher who wishes to study him; far from creating a block to the reporting task, it is an integral part of the reporting.

A Profile of the Accused

In terms of charging patterns, there were no substantial differences between those accused interviewed and those we were unable to interview. In relation to the total sample of 131 accused, 295 charges were laid, meaning an average of slightly more than 2 charges against each accused person. However, 72 accused had only 1 charge against them. Among the others, 27 had 2 charges, 15 had 3 charges, and 17 had 4 or more charges. These figures do not include the total number of charges brought together for trial; by then, charges may have been added, dropped, or replaced with other charges as the accused and/or the police continued in their activities. Property offence charges were by far the most frequent (59 per cent of the 295 charges), followed by traffic-related offences under the Criminal Code (12 per cent), violent offences (12 per cent), public order offences (8 per cent), narcotics offences (4 per cent), sex offences (3 per cent), and others (2 per cent).

In response to a question asking the 101 interviewed accused to enumerate all previous convictions, 46 said they had none, 12 said 1, 8 said 2, 5 said 3, 7 said 4, 5 said 5, 7 said between 6 and 10, and 5 said between 11 and 20. For 6 accused we were unable to determine the number of previous convictions.

Almost one-half of the accused claimed to have no previous convictions. Among the remaining 55, 22 said they were previously convicted of the same offence as the one they were currently facing, 16 said they had convictions for offences in the same offence category (e.g. property) although not the same specific charge, and 17 said their previous convictions were unrelated to their current types of offence.

While 46 members of the sample claimed to be conviction-free, there were few who said they were complete novices to the criminal control process. Only 29 said they had never previously been charged with an offence by the police and only 10 claimed to have had absolutely no contact with the police, let alone a charge. Among the members of the interviewed sample, 14 said they had been incarcerated once before, 7 twice, 5 three times, 1 four times, and 1 five times. In sum, 30 per cent of the sample said they had extensive previous experience in the process including a period of incarceration, and 90 per cent of the sample claimed to have had at least entered the 'front end' of the process through interactions with the police.

The interview sample consists of 90 men and 11 women, providing a ratio of men to women just slightly higher than that available from other Canadian data (Fox and Hartnagel, 1979). They range in age from 16 to 57, with 40 being 16–21 years, 21 being 21–25 years, 15 being 26–30 years, 17 being 30–40 years, and 8 being 41 years or more. Almost one-half (48) were single; among the rest, 26 were married, 14 lived common-law, 8 were separated from their spouses, and 5 were divorced. Most (85) had spent the majority of their lives in Canada. At the time of the alleged offence, 32 were unemployed. A further 14 were full-time students and/or persons employed at intervals throughout the year, while the remainder (55) were in full-time employment. The usual type of employment held when they were working ranged from unskilled labourer (56), to technicians and semi-skilled (30), to professional (3), excluding 12 persons who, as students or housewives, are not traditionally considered to be part of the labour force.

These accused persons function as our guides as we proceed to explore in subsequent chapters how the criminal process is ordered. In chapter 2 we examine transactions between the police and the accused, focusing especially upon compliance of the accused with police orders and the ways in which much of the case becomes sealed at a very early stage in the process. In chapter 3, the accused's decision to engage a lawyer, and the nature of relationships with lawyers, are documented from the perspective of the accused. In chapter 4, we use data derived primarily from other studies in the wider research program to describe and analyse the process of plea transaction. Lawyers' accounts of this process and case examples are used to argue that it is typically in sessions held out of court, from which the accused is excluded, that the 'trial' is conducted and the outcome decided. In chapter 5 we contrast this knowledge of the order out of court with the accused's perception of it, especially as it relates to his decisions about a guilty plea. In chapter 6 we out-line both the order in court as it is physically and linguistically constituted to confirm the ideals of formal legal rationality and the dependent position of the accused. In court, trials are a rare occurrence which can be conceived as an appeal from the plea transaction 'trial'; most often, the only remaining issue is sentencing. In the final chapter, we briefly review our findings and our thesis as they pertain to questions of reform. We analyse critically the various policies and programs often suggested and occasionally implemented to reform the criminal process and conclude that none of them can effect funda-mental change of the dependent position of the accused within the ordering of justice. Our findings and our policy analysis raise some fundamental ques-tions about the criminal process, showing it to be a rigorously ordered mech-anism for social control at a considerable distance from an adversary system of justice.

2

Police Orders

Watch out for the fellow who talks about putting things in order! Putting things
in order always means getting other people under your control.
> Denis Diderot, *Supplement to Bougainville's 'Voyage'* (1796)

So full of artless jealousy is guilt,
It spills itself in fearing to be spilt.
> Shakespeare, *Hamlet* (1600)

The police command a pivotal position in determining the outcome of
criminal cases. They are backed up by a host of enabling rules which allow
them to justify a range of alternative decisions about investigation, charging,
and the construction of evidence. Several researchers have concluded that
conviction and even sentencing outcomes for accused persons are fundamentally influenced by the police. This conclusion has been reached through
interviews with accused persons (e.g. Casper, 1972; Klein, 1974; Bottoms and
McClean, 1976), through observation of police practices (e.g. Skolnick, 1966;
Medalie et al, 1968; Chevigny, 1969; Chatterton, 1976; Sanders, 1977; Helder,
1979; Ericson, 1981, 1982), and through a scrutiny of the legal rules ordering
the entire criminal process (Chambliss and Seidman, 1971; and especially
McBarnet, 1981).

The investigation of citizens is not carried out entirely at the whim of the
police. Rather, the police have a powerful array of enabling structural resources to justify a range of possible actions. These resources include enabling
procedural rules relating to arrest, search, and interrogation; 'all-purpose'
charges in the Criminal Code; and 'low visibility' and even secretive conditions of work (Ericson, 1981: especially chapter 6). Once the police decide
they can legitimate action within this enabling framework, the candidate for

accusation has very few options available to counter police efforts. Most accused simply comply with police efforts and hope for some amelioration along the way. At this earliest point in the criminal process the accused begins to appreciate his dependent position, a position which sets him up for subsequent transactions with his lawyer and in court.

Arrest

Once the police are in a position to show 'reasonable and probable' grounds for suspecting that a person has commited a criminal offence, they can approach the person and initiate an investigation directly with him through search, questioning, and/or interrogation. The police can usually back up their investigative actions with the power of arrest. In Canada, the legal definition of arrest is problematic because a person can be deemed to be under arrest even if he is not told he is, and is not physically taken hold of.[1] The test is a subjective one from the viewpoint of the suspect: does he feel free to leave the presence of the police officer? If he does not feel free to leave, he can consider himself to be under arrest even if there have not been direct verbal or physical restrictions on his freedom.

Among the 101 accused people we interviewed, 74 believed that they had been arrested by the police for the incident which brought them into our sample. It is particularly noteworthy that in this area, more than any other, the accused were highly perceptive of the legal reality of their situation: the vast majority defined arrest in general, and arrest in their own case, according to the restrictions on their freedom and/or being told by a police officer that they were under arrest.

In Table 2.1 we categorize definitions of arrest by the accused, and relate these to their reasons for believing they were or were not under arrest in the particular case which brought them into our sample. Among the 101 accused, 58 defined arrest in terms of 'restriction on freedom.' This category includes those who referred to being taken to the station (19), being detained at any point (17), being detained in a police car (12), and being detained at the police station (10). For many of these people, the meaning of arrest is obvious in the context: it comes when the suspect realizes that the officer has asserted total control over the situation: 'I would feel I was under arrest at the point where he quit discussing with me the problem and just took over the situation ... Like, say if he approached me and said, "Well, listen, you are [accused of] stealing this stuff," and I'd say, "Well I didn't steal it," and he'd say, "Yes you did, you are coming down to the station anyways." I'd feel under arrest because he's exercising his right to take me to the station against my will, which puts me under his power, which is what we would call actually under arrest although he didn't say the actual term, "You are under arrest."'

Among the 58 who defined arrest generally in terms of restriction on freedom, 44 said they felt under arrest in their own case. Their explanations

TABLE 2.1

Definitions by the accused of arrest and reasons why they felt they were or were not under arrest

Accused definitions of arrest	N	Why accused felt under arrest								Why accused did not feel under arrest					
		Restriction on freedom		Police told		Charged/ caught		Other		Police did not tell		Charge not serious		Other	
		N	%	N	%	N	%	N	%	N	%	N	%	N	%
Restriction on freedom	58	22	78.2	11	42.3	3	25.0	8	88.9	5	35.8	5	83.3	4	67.7
Police told	16	0	0.0	9	34.6	1	8.3	0	0.0	6	42.9	0	0.0	0	0.0
Police presence	15	6	21.8	3	11.5	3	25.0	0	0.0	1	7.1	0	0.0	2	33.3
Charged/ caught	7	0	0.0	1	3.9	5	41.7	0	0.0	0	0.0	1	16.7	0	0.0
Other definition	2	0	0.0	1	3.8	0	0.0	1	11.1	0	0.0	0	0.0	0	0.0
No information	3	0	0.0	1	3.8	0	0.0	0	0.0	2	14.2	0	0.0	0	0.0
Totals	101	28	100.0	26	100.0	12	100.0	9	100.0	14	100.0	6	100.0	6	100.0

concerning why they did or did not feel under arrest are enumerated in Table 2.1.

A further 16 defined arrest as occurring only when the police specifically tell the person he is under arrest. Among this group, 10 felt they were under arrest in their own case: 9 because they were told they were under arrest and 1 because he was immediately charged. In response to a separate series of questions, the accused frequently indicated that they were not told they were under arrest or given the reasons for arrest. Only 37 of the 101 interviewed accused said that the police told them they were under arrest. Five said they asked the officer if they were under arrest and were told nothing in return. Only 29 accused said that they were given reasons for their arrest, including 6 who said they were given a reason only after they asked for one. A further 6 said they asked for an explanation but were refused by the officer. In general, the perception of the accused that the police frequently do not state that the person is under arrest or give reasons for arrest is supported by our observational studies of police practices (Ericson, 1981: chapter 6; Ericson, 1982: chapter 6).

Returning to Table 2.1, we find that a further 15 accused defined arrest as occurring as soon as one comes into the presence of the police. In general, these persons felt that one is not free to resist any form of police probing and is under police control from the point of contact. A further seven accused defined arrest as occurring when one is caught in the act of committing an offence and/or is being charged at the point of contact (e.g. being searched on suspicion and found in possession of stolen articles, narcotics, etc).

We did not systematically question the accused as to why they decided to go along with the police once they felt they were under arrest. We do know from the data from the police studies (Ericson, 1981: chapter 6; Ericson, 1982: chapter 6) that suspects and accused people routinely complied with the police, and in only one instance (two accused in one case in our sample) did they successfully resist an attempt by a police officer to arrest them. In this case, the police officer returned to the station and had the victim take out a private information against the suspects, which in turn provided the basis for obtaining arrest warrants which were ultimately executed.

Many of the accused we interviewed addressed the issue of compliance during the course of their conversations about the arrest process. For several of them, the very question of why they complied with the arresting officer was absurd since, to them, there was absolutely no choice. For example an accused who was under arrest for driving while impaired was asked why he went along with the police to the station. He replied, 'Well, what was the alternative?' His curt answer indicated his view that there was no decision for him to take. Others gave more extended answers, but essentially made the same point. In the words of an accused charged with theft under $200, 'You're not going to go nowhere if they're going to take you with them ...

You're not going to argue with any kind of law, you're just supposed to assist them.'

For many suspects, compliance at the point of arrest had implications for compliance during the entire course of transactions with the police. The feeling of having lost power at the point of arrest was generalized to the feeling that nothing else could be done to ameliorate whatever the police decided to do with them. As one accused expressed it, "He was doing what he was going to do and there was nothing I could say that was going to stop him.' On this basis, many allowed subsequent searches, gave information, confessed, did not bother calling a third party, had their fingerprints and photographs taken, and signed their release forms.

For some accused the processing was so routine that they barely paid attention to it. Thus, an accused who claimed innocence persistently in relation to a mischief charge and who eventually had his charge withdrawn by the Crown, nevertheless submitted to everything the police asked of him short of confession. To him, the matter was routine; for example, he said he did not even bother reading the forms for release but just signed them, arguing that there was little else he could do if he wanted to go home.

For most accused, compliance was an obvious necessary element in routine dealings with the police. The persons we interviewed had a very realistic perception of the situation, including a knowledge that police authority is extensive enough to allow them to worsen a situation through more charges (e.g. 'obstruct police,' 'assault police,' 'cause a disturbance') or even more summary forms of punishment if the accused resists (see McBarnet, 1976, 1979; Freedman and Stenning, 1977: chapter 3). They knew that these charges could be used as the functional equivalent to 'contempt of court' charges, even if they are officially formulated in other terms. One accused said: 'Well, I figure [arrest is] just at that time you're in their power. If you do anything against it, you're automatically committing yourself to another charge. They're the boss, when they tell you to do something you got to do it, so you're more or less under arrest. You're under their power, so what's the difference?'

It should be stressed that while accused invariably felt the need to comply with police orders, they occasionally complied in a manner that was of potential stategic benefit to themselves. For example, an accused wanted for questioning in relation to indecent assault (male) allegations, said that he agreed to go to the police station after a detective telephoned him and asked him to, because he wished to avoid the possibility that the police would come to his home and embarrass him in front of his wife and neighbours. Two accused in one case eventually 'volunteered' to go to the police station once they had learned that they were 'wanted' because they felt that their role as informants would allow them to talk their way out of charges. Of course, these strategies were worked out *within* an order created by the police. This meant that there was no real decision concerning compliance with arrest, only a decision of how to deal with the police once under their control.

Search

Almost identical conclusions can be reached in examining 'decisions' by the accused about other police actions, including searches. In the interviewed sample, 49 said they were searched. These included searches of the person (17), of residence (11), of a vehicle (5), of the person and residence (6), of the person and vehicle (8), of the person, residence, and vehicle (1), and of the residence and vehicle (1). Only 5 respondents said that the police produced a search warrant in connection with the search(es) in their cases, all of which were residential searches. The infrequent use of search warrants is in keeping with the findings from our observational research on the police where consent searches were more frequent than searches with warrants (Ericson, 1981: chapter 6; Ericson, 1982: chapter 6). No accused person in our entire sample claimed to have successfully resisted an attempt by a police officer to conduct a search. This again accords with the findings in our police observational studies.

The 49 persons who said that they were subject to searches were asked on a systematic basis why they complied with the police effort to search. Twenty-five said they complied because they believed the police had the general authority to search whenever they wanted; that is, they saw the power to search invested in the police themselves, precluding any effective objection the accused might raise. Thus, when an accused was asked why he allowed a frisk search he replied, 'He's a police officer. Do I have a right not to let him?' Four additional persons said they submitted after the threat of physical force by the police. Two persons referred to the general legal authority of the police to conduct a search incident to arrest, two said they deferred because the officer's request was backed up by the legal authority of a search warrant, and one said he conceded after the officer threatened to obtain a search warrant. Seven persons indicated that they allowed the search because they believed the police would find nothing anyway, while five gave other idiosyncratic reasons, and three gave no reasons (including two where the residential search was conducted in their absence).

It should come as no surprise that the accused defer so readily to police efforts in the area of search. They exhibit a clear understanding of the legal fact that the police do have extensive powers of search, especially in relation to a person who is likely to be accused. As McBarnet (1976: 177) argues, we must focus upon 'the procedural powers and legal definitions which enable, indeed invite, the police to use their discretion in this way' (see also McBarnet, 1981: 39 – 40). As we have shown in our observational research on the police

(Ericson, 1981, 1982), the police routinely conduct searches with the consent of suspects, even in situations which are no more than stops on general suspicion. Moreover, they are just as routinely able to obtain search warrants from justices of the peace if they wish to take the trouble to do so. There is a general authority to search incident to arrest, as well as particularly enabling provisions in the Ontario Liquor Licence and Control Act and the federal Narcotics Control Act (see generally Freedman and Stenning, 1977: chapter 3). Given this legal arsenal in the command of the police, in most situations an accused would be ill advised to offer any resistance.

For many, the question of why one would comply with a search was as absurd as the question of why one would go along with the police at the point of arrest. For example, an accused whose residence was searched after he had been interrogated but refused to confess to 'shoplifting' allegations, was asked why he allowed the search. He replied, 'Well, how can I say no?' This was a particularly interesting response because our police observational data informs us that this search was conducted without warrant after the accused had persistently refused to consent to it (Ericson, 1981: 155).

As we discussed in relation to arrest, accused people frequently explained compliance in terms of a belief that resistance would incur further assertions of police power. Police power is taken for granted by the accused so that its exercise becomes routine. Thus, in describing the personal and vehicle searches incident to his arrest for serious allegations, including illegally discharging a firearm, an accused stated:

A: They just frisked me.
Q: Why did you let them?
A: I got no choice.
Q: OK. Did they search your car?
A: Yea.
Q: And did they ask for that?
A: They found the gun on the – No.
Q: They didn't ask?
A: They *don't* ask!

In another case, patrol officers were called to the residence of the accused on a 'domestic' complaint initiated by his neighbours. Once admitted to the house, the officers discovered some hash pipes and asked if they could conduct a search. The suspect consented, and the search eventually turned up what the officers believed to be hash oil. A charge was laid, but later withdrawn when the analysis revealed the substance was perfume (as the accused had contended all along). The accused's rationale for consenting is revealed in his extended discussion of the search:

Q: He took the pipes?

A: Yes, he just stuffed them in his pocket and walked away and then he said, then he turned around and said, 'Do you mind if we look around?' And I figured, well, if I say no you can always get a search warrant and come back anyways, and I've got nothing to hide, so sure, go ahead.

...

Q: Did he say why he wanted the pipes when he took the pipes?

A: No he didn't, he just said, 'I'm taking them.'

Q: And you let him take them?

A: Well, what can you do?

Q: Yes, but why did you let him take them?

A: Because I felt very persecuted by him. Like I felt, like, well, if I say no he is going to get excited about the thing and make trouble or something. Because I have seen circumstances where they have made trouble for people to the extent, like, they can search your home and then again, they can *search* your home. In other words, like they can actually go in and wreck the house if they wanted, if they have reason to believe that they can find what they are looking for. They have legal right to anything, I have seen this go on before.

Several accused had similar perceptions, believing it was best to allow a search and follow other police orders, even though they felt there were no grounds for it or they actually protested their innocence. An accused stated that he complied with a personal search because he believed that otherwise he would be charged with 'resisting arrest.' He gave similar reasons for complying with other police orders, including signing a statement of confession: refusal would simply have made the police take more power over him, including delaying his release. This accused subsequently defended himself in court. He was successful in having the statement of confession ruled inadmissible, and he was found not guilty on one charge of possession of stolen property and had a second count dismissed.

As we shall illustrate in subsequent chapters, this attitude of compliance was, most often, enough to seal the accused's fate by precluding defence options at later stages in the process. By the time they reached court, the accused usually had very little left to fight with.

Some accused argued that compliance with police orders regarding search was strategic in setting a tone of co-operation which might eventually yield some leniency. One accused who was a lawyer charged with 'impaired driving' and 'over 80 mg,' said he co-operated with the search and every other part of the police investigation in the hope that it would buy him leniency in court in the form of the police not objecting to considerations of charge and sentence leniency. While he was the only accused in our sample who was a lawyer, he did not need to be a lawyer to realize, along with the others, that he

had no choice anyway. The police had their reservoir of legitimate justifications to secure their order; the accused only had his reserved demeanour to
keep open the possibility of future leniency.

Interrogation and Confession

Compared with the legal and situational powers of the police in relation to
arrest and search, their powers for securing confessions are apparently more
limited. For example, in Canada there is a legal right to silence available to
the accused. This right comes about through the absence of a right of the
police to compel legally an answer to their questions, not through a privilege
against self-incrimination (Law Reform Commission of Canada, 1973: 6). Of
course, as we shall soon document, the police have an array of interrogation
strategies and tactics which mean that this right to silence is usually negated in
practice (McBarnet, 1981: 53 – 9). As Greenawalt (1974: 236 – 7) argues, there
is no such thing as a 'perfect' right to silence because, among other things, the
suspect is likely to have a 'natural feeling that his chances of appearing
innocent may depend on his explaining himself [which is] reinforced by the
predictable police response to silence.' Under these circumstances, silence
may signify yet another symptom of suspicious behaviour, or of 'guilt.' In
practice, the police will deploy their repertoire of power resources to secure
the confession they want, and the suspect's resistance must be viewed in this
light. At best, the rules and practices relating to police interrogations support
the stronger rather than the weaker (Law Reform Commission of Canada,
1973: 11; Greenawalt, 1974: 266-7; Zander, 1978; Morris, 1978).

Many researchers and commentators have observed that interrogations
and confessions are not often crucial to the police in terms of laying charges
and securing convictions. Thus, Blumberg (1970: 280, 289) cites some early
American studies which give figures indicating that only 6 to 10 per cent of
indictments involved confessions to the police prior to indictment. Blumberg
states that his own observations confirm these data. Similarly, in a study
conducted in Pittsburgh (Seeburger and Wettick, 1967), the researchers esti-
mate that confessions were necessary to secure conviction in only 20 per cent
of the cases they examined. Wald and associates (1967: especially
1581 – 8, 1591) judge that only 3 of 90 interrogations were 'essential' to the
cases they studied, while a further 12 of 90 were 'necessary.' Wald and
associates also had detectives do evaluations, and in 57 of 70 cases the
detectives judged interrogation to be 'unnecessary.' Reiss and Black (1967:
55) produce data to show that in field patrol settings, officers *always* had
evidence other than confessions to support their decisions and to induce
confessions. Some authors (e.g. Ayres, 1970: 275; Wald et al, 1967: 1554)
argue that while interrogations and confessions have little effect on case

outcome for the accused, they are useful in gaining intelligence about other crimes and criminals and for gaining the prosecutor's approval for proceeding with the case to the court stage. More recent research in Britain by Baldwin and McConville (Royal Commission on Criminal Procedure, 1980b: 35) 'indicates that there is such a close correspondence between the existence of a confession and eventual conviction at trial that one must not underestimate the importance of the first stage of the criminal process.' Baldwin and McConville found that while in one-half of the cases the accused's statement was considered to have little bearing on the strength of the crown's case, in one-fifth of the cases the crown's case would have been 'fatally weakened' if the accused's statement was not taken into account.

Many of these studies fail to provide detail about the nature of the independent evidence that the police can use to induce confessions and/or proceed with charges without confessions. Obviously, statements of confession are unnecessary in some types of offence where there are well-established independent sources of evidence (e.g. breathalyser tests for drivers who are apparently impaired; drugs possessed in violation of the Narcotics Control Act), while in other areas (e.g. interpersonal offences such as indecent assault; the theft rather than possession components of property offences) the securing of confessions is usually important, and sometimes crucial. Police manuals (e.g. Inbau and Reid, 1967: 213) sometimes stress that confessions are important even in routine cases because much police work does not involve Sherlock Holmes-style production of physical evidence leading to the apprehension of a suspect, but rather processing of persons prior to any detailed investigation (for supporting empirical evidence, see Greenwood et al, 1975; Bottomley and Coleman, 1980; Royal Commission on Criminal Procedure 1980, 1980a; Steer, 1980; Ericson, 1981). From the perspective of the police, confessions are often only 'icing on the cake' and/or a means of reducing the volume of investigative work a police officer would otherwise have to undertake. However, they are also sometimes the only means of legitimating charges where other evidence is lacking.

From the perspective of the accused person, the decision about whether to confess to an offence is one over which he does have some control. If he can withstand the manipulative and coercive techniques of police interrogators, and if he does not perceive strategic advantage in co-operating, he can legitimately resist in a way that is usually impossible in relation to arrest and search.

Many accused said they gave verbal statements in field settings during preliminary questioning and prior to interrogation (defined as in-custody questioning): 57 said they gave some form of verbal statement at this point while 41 said they did not. Most frequently a verbal confession was forthcoming in circumstances where the police had other evidence (e.g. a youth who was searched and had marijuana found upon his person admitted that it belonged to him). Nineteen persons said they confessed in these circumstances. A further 9 said it was strategic to co-operate because it would bring reciprocal lenience from the police. Another group of 8 said they wished to provide their own version of what happened and did so even if there was no other evidence against them. Another group felt they had nothing to hide by giving a verbal statement, including 7 who did not explicitly deny the offence and 5 who did. A further 6 persons gave idiosyncratic reasons, and 3 gave none.

Given that the police have no right legally to compel answers to their questions, it may be surprising that so many accused gave verbal statements. However, there are obvious factors against silence even at the beginning of a transaction with the police. First, there is a strong tendency to want to explain oneself if serious allegations are being made, especially if these allegations are backed up with apparently cogent arguments by the police that they have strong independent evidence. Second, there is the factor of ignorance on the part of the suspect. As we document shortly, cautions about rights are not usually given to suspects at the initial point of apprehension, and some of our respondents reported that the thought of not answering police questions never entered their minds. As one person related in discussing whether he had a choice not to answer police questions, 'I never thought of it that way ... I just answered them.' Third, countering the police by refusing to answer their questions can pose the same problems as unco-operativeness at any other stage in the criminal process: it can be taken by officials as a sign of unwilling-ness to accept what the officials see as 'obvious' guilt and can therefore open up the possibility of more severe official action to ensure that the person realizes the gravity of the circumstances and his guilt. Fourth, as Ayres (1970: 277) states, suspects sometimes think they can escape charges by 'talking their way out' with police, but they often end up sealing their own fate. In the eyes of both the accused's lawyer and the accused himself, this often occurs when he fears that co-suspects are unfairly putting the blame on him. The suspect attempts to clarify his own position and ends up condemning everyone, including himself.

Among the 41 who said they did not give a verbal statement during field questioning, only one-half gave reasons indicating that they were exercising their right to silence. Among these, 16 said they refused because they did not wish to incriminate themselves, and 4 said they did not feel obliged to offer a statement even though one was demanded. A further 18 said there was no police request for a verbal statement and they did not volunteer one. In summary, of the accused who gave reasons as to why they did or did not make a verbal statement to the police at this stage, 59 said that the police had asked them for one. Of these 59 accused who were asked to make a statement, only 14 (24 per cent) actually refused to give one.

Among the 81 respondents who said they were subject to some form of in-custody questioning, 40 said they gave written statements to the police. If we eliminate the 22 who said they did not give a written statement because the police did not ask for one, we find that 19 of 59 who were asked to give a written statement successfully refused. The articulated reasons for refusal included not wishing to incriminate oneself (7), maintaining innocence (5), a simple refusal to co-operate with the police (3), other idiosyncratic reasons (3), and no reason given (1). As with verbal statements, only a small minority refused what the police wanted, hoping that it would serve their strategic advantage.

The apparently low level of resistance to police efforts at gaining some form of co-operation through confession is in contrast to the findings of others who claim that suspects are very unlikely to confess (e.g. Reiss and Black, 1967: 54; Wald et al, 1967: 1562). However, more recent studies provide data to document the high proportion of confessions to the police (e.g. Bottoms and McClean, 1976: 115; Royal Commission on Criminal Procedure, 1980, 1980a, 1980b). Our own observations of how the police dealt with the suspects in our sample as well as other suspects who were part of the observational studies of the police confirm that most suspects do not successfully resist giving a confession (Ericson, 1981, 1982).

The accused gave a variety of reasons for providing the police with a written statement. Eight said that the police had sealed the case with other evidence. The same number of respondents said they gave a statement because it was part of an exchange for leniency. These persons were involved in transactions with the police that included a bargaining element. However, as we consider later in this section, these 'bargains' were almost always police-initiated and carried much more advantage to them than to the accused. A further one dozen respondents said they were coerced into a confession through fear of the police; this fear was of police use of force (seven), or of further investigation which might make matters worse (five). Only three said they confessed because they had committed the offence and wished to 'come clean.' A further nine gave idiosyncratic reasons for their decisions to comply. Two accused in separate cases signed statements and co-operated with the police against the explicit advice of their lawyers.

The research conducted by Wald and his associates (1967) indicates that in the opinion of lawyers the accused should not give any statement at the time of arrest. The vast majority (51 of 55) of the lawyers they interviewed said they would normally advise a client against giving a statement at the time of arrest. Wald and associates also provide data to support the argument that later negotiations about plea and sentence were more successful if there had not been a confession. We have no systematic data on the topic, although many of the lawyers who represented the accused in our study expressed similar opinions, while a few felt that a confession might be beneficial as a sign of co-operation in an otherwise tight case from the viewpoint of the prosecution.

Some accused said they simply conformed with every aspect of police orders because they felt they could not do otherwise. For them, police authority was the same throughout the process, no matter what action it was they were undertaking. Thus, an accused said he signed a written statement, 'Because I was told to sign it,' full stop.

Some accused said they did offer resistance to a full confession for a period but then 'caved in' under police pressure. For example, an accused was caught fleeing from the scene of a residential break-in and eventually confessed to this offence as well as to others in the same area. The detectives then did further investigations and treated him as a suspect for several additional break-and-enter offences, eventually re-arresting him. As the suspect said, at this stage the 'game' was clearly over and there was no use in pursuing it beyond the obvious checkmate advantage held by the police. The accused said that at this point he confessed to everything he could remember: 'If it was up to 17 it could have been 1700, it wouldn't have made much difference.' It is worth mentioning that this accused ultimately pleaded guilty to all charges read out in court, including several he said (in interview) he was unsure of. It did not matter to him because his lawyer had worked out a satisfactory arrangement about sentence with the crown attorney, so that the number of convictions was irrelevant to sentence (he apparently did not think of his criminal record). His lawyer stated in interview that without the statements to the police, there was no case on 15 of the 17 counts against the accused.

Other accused at least hinted at a strategic element in their decision to give a confession. As already mentioned, the strategy employed most frequently was based on the belief that co-operation would yield some immediate or future form of police leniency, e.g. charge reduction, not charging certain counts, not blocking bail, earlier release from police custody, a favourable report to the crown attorney and in court, not pursuing further investigations against the accused and/or his friends.

Among those who did not give statements, there was rarely any strategy except the desire to avoid obvious condemnation of oneself at an early point in the criminal process. Some accused who refused to give statements offered unique rationales for their decisions. For example, one said he did not know what the proper procedure was, and that this was reason enough *not* to sign a statement. Another respondent said he did not provide a statement because 'They're just out to hang you' and later furthered his views by saying, 'The police don't go around saying you're not guilty and put you in jail [awaiting trial].' In other words, the police are committed to the view that the person they suspect is guilty and their every effort is directed toward constructing and establishing that fact. One of the very few resources available to the accused is to refuse to commit himself to the police view from the beginning by giving them a confession.

Access to a Third Party

Another potential resource at the disposal of the suspect is to contact a third party for advice and assistance in dealing with the police. Although there is no legal requirement on the police to inform the person that he can call a third party,[2] the Canadian Bill of Rights states that a request from a suspect to make a call should not be denied.[3] Among our respondents this resource was rarely employed to strategic advantage.

Among the 81 interviewed accused who said they were subject to in-custody questioning, 41 said they requested access to a third party. Of the 18 who said their request was for a lawyer, 16 wanted advice, 1 was told to call by the police, and 1 wanted to let someone know his whereabouts. Of 20 who said they wished to call a relative or friend, 13 wanted to let someone know their whereabouts and 7 wanted advice. In some situations the accused wished to call a relative or friend, hoping in turn to ask that person to contact a lawyer.

Among the 40 who did not request a call to a third party, 19 said they felt it would be of no benefit, 8 said they did not know who to call, 6 said they never thought of it at the time, 4 gave idiosyncratic reasons, and 3 gave no reason. Some of these persons indicated that they felt they had no right to request anything because they were completely powerless in the face of police authority. As a respondent expressed it, 'I didn't feel to [call anyone], I just spoke to whoever wanted to speak to me.' For many, it was useless to get a lawyer because they had already decided that the matter was foreclosed and that a lawyer would be an unnecessary cost. Thus, an accused charged with 'break, enter and theft' stated, 'I signed a statement, a plea of guilty, so I figured there's no sense in getting a lawyer up here, costing me money which I can't afford, because this is why I pulled the job off in the first place, because I needed money.'

Several respondents gave less obvious reasons for not requesting access to a third party. The most unusual situation was that of an accused who voluntarily went to the police station to confess to three break, enter and theft occurrences and implicated a co-suspect in the process. Against her lawyer's wishes, she repeatedly assisted the detective by successive confessions, the recovery of stolen property, and acting as an informant. She said that she co-operated because she trusted the detective, and she apparently felt that her relationship with the detective obviated the need to mobilize other resources. She placed all her faith in the detective; indeed, she equated her confession to him with confession to priests.

Other accused said they did not call a lawyer because they did not know one, and they did not call friends or relatives because they wished to keep their troubles private. One accused said he never planned to call a third party because he had never planned to give a statement to the police and felt quite capable of resisting police pressure on his own.

A few accused had third-party contacts even if they did not request one. This was most likely to occur when the investigating officers decided to conduct a residential search with the suspect present in their custody, and contact was made with other residents (e.g. a roommate or spouse).

According to the 41 respondents who said they made a request, only 7 of 20 requests for calls to relatives/friends were granted; 5 of 18 requests for calls to lawyers were granted; and 1 of 3 requests for calls to other people was granted.[4] Moreover, 7 of 13 requests granted were only granted after delay, usually after the accused had already confessed. Furthermore, while 12 of 13 of those accused who were granted calls said that they were able to complete them, only 3 said that they consequently received explicit advice to remain silent in the face of police questioning. In only one case did the lawyer's advice lead to the cessation of the police interrogation and no statement; in this case, the lawyer called the police station and asked to speak with his client, having been alerted by the client's girlfriend that the accused had been arrested.

These data clearly inform us that the police did not regularly allow the accused the advantage of third-party access. Moreover, our observation data on the police inform us that when access was allowed it was most often when the case was 'tight' from the police viewpoint (Ericson, 1981, 1982). Furthermore, when the accused themselves decided to request access, it was more often than not to a person who was not a lawyer, for purposes other than legal advice. Many respondents said they were more concerned that their friends or relatives would be worried by their absence than they were about their own legal position with the police.

Some respondents who were able to contact their lawyers simply received advice on matters where no choice existed. For example, an accused said he refused to sign the form of release until he could call his lawyer. The police then allowed the call, but the accused said that his lawyer simply told him to sign the form, indicating that there was no choice given the formal rules relating to release procedures. Another accused actually consulted with his lawyer prior to turning himself in to the police. The accused said his lawyer did not deem it necessary to accompany the accused to the station, and he was unavailable for advice when the accused ran into difficulty over signing a written confession.

Cases like this confirm the views of other accused that there was little use in mobilizing support because the situation was already decided. Indeed, some felt that trying to gain assistance might antagonize the police to his or her ultimate detriment. For example, an accused claimed that as soon as he demanded a lawyer he was placed under arrest.[5] He believed that if he had not made this demand at the outset he might have been able to 'talk his way out' during the preliminary questioning.

In sum, while access to a third party was a possible strategic resource of the accused, they did not or could not use it to their advantage except on rare occasions.[6] Like other elements in transactions with the police, this resource was seen to be of limited value in the face of the power resources of the police, which could be used effectively to neutralize it, overcome it, or simply ignore it.

Right-to-Silence Cautions

Another apparent protection for the suspect is the requirement that the police tell him about his right to remain silent and that anything he does say may be taken down in writing and used as evidence in court. The Canadian procedure is linked with the Judges' Rules in the United Kingdom; these rules serve as guidelines for the police and do not have the status of law (cf Kaufman, 1974). Moreover, failure of the police to caution a suspect, who subsequently provides a written statement of confession and is charged, does not in itself make the statement inadmissible as evidence in court; rather, the fact that there was no caution is but one factor which the judge takes into account in ruling on whether the statement appeared to be voluntarily given. Legally, this places the Canadian police and the suspects they confront in a very different position than their American counterparts, who are subject to the *Miranda* ruling and related decisions that have followed it. Practically, the police are able to circumvent the rules, whether or not they have the status of law (cf Medalie et al, 1968; Morris, 1978; Zander, 1978), and because the vast majority of cases are disposed of by guilty pleas without inquiry into police practices (Grosman, 1969; Klein, 1976).

In Table 2.2 we present the responses of 81 persons who said they were subject to interrogation concerning whether or not they were cautioned, when they were cautioned, and whether or not they gave a written statement of confession. The fact that over one-half report not having been cautioned accords with American studies on the subject which followed the *Miranda* decision (e.g. Wald et al, 1967; Medalie et al, 1968; Ayres, 1970), and with more recent research in America (e.g. Arcuri, 1976: 178). However, there is an anomaly in our data when we compare it with findings from observational research on the police (Ericson, 1981, 1982). It was the standard practice of the police in the jurisdiction to have the right-to-silence cautions printed at the head of each statement-of-confession form. Therefore, even if the cautions were not verbally stated to the suspect, they were invariably present in written form if the suspect ultimately gave a written statement of confession. It is therefore remarkable that 12 people who said that they gave written statements of confession said that they were not cautioned. Of course, this

TABLE 2.2

Whether and when rights' caution given by the police and whether or not written statement of confession given to the police

Whether and when rights' caution given by the police	Total		Written statement of confession		No written statement of confession	
	N	%	N	%	N	%
No caution	45	55.5	12	30.0	33	80.5
Caution before anything said about alleged offence	4	4.9	2	5.0	2	4.9
Caution after some discussion about alleged offence	12	14.8	8	20.0	4	9.8
Caution after a verbal statement of confession	14	17.3	13	32.5	1	2.4
Caution – unable to recall when given	2	2.6	2	5.0	0	0.0
Unable to recall whether caution given	4	4.9	3	7.5	1	2.4
Totals	81	100.0	40	100.0	41	100.0

procedure, to be effective, requires that the suspect has read it and understood it. Moreover, even if these two conditions are met, the procedure does not protect the accused from giving a statement in the first place. It only protects him from signing the investigating officer's written version of his verbal statement if he reads it and comprehends it.

American research on the topic has consistently referred to problems of suspects understanding the warnings. Medalie and associates (1968: 1374) report that 15 per cent of their sample of 85 'post-Miranda defendants' did not understand the right to silence warning. Wald et al (1967: 1573) directly observed transactions between the police and suspects and noted: 'On several occasions ... a suspect seemed to be thrown off guard by the warnings. He apparently thought that if the police could give these warnings they must have him. In such cases – albeit a small number – warnings may actually have aided in obtaining a statement.' Ayres (1970: 276) reports that even on the rare occasions when the detectives he observed did give all the *Miranda* warnings, 'the advice was often defused by implying that the suspect had better not exercise his rights, or by delivering the statement in a formalized, bureaucratic tone to indicate that the remarks were simply a routine, meaningless legalism' (for supporting evidence in England, see Royal Commission on Criminal Procedure, 1980, 1980a).

The reports of many accused who did recall being cautioned confirm the view that there may have been problems of understanding. Interestingly, many accused described the caution in terms more similar to the American than the Canadian situation. For example, one person described his rights as 'what you hear on the cop shows, a right to an attorney and all that.' Other accused referred to the specific context of the caution as being similar to other 'legalese' they had heard through the course of their experiences in the criminal process. For example, when asked what the police officer said in cautioning him, one accused replied, 'He said all those mumbo jumbo words and he read to me, la la la la la.'

As indicated in Table 2.2, a substantial number of persons who were charged said they were not cautioned. Among the 33 persons who said they were not cautioned and did not sign a written statement, 19 gave as the reason for not signing a statement the fact that the police did not ask for one. Among the 32 persons who recalled being cautioned, only 4 said the caution was given before anything was said about the alleged offence. Obviously it was not the practice of the police to interrogate in accordance with the English Judges' Rule that 'persons in custody should not be questioned without the usual caution first being administered.'

Among the 16 who said they did receive some form of caution before confession, 10 said they gave written confessions: 3 because the police had other evidence, 2 because they feared other police investigation, 2 because of possible leniency offered by the police, and 3 for other individualistic reasons. Thus, the police were more often than not successful in securing a written confession even on the rare occasions when they gave cautions in advance. Wald et al (1967: 1562) have also commented on the fact that interrogations are particularly 'successful' for the police when cautions are given. Perhaps the police give advance cautions only in cases that are otherwise secure.

Some accused treated the cautions about the right to silence in the same way as other resources (e.g. access to a third party): it was meaningless because they had already decided to admit to whatever allegations were being made aginst them. Thus, an accused charged with multiple counts of theft from cars in a parking garage said there was 'no sense' to a caution when one is caught 'red-handed' and that to exercise the right to silence would have only made matters worse in his own case:

Q: Did the police ever caution you about your rights?
A: No.
Q: Do you know what your rights are?
A: Pretty well, I think, yeah.
Q: What are they?
A: Like, the right to remain silent and all that?
Q: Uh-huh.
A: Yeah, well, I know pretty well all that, but there's no sense in it.
Q: Could you tell me what you think they are?
A: Well, you've got the right to remain silent, you, until you can have an attorney present, if you want, during questioning and, I don't know. That's about it that

I know of. But, like [there's] no sense really in doing something like that if you're caught red-handed.

Q: Why?

A: Because you know you're caught and it's easier. Well it just seems to go easier if you say something. If you tell them.

Q: Easier in what way?

A: Oh, just in the way the police act toward you, the way you're treated.

Certainly, the view of researchers and commentators on the police (e.g. Wald et al, 1967; Ayres, 1970; Morris, 1978; McBarnet, 1979, 1981; Zander, 1978; Ericson, 1981, 1982; Royal Commission on Criminal Procedure, 1980) is that it matters little whether there is a legal rule like *Miranda* or guidelines like the Judges' Rules. The police can work the rules to their advantage. The accused left us with the impression that the right-to-silence caution is a legal formalism that they see as largely irrelevant to their circumstances, or is simply not mentioned at all. The accused certainly did not see it as a possible resource to be used to justify silence. The vast majority were more interested in the problem of how to deal with the police in order to obtain early release and to convey a spirit of co-operation which might be to their benefit later in court.

Dealings between Police and the Accused for Information and Confessions

In addition to manipulating whether and when they would give right-to-silence cautions, the police had a reservoir of threats and promises which they could use to ease their task of securing a confession and ultimately constructing charges. As Klein (1976: 124) has argued, the police significantly shape what he calls the 'negotiation process' (i.e. dealing over charges and sentences and other forms of apparent leniency). In Klein's study, 'The police were involved in 79% of the 202 cases of bargaining described by our informants. In fact they were the only officials directly involved in conducting the negotiation with the offenders in 52% of these cases.'

Our research confirms the view that the police play a pivotal role in negotiation, although, as we shall consider later, the process is often characterized by manipulation and coercion rather than negotiation (cf Strauss, 1978). Much of this influence is not visible to the accused, and the accused is either unaware of it or receives his information at second hand through his lawyer. However, the accused does have direct knowledge of police 'bargaining' and 'dealing' to the extent that these occur in investigations and interrogations.

Thirty-nine accused said they received promises or threats regarding 'co-operation' in the form of giving statements, supplying information of potential use to the police, or both. In exchange for co-operation, the police were said to have offered one or more of leniency over charges, i.e. reduced charge(s) and/or no charge(s); leniency over release (not opposing bail and/or earlier release from police custody); court recommendations (emphasizing with the crown attorney and/or judge that the accused had co-operated); no further investigation (against the accused and/or his associates); and abstaining from the threat of, or use of, physical force. The types of offers said to have been attempted by the police, and whether agreement was reached, are enumerated in Table 2.3. The extent of dealing reported by our respondents is higher than that documented in some studies (e.g. Wald et al, 1967: 1545), but supports the impressionistic observations of other authors (e.g. Bottoms and McClean, 1976: 230).

Promises and/or threats regarding written statements alone were the most 'successful' from the police viewpoint: 17 of 20 of these resulted in agreement, compared with only 2 of 5 for information alone and 8 of 14 for both a written statement and information. This indicates that the accused were less willing to inform on others than on themselves.

Other accused believed that while informing on an accomplice or about other criminal activity could yield some minor personal gains, it could also open up the possibility of future repercussions from these others. Moreover, several believed that while the police were often full of promises when making arrangements in exchange for information, they frequently reneged on their promises so that what at first appears to be a deal could turn out to be no bargain at all.

Some accused saw their options as foreclosed because they believed that even if they did not sign a statement they would be charged anyway. They concluded that it was simply easier on everyone concerned to give the police what they wanted. In many respects, this situation is similar to the one the accused faces at a later stage when he must decide upon a plea: if he perceives the odds as stacked against him if he goes to trial, he is likely to accept an arrangement for a guilty plea in the hope that he will be rewarded for his co-operative disposition.

In general, the impression left by our respondents was that offers by the police were not often bargains, but rather threats which reflected police omnipotence, or manipulative promises which offered only an appearance of advantage. Only one accused said he initiated the attempted agreement; the other 38 attempted agreements were reported to be on the initiative of the police. The accused appreciated that the police would not initiate these practices with the intention, or predicted effect, of making major concessions to the suspect. One accused provided the analogy of the police as loan sharks whose currency is information rather than money; he observed that the police are able to back up their demands with similar techniques used by other loan sharks, but additionally the police have the advantage that their role is legitimated by the state.

TABLE 2.3

Police promises/threats to induce co-operation by the accused

Police promises/threats	number agreement reached / number agreement attempted
Regarding written statements only	
Charge and release leniency	6/6
Court recommendation and release leniency	5/6
Release leniency	1/3
Charge leniency	2/2
Charge and court recommendation leniency	1/1
Court recommendation leniency	1/1
Court recommendation leniency and no further investigation	1/1
Total	17/20
Regarding information only	
Charge leniency	1/2
Charge and release leniency	1/1
Release leniency	0/1
Court recommendation leniency	0/1
Total	2/5
Regarding written statements and information	
Court recommendation of leniency and no physical force	3/4
No physical force	1/3
Charge leniency and no physical force	1/2
No further investigation	1/1
Court recommendation and charge leniency	1/1
Release and charge leniency	1/1
Charge leniency	0/1
Release leniency and no physical force	0/1
Total	8/14
Overall total	27/39

Consideration of accounts by the accused of some of these transactions, and the factors that they said influenced their decisions, further illuminate the situations they faced.

The threat of delayed release, or of holding an accused for a bail hearing, is a powerful weapon in the hands of the police. Other research has documented both the extent of 'bail bargaining' (e.g. Bottoms and McClean, 1976: 200ff) and the fact that police threats in this area are cogent because the police have been shown to have a significant influence on magistrates' bail decisions (for a review of relevant studies, see Bottomley, 1973 especially 84 – 103; see also Bottoms and McClean, 1976: 196). As recorded in Table 2.3 a total of 19 attempted agreements were said to involve an element of 'release leniency,' and in 14 of these, agreements were reached.

One accused who stated explicitly that he offered a statement in relation to leniency over release had been arrested along with three accomplices, for a series of thefts from automobiles in an underground garage, after uniformed officers caught them in the garage. The evidence seemed to be against the accused whether he confessed or not, and a statement seemed an expedient way of gaining early release:

Q: When you were at the police station, who first mentioned release, was it the police or you?

A: Police.

Q: What did they say?

A: You'll get out a lot faster if you co-operate with us.

Q: And what did 'co-operate' mean?

A: Give us, to sign our statements.

Q: Did they say that specifically, or?

A: Yeah. 'Cause he says, like I wasn't going to sign my statement and they were just going to put me back in the cell and forget about me. So I decided to sign my statement. So I signed it.

Among those who did not yield to pressure to give the police what they wanted in exchange for release leniency was a person who had allegedly caused damage to a field by driving a car through it, providing grounds for a 'mischief' charge. The essence of the proposed arrangement was that the accused would not be held for a bail hearing if he gave a statement which named the driver of the car. He declined the offer and was held for a bail hearing. The accused summarized the interrogation as follows:

A: He just said, 'Tell me who was driving the car, or you are going to — jail.' He says, 'If you tell me who was driving the car you can be let out on personal bail from the police station.' I told him, 'No, what can I do? I don't know, can't remember. — jail.'

Q: Oh, I see, so in other words they wanted you to make a statement about the driver and then they would release you?

A: Uh-huh.

Q: Do you think they were being honest, I mean would they have released you if you gave them the name?

A: Probably.

Q: Then why didn't you give them the name?

A: Because I just don't sign statements, it's just something you don't do.

Q: Why is that?

A: 'cause you just don't, you don't get anybody charged for anything.

A total of 17 attempted arrangements involved the element of 'charge leniency,' with 14 resulting in some agreement. In the case of one accused, detectives searched his house after an accomplice had informed on him regarding a series of three break, enter and thefts that they had allegedly committed together. During the search, the detectives discovered a small amount of marijuana as well as some property that the accused admitted to stealing even though it was unconnected with the alleged break, enter and theft. The detectives told the acuused that he would not be charged under the Narcotics Control Act or for the possession of stolen property, if he co-operated in giving statements regarding the break, enter and thefts and informed on someone who had allegedly stolen an automobile. The accused gave statements on the break, enter and thefts and was not charged for the narcotics or stolen property.

In contrast, a co-accused in another case made the decision not to provide a statement or inform on accomplices. The detective planned to charge him with a break, enter and theft as well as an 'unlawfully at large' charge, but in addition interrogated him regarding two 'purse snatchings' that his accomplice said he was involved in. According to the accused, the detective said that if he provided written statements on the purse snatchings as well as information about the activities of his accomplices, he would be charged with attempt theft and not attempt robbery. The accused denied having committed these offences and refused to give the information on his accomplices. The detective showed him a statement from an accomplice which implicated him in the purse snatches:

A: I told him it was a bunch of crap, right? He says 'OK, I'll give you the same
     chance, you'll tell me what happened.' He says, 'I'll drop the charge [to]
     attempt theft.' I says, 'I don't know what you're talking about.' So he says, 'OK,
     two attempt robberies.'

     ...

     [Later]
A: They said if I signed a statement, that they would drop it. The two attempted
     theft – and, if I ratted on some more people.
Q: Now, which one did they want you to sign a statement on?
A: Uh, all of them.
Q: All of them? And they would drop it all to one attempt theft, or?
A: Two attempt theft.

The detective charged the accused with two attempt robbery occurrences. It is noteworthy that one of the accomplices for some offences in this case was never charged after he provided detailed statements regarding the alleged activities of his associates.

A total of 15 attempted arrangements were said to involve the element of 'court recommendation leniency' i.e. the police officer said he would inform the crown attorney about the accused's co-operation as part of an argument for recommending leniency in sentencing. Among attempted arrangements in these terms, 12 resulted in agreements. These offers involving court recommendations were reported to be the most vague and least reliable of any type of offer made by the police. Several accused complained that the police did not keep their part of the arrangement when the case came to court. For example, an accused said he gave homicide detectives information about a homicide in exchange for a promise of a recommendation for a lenient sentence in his own case, but nothing was forthcoming from the detective at the sentencing hearing, and the accused ended up with the statutory maximum sentence.

Only two accused mentioned transactions involving a promise from the police that there would be no further investigations against the accused if he co-operated. One of these persons, under investigation for indecent assault (male), related his experience as follows:

Q: OK, now you said you sat there for an hour and they tried to convince you to come clean, that they would put a report in to the crown attorney saying you were co-operative. What happened after that?

A: Well, they also, I don't know what you want to call it – threat or not – but they said that they, that if we couldn't get it settled here now, right now, that they would have to do more investigation which would involve people who live in apartments around me. They would have to talk to my relatives, my employer and so on and so forth.

     ...

Q: Can you tell me what exactly motivated you to sign that statement?

A: Fear.

Q: Fear?

A: Yeah, the main thing that was going through my mind was that they were gonna carry on the investigation and they were going to talk to my work, you know, and people in the apartment, and if, for no other reason – my embarrassment it would be, and losing my job, it would be quite embarrassing to my family.

Q: Did the offer that, of speaking to the crown, make any impact on you?

A: Yes it did.

Q: Do you think that was a factor that affected you – to sign it?

A: Yeah.

Ten accused stated that they were asked to give written statements and serve as informants in exchange for agreement not to press their threats of physical force. The threat of physical force was said to have resulted in co-operation in only five instances and was therefore the least 'successful' technique from the police viewpoint.

It is remarkable that 10 of 101 accused claimed that the police threatened and/or used physical force to induce a confession and gain information. Other research (e.g. Wald et al, 1967: 1549; Royal Commission on Criminal Procedure, 1980) has shown that the police usually have enough independent evidence and/or manipulative techniques for gaining what they want so that the threat or use of physical force is unnecessary: why use the stick when the carrot is available and works? Moreover, as Carlen (1976: 106) has pointed out, extensive use of force can detract from the authoritative symbols of the criminal process which allow so much work with potential conflict to go on without manifest conflict.

Among this group of ten, one lodged an official complaint through his lawyer with the police citizen complaints' bureau concerning the alleged beating. This accused, charged with rape, abduction of a female, and possession of a restricted weapon, unsuccessfully challenged the police written statements at a supreme court *voir dire* hearing. Two accused in another case said they lodged a complaint of 'brutality' with the citizen complaints' bureau but did not use this to challenge the police case in court. Another accused said that he was initially refused a third-party telephone call to his lawyer and was assaulted by detectives when he persisted in his request and refused to provide a confession. He said he complained to a justice of the peace about the assault and asked the justice if he could put the complaint on recording tape; in response, he was passed some adhesive tape. Two accused in separate cases said they informed their lawyers about the physical intimidation that they had been subjected to, but for various reasons the lawyers decided to take no action. The lawyer for one of these people stated in interview that he knew the accused had been physically abused during interrogation, but said they were not contemplating charges against the police because his client was fearful that such a challenge would invite further police investigation of his activities.

Whether or not they were subject to police promises and threats, most accused viewed police efforts at gaining information and written statements as a routine part of the process which they could do little to counter. Some accused believed that written statements were inconsequential to the outcome of their case and easy to challenge if necessary. Thus an accused apprehended for dangerous use of a firearm after allegedly firing a shotgun at the front window of his ex-girlfriend's house, said he gave a written statement because: 'I didn't really have no choice really. But it was OK, I didn't really care ... It isn't going to mark on how much time I'm going to get. They don't really use statements ... It's not really that important because it's easy to get out of it. Just say that you didn't sign it on your own or something like that.'

It can be argued that the reality of the situation is quite different (cf Royal Commission on Criminal Procedure, 1980b). Only one accused was successful in having a statement ruled inadmissible. Moreover, as we consider in detail in chapter 4, statements were often used by the crown attorney and accepted by defence lawyers as grounds for an arrangement for a guilty plea. The lawyers apparently predicted the value as evidence of the statement, rather than testing it out in court, and used their prediction to justify to the accused the 'necessity' of accepting a guilty plea arrangement.

The strategies at the disposal of the police to gain information and secure confessions made the reality of their powers in these areas similar to what we have previously discussed regarding arrest and search practices. The vast majority of accused referred to the fact that the police have the 'upper hand' in everything they do. Even those who were not required to give written statements of confession viewed themselves as in a relatively powerless position to combat the case the police were constructing against them. For example, several persons charged with impaired driving or impaired care and control pointed out that they were not able to read the breathalyser machine because the recording panel was visible only to the operator. One of these people stated in interview:

> [The machine operator] told me I blew two forty, point two four o. And he said I had to wait fifteen minutes to take another test. Then he said that if there was twenty points difference, that meant there was something wrong with the machine or something. So I heard, I honestly heard him say to another officer, he says 'Well it's nineteen, close enough!' So that's what I say – that's the only thing I had against – I never said anything to them at the time. That's the only thing I have against breathalysers – I can't have someone there that can represent me that knows how to read that machine also ...
>
> [Why not question the operator?]
>
> What's the sense? What are they going to say? 'Do you know how to read it? We know how to read it!' So I figured, what's the sense? You'd get in an argument.

Thus, even in an area where the evidence is apparently more objectively produced, the police control its production by excluding the opportunity for other interpretations.

As one perceptive accused pointed out, police orders are so overwhelming that potentially excusing conditions for the accused may also excuse the police. For example, if the accused claims an excusing condition (e.g. drunkenness) as a defence, the police could argue that his condition also prevented him from rationally assessing the methods the police used in dealing with him, thus neutralizing any possible challenge to their actions.

The accused enters the maze of police processing with some hope that there are alternative routes. However, as we have seen, he quickly learns that what initially appear as alternative routes are in reality dead ends. There is usually only one possible route and one end point to the maze. These are skilfully designed by the architects of the criminal process and engineered by the police.

We are not arguing that the accused is invariably disadvantaged in his dealings with the police, although he often is. Some accused gained clear advantage in their dealings. For example, an accused managed to avoid a 'harassing telephone call' charge by promising to turn in a machine-gun and to provide information about a homicide. To our knowledge, the accused never provided the gun and the police already had the information he supplied, but he nevertheless escaped the charge. Three co-accused in one case all managed to obtain withdrawal of mischief charges by the fact that one accused was an informant. One of the co-accused said that her experiences in this case had changed her attitude toward the police: 'I know now that [if] I deal with them that they're kinda good to you.' Moreover, those who did deal for charge reductions and/or a lesser volume of charges were able to lessen the seriousness and length of their official criminal records, producing the opposite effect to 'clearing the books' deals described by Skolnick (1966) and Klein (1976).

Forty-six accused stated in retrospect that they would have dealt differently with the police. Among the 40 who gave written statements of confession to the police, 14 stated that if they had the opportunity to do it over again they would not provide written statements. Included in this group of 14 are 5 who said that they had requested a third-party contact with a lawyer: 2 were denied outright, 2 were delayed and the accused never made contact, and 1 was granted outright but the accused was unable to make contact. Among the 8 who said that they had signed a statement of confession to 'get it over with,' 6 said that in retrospect they would deal with the police differently, including 4 who said they would not sign a statement.

Fifty respondents said they would not do anything differently with the police if they had the opportunity to do it over again. Among this group, 9 did not give a reason. A further 9 said that another strategy would not have made any difference, indicating a general feeling of powerlessness in face of police practices. The remaining 32 gave reasons indicating that they dealt with the police the way they wanted to and/or that they were satisfied with what happened throughout the case. Thus, only 32 members of the entire sample indicated in retrospect that they had no complaint about their transactions with the police. Of course, it is usually easier to think of alternative responses in retrospect when one is removed from the situation than it is when actually confronting the orders in question.

Legitimacy of Charges

In order to appreciate the nature and function of charging practices by the police, it is instructive to consider how legitimate the accused and their lawyers see them to be.

We did not ask the accused directly about the legitimacy of the charges against them, but we did ask them if they were guilty of the charges and the reasons for their guilt or innocence. This allows us to ascertain indirectly their views on the legitimacy of the charges. Among the 101 accused, 50 said that no charges were questionable or illegitimate (i.e. they were guilty of them), 33 said that all charges were illegitimate (i.e. they were not guilty), 11 said that some charges were questionable (i.e. they were guilty to some and not to others), 4 said all charges were questionable (i.e. they were guilty of something, but not as charged), and 3 said they were uncertain.

Some types of charges in particular were usually viewed as legitimate without question. For example, most persons charged with possession of marijuana accepted that the evidence was against them and that the police were at least operating with legal legitimacy in laying the charge. While many of these persons mentioned that the law itself was questionable, or referred to selective enforcement practices, they knew the police officer laying the charge was 'legally covered.' The only exception was the previously mentioned case in which the accused claimed the substance was not a narcotic; his position was confirmed in the official analysis of the substance, and the charge was eventually withdrawn.

Among the persons who viewed the charges as illegitimate there was an overrepresentation of non-property-related offences, especially 'order maintenance' or police-constructed charges. When the police laid charges in 'order maintenance' situations, essentially using the law as an 'all purpose control device' (cf Bittner, 1970; Chatterton, 1976; Ericson, 1982), the accused was particularly likely to see the charges as illegitimate. Such was the case with an accused charged with obstructing police after arguing with a police officer who had stopped him for an alleged traffic violation. In another case, one accused was charged with 'assault police' after the police initiated an altercation to construct a charge that would allow them to handle a hostile domestic situation, while his wife was charged with two counts of 'obstruct police' for allegedly attempting to intervene physically to prevent the arrest of her husband. As the wife expressed it, 'It wasn't a real charge, and they could, ah, use the law to their own advantage.'

Complete illegitimacy was also attributed by some accused people involved in quite different circumstances. People arrested and charged only for investigative purposes challenged the legitimacy of charging and of the police in general. For example, two accused were arrested after they had been proactively stopped by a uniformed officer and a vehicle search revealed a fishing knife, a starter's pistol, silk stockings, and a hypodermic needle in their possession. They were turned over to detectives, who interrogated them as if they were suspected of being out to commit a robbery. They were ultimately charged with possession of a dangerous weapon with intent to commit an indictable offence (robbery). Both accused were held in custody for seven weeks before being released on bail. One accused faced the additional burden of parole revocation if convicted, and for a brief period during the 15 months awaiting trial he did have his parole suspended. In the end, both accused were acquitted. In interview, one accused related that when they had initially been stopped by the uniformed officer on the night of their arrest, they expected a traffic summons for a moving violation. Not surprisingly, the accused failed to attribute any legitimacy to the charge, or to the constraints he experienced in the 15-month period subsequent to the charge.

Illegitimacy of charges was also attributed by people who believed that the police had personally decided to 'get them off the streets' or otherwise place extra legal controls on them. For example, one accused was under surveillance by the police intelligence unit because he was believed to be a potentially dangerous sex offender. The police continually looked for circumstances in which they could charge him, and were eventually successful in finding 'status offences' which did the job. The accused was charged with three counts of 'vagrancy E' – Criminal Code, sec 175(e) – which pertains to certain categories of convicted sex offenders found loitering in public parks, school-grounds, etc, and two counts of breach of probation (pertaining to an outstanding probation order which prohibited him from communicating or associating with any male person under the age of 21). The accused was ultimately convicted on the two counts of breach of probation after the three 'vagrancy E' charges were withdrawn, and he received a one-year prison term after being sentenced consecutively to the maximum term on each count. Needless to say, the accused realized the discretionary latitude available to the police in using 'status offences' of this type. His view was that these were illegitimate laws used in an illegitimate way. As he succinctly expressed it in referring to the police actions, 'I think they just wanted me off the street, period.'

Another type of situation in which illegitimacy was imputed concerned the use by police of criminal charges to handle what the accused viewed as a non-criminal dispute. For example, an accused was charged with theft over $200 after he refused to return previously shared property to his former common-law wife. The accused claimed that his former common-law wife had taken many valuable items belonging to him, and that he had sold off some of her possessions in order to obtain partial reimbursement. Detectives obtained a search warrant for the accused's residence, and in his absence allowed the 'victim' to select out for removal any item which she said belonged to her. The detectives then secured an arrest warrant against the suspect and ultimately arrested and charged him. The charge was subsequently withdrawn after the accused agreed to return some property to the victim. In the accused's eyes, the police were *using* the criminal process for illegitimate purposes, and the charge was only a 'lever' to secure compliance. The accused called the police actions 'improper' and believed they never intended to have the case reach court because they would not want their 'improper' actions to be revealed.

It should be stressed that our respondents were generally perceptive about both the intentions and effects of police practice. As we have documented in our studies of the police (Ericson, 1981, 1982), the police frequently charge with other ends in mind than the simple conviction of an accused. At times a conviction is irrelevant to police purposes; at times the police aim not only for a conviction but also a specific sentence; at times a conviction on any charge will do. As the accused related to us, one cannot judge police 'success' in charging simply by reference to the tally of convictions secured.

The 11 accused who said they were guilty to only some of the charges laid against them were all involved in multiple charges; they felt that the police had 'overcharged,' i.e. laid every charge legally possible when it was evident that convictions were unlikely and/or unnecessary on some of the counts. Included in this group are the four accused in one case who were each charged with ten counts of theft under $200, one count of possession of stolen property over $200, and one count of mischief. The theft and mishcief charges all arose out of a series of alleged attempted and actual thefts from cars in an underground parking garage on one occasion. There was consensus among both the accused and their lawyers that fewer charges could have been laid, e.g. one charge of possession of stolen property over $200 to cover the one connected incident.

Most of these people were not particularly concerned about it except its effect on sentencing. Our respondents rarely mentioned the effect of having multiple charges on their police record. Indeed, many accused never bothered to learn about the basis of each charge, or even how many charges they faced. For example, one of the accused in the case cited above never bothered to link his charges with specific acts, and accepted at face value that the number of charges must have had a direct relationship to the number of items actually stolen: 'Well, they had 48 charges between four of us, so there must have been at least forty-eight things.' When asked after the disposition of his case how many theft under $200 charges were laid against him, a co-accused replied, 'I don't know, no idea.'

The four persons who questioned all charges against them each believed that the police had charged up to a higher category than they could legitimately sustain. Among the three persons who said that they were uncertain about their guilt in relation to the charges constructed by the police against them, two said they were too 'stoned' to remember whether they had done what the police alleged, and the other one complained that since he was unable to read the breathalyser recording device he could not say whether the charges of impaired driving and over 80 mg were legitimate or illegitimate.

It is obvious from these data that questions of which charges, and how many, are seen to be very much in the control of the police. Similar to other steps taken by the police against the suspect, the matter appears to be largely foreclosed, and at this early stage the accused are already looking ahead to court outcomes. Of course, our study includes only those suspects who were unable to escape police efforts at getting a charge and thus ended up as accused persons. Our police studies (Ericson, 1981, 1982) do include isolated examples of suspects who successfully negotiated their way out of charges by offering the police some valuables in the currency in which they traffic, e.g. return of stolen property, information on accomplices, and information on other criminal activity. Our police research also informs us that, in intention and effect, the police decide to charge with an eye toward outcomes in court. They 'frame' the limits as to what is negotiable, and produce conviction and sentence outcomes, by 'overcharging,' 'charging up,' and laying highly questionable charges. Needless to say, our accused were aware of these practices and highly sensitive to the consequences they entailed.

The sub-study of defence lawyers (Macfarlane, 1982) included systematic questions about the legitimacy of charges. We studied the responses to these questions from the lawyers for the 81 accused persons who had lawyers who were available for interview.

Lawyers for 44 of 81 accused persons stated that the charge(s) against their clients were not illegitimate or even questionable in any way. They felt that the one or more charges laid by the police were all proper given the information they had at their disposal. In the main, these lawyers were defending accused persons facing single charges, often of a minor nature (e.g. theft or possession of stolen property under $200); multiple charges where the police routinely laid two charges even if conviction was unlikely or legally impossible on both ('impaired driving' or 'impaired care and control' and 'over 80 mg'); and multiple charges involving clearly separate incidents, where the lawyer's main effort was directed at negotiations about sentence recommendations.

Lawyers for 37 of 81 accused persons viewed some or all of the charges against their clients as illegitimate or at least questionable. Among this group, lawyers for 11 said that some charges against their clients were illegitimate while some were legitimate. For example, the lawyer for one accused felt that the police had illegitimately 'overcharged' his client. His client was allegedly involved in an incident at a discotheque with three co-accused; a window was broken, and two of his accomplices apparently had a baseball bat and what the police described as a 'sawed-off hockey stick' to use potentially as weapons in a fight. The police charged all four with 'weapon dangerous,' 'mischief,' and 'causing a disturbance.' The lawyer said that his client neither had a weapon nor broke the window and should have been charged with causing a disturbance only: 'I do not think he should have been charged with the three offences. There is a policy now with – as a result I gather of increased plea bargaining – of ... police officers overcharging .... In my opinion he should have been charged only with causing a disturbance. As it appeared there were not enough facts to convict him of the weapons charge and there were not enough facts to convict him of the mischief charge ... Overcharged him is what they did, and that's common, and then they end up plea bargaining to the charge that could stick. It would have been much simpler if they had just charged him with the lesser charge [causing a disturbance] at the outset.'

The lawyers for a further 11 viewed all charge(s) against their client as illegitimate. Seven of these involved 'order maintenance' charges. For example, the lawyer representing an accused charged with obstruct police after he argued with a police officer over an alleged traffic violation said that the police had clearly overreacted and that the charge was illegitimate. The lawyer also believed that his client was illegitimately convicted, mainly because the judge appeared to accept the evidence of the police witness more than the evidence of the defence witness. From the perspective of both the lawyer and the accused, it was clearly a case of the police *using* the law to reassert their authority, and the judge backing the police up for the same purpose.

The lawyers for another 11 accused persons regarded some of the charge(s) against their clients as questionable, although not illegitimate; that is, they felt that the police had the necessary evidence 'covers' for their charge(s), but regarded the evidence as weak and/or the charges as being largely motivated by the police policy of multiple-charging for purposes of plea and sentence negotiation. For example, all three lawyers representing four accused had this view regarding the ten theft under $200 charges laid against each accused after they were caught in one incident of allegedly stealing from cars in an underground garage. In the words of one lawyer:

> The police use this tactic, you know, hit 'em with so many and negotiate, you know, negotiate out so you drop out some ... We probably could have successfully defended at least four or five of them ... Half would have gone to trial, we would have been able to defend probably four or five of them ... Some of the stolen merchandise was not stolen merchandise whatsoever, it was merchandise taken out of one of the co-accused's car and it actually belonged to him ... They came in and cleaned his car out [and] ended up taking his tapes and his tape recorder and his tape deck and this sort of thing, and they were charging them with theft of those items even though they didn't, they couldn't link it to anybody ... What I don't like ... if he runs into problems again, even if they may be of a minor nature again they'll look at his record sheet and it'll be a full sheet even though it was virtually taken from the one offence. It's similar to if you want to charge a bank robber going into a bank, charge him for each till he cleans out ... The police have a great habit of charging you with as many things as possible, hoping you're going to negotiate some of them off and take, plead guilty to the others to save their time and their investigation, because this course [not guilty pleas] would have meant a lot of investigation for them and calling, summons in a number of witnesses to get them all in.

There were lawyers for four accused persons who questioned all charge(s) laid against their clients. Included in this group are the two lawyers for the accused who were charged with possession of a weapon for the purpose of committing an indictable offence (robbery), after a proactive search of their vehicle (see above, pp 68–9).

Lawyers gave one of three major reasons for judging charges against their clients illegitimate or questionable. These included 1) suspicions about the quality of evidence for the prosecution, 2) a judgment that the police were unnecessarily overzealous in their charging (especially in the case of multiple charges), and 3) an assessment that the strength of the charge was based solely on issues of credibility/respectability. We have already touched upon these reasons in our discussion of case materials to this point; however, further examples will provide additional insight into the lawyers' concerns about charging practices.

As in the case cited above, there were cases in which the lawyers decided that the evidence available to sustain the particular charges laid was extremely weak or non-existent. Other challenges were in terms of the particular charge laid rather than a belief that no charge at all should have been laid. For example, a lawyer pointed out that his client had been improperly charged with 'impaired driving' when it should have been 'impaired care and control.' Another lawyer stated that his client had been improperly charged with 'break, enter and theft,' and 'taking a motor vehicle without the owner's consent,' because he had entered a garage compound to recover his own motorcycle which had been impounded at the garage by the police. As we show in detail in chapter 4, correctives to these questionable charges were often made during out-of-court discussions among the lawyer, police, and crown attorney.

In cases where the prime police evidence was a written statement of confession, the lawyers sometimes viewed this evidence as illegitimate because of the way it was believed to have been constructed. For example, a rape charge against an accused was primarily based upon a written statement of confession since physical evidence was poor, due to the time lapse in reporting the offence and the fact that the victim had taken two baths before reporting the offence. The lawyer believed that the detectives had physically assaulted his client to secure the confession, and he unsuccessfully challenged the statement at a *voir dire* hearing within the trial in the Supreme Court of Ontario.

Lawyers' views that the police were overzealous in charging came mainly in cases where the police laid every conceivable charge against every conceivable person. The tendency of the police to lay multiple charges in this way was a very common source of complaint among the lawyers interviewed.

In isolated cases, lawyers imputed overzealousness to the police in laying single charges. For example, an accused was charged under the Narcotics Control Act after a proactive stop and search revealed that he was in possession of one marijuana cigarette. The officers involved were suspicious of the fact that the youth had $200 in cash in his possession and his vagueness about his activities in the early hours of the morning. They decided to use the possession of marijuana charge as a justification to take the accused into custody for investigation, and he was held for a bail hearing. In his lawyer's eyes, the accused should not have been charged in the first place let alone held in custody for a bail hearing. He had no doubt that the charge and the procedures used could be legally legitimated, but he saw the police actions as being extremely petty under the circumstances. An indication that the purpose of the charge was to legitimate police investigations with the suspect in custody is the fact that the police and crown attorney willingly obliged the lawyer's request to have the charge withdrawn when it reached court.

A third basis for questioning police charging was the view that the charges were sustainable only through credibility issues. For example, a lawyer said that in his opinion a charge of threatening death by telephone was illegitimate because the complaint was laid by the separated wife of the accused and she had a notorious reputation for laying questionable complaints against her husband as well as against other parties. The lawyer believed the police could legitimate the charge if challenged, but his own view was that the victim's lack of credibility should have been used to justify not charging.

In several cases (e.g. as described at pp 64ff above), the question was one of the credibility of the police versus that of the accused. Predictably in these cases the police, with their higher station in the hierarchy of credibility, had their version accepted, thereby reproducing the commonly held assumption by the courts and the public that the police are effective and efficient screeners of guilty persons.

Lawyers often indicated that they believed the accused's version, in spite of out-of-court and in-court decisions which publicly certified that the accused's version was not credible. In one case the police charged the accused with two counts of attempt robbery rather than two counts of attempt theft, apparently because the accused refused to give a written statement and to inform on other culprits.[7] The accused eventually pleaded guilty to these charges reduced to attempt theft even though his lawyer believed his private protestations that he was not involved. The accused related in interview that he 'took the rap' in order to protect the person who was involved and because he believed it would not affect his overall (concurrent) sentence in relation to other convictions he was being sentenced on at the same time.

In most cases, both the lawyer and the accused he represented knew that the police could legitimately 'cover' the charges they laid in the face of a challenge; that is, the police could give excusable reasons for the charges, even if they were challenged during out-of-court negotiations or at trial. Thus, the question for lawyers and their clients was not whether the police could legitimate their actions, but rather a personal sense that some charges were 'cheap,' 'unfair,' or 'harassing.'

Further, many of the charges which lawyers viewed as illegitimate did not result in convictions. Among the 22 accused whose lawyers said some or all charges were illegitimate, 9 were not convicted on any of the charges seen as illegitimate, 7 were convicted on some but not on others of the illegitimate charges, and 6 were convicted on the illegitimate charges. As we document in chapter 4, many of these charges were successfully challenged by lawyers during out-of-court plea discussions. The police expected this to occur during out-of-court discussions; indeed, they laid the charges with the '*frame*work' of these discussions in mind (Ericson, 1981: chapter 6; Ericson, 1982: chapter 6). Moreover, the police could anticipate that some of their charges would not be questioned, or at least successfully questioned, by the lawyer, resulting in a greater number of convictions.

From the perspective of the accused, police investigation and charging practices are based upon a stimulus-response model: the police order a certain response and the accused obliges. The period during which the accused is directly subject to police ordering is not a time for raising fundamental issues of rights, for being obstreperous, or even for bickering over details of what charges are the proper ones. Given the structure of resources which enable the police to get a charge, accused persons under police orders are highly perceptive (and wise) in showing a tendency to follow the course of least resistance.

It is extremely difficult to object *legitimately* to arrest or search initiatives by the police. It is ideally possible to legitimate a decision to remain silent to police questioning, but practically it is extremely difficult to do so. Similarly, the accused can decide to mobilize a third party to assist him in dealing with the police, but as our data illustrate, this is most often not thought of, deemed unwise, or actively circumvented by the police.

It is only at the point of release from police custody that the accused can make a relatively autonomous decision: in planning his defences, he can decide to engage a lawyer. We now turn our attention to this decision and the consequences which follow from it, including the fact that once a lawyer is engaged it brings the accused into another forum of legal ordering.

3

Lawyers' orders

The lawyer's truth is not Truth, but consistency or a consistent expediency.
Thoreau, *Civil Disobedience* (1849)

We do not get good laws to restrain bad people. We get good people to restrain bad laws.
G.K. Chesterton, 'Thoughts around Koepenick,' *All Things Considered* (1908)

The Relation between the Accused and the Lawyer

One of the few relatively autonomous decisions available to the accused concerns the acquisition of a lawyer. The potential benefits of engaging a lawyer include his or her superior specialist and 'recipe' knowledge and his or her access to other criminal control agents to negotiate settlements. The potential costs include the obvious financial burden if a private lawyer is chosen and the loss of control over decision-making. As we show in this chapter, these and other factors enter into the decision about whether or not to have a lawyer. Among the accused we interviewed, three-quarters made the decision to engage a lawyer.

The ordering which the accused confronts in and out of court varies according to whether or not he has a lawyer. The professional status and experience of lawyers gives them a superior position to control the direction of a defence, including the making of recommendations for plea which their clients are usually unable to reject.

Many of our respondents said they left all decisions to their lawyer because, to them, that was the very thing their lawyer was engaged to do. Responsibility was thereby displaced to lawyers. If they were successful in obtaining an apparently lenient outcome, then they were judged to have done a competent job; if not, then they were deemed to have neglected their responsibilities to a degree. As Casper (1978) states, 'Defendants are not some idiosyncratic criminal subculture, but very much like the rest of us. Their judgments are the product of an amalgam of self-interest, notions of equities, and a sense of whether the process has been one in which their interest and concerns have been heard and considered.'

The central questions addressed by researchers studying legal representation of accused include the competence of lawyers and whether lawyers demonstrably bring advantage to the accused. Blumberg (1967) was one of the first to provide a major sociological treatment of the subject. He argued that much of the lawyer's efforts and product is difficult for the accused to assess, and that the lawyer is sometimes more concerned with his own personal interests and/or the interests of ongoing participation in the criminal control organization than with the immediate concerns of any client.

The assessment of the quality of legal representation has proven as difficult for the social scientist as for the accused. For example, there have been attempts to measure the quality of legal representation with indicators such as when the lawyer was first contacted and the length and frequency of meetings between lawyer and accused (e.g. Arcuri, 1976: 179). Assessing quality with these quantities obviously ignores many important elements of the *process* by which lawyers work. Arcuri's criteria of 'quality' could just as readily be taken as indicators that a lawyer does not have enough 'recipe' knowledge and access to negotiate out-of-court settlements that would bring a case to a quick and effective solution, or that he is doing extra work for his own financial gain. Lawyers who supposedly gave better 'quality' were more likely to be privately retained.

Blumberg (1967: 112) argues that the accused's perceptions about outcome are sometimes manipulated by lawyers, who develop and use techniques for 'setting up' their client's expectations and cooling them out if something goes wrong (see also Baldwin and McConville 1977: 49ff).

The accused usually lacks the requisite specialist and 'recipe' knowledge to assess the lawyer's actions and to challenge his judgments. Furthermore, he is usually excluded from the arenas in which outcomes are arrived at. He is rarely present when lawyers discuss with the police, the crown attorney, and/or the judge the possibilities of concessions. He is dependent upon a verbal report from his lawyer concerning what the limits to negotiation were without any independent means of ascertaining how these limits were arrived at vis-à-vis what was possible. Short of not having a lawyer at all and thus not having the potential advantage of an out-of-court bargaining agent, the accused has no option but to act on faith.

We are not arguing that the lawyer has much scope to act otherwise. While he may appear to be functioning in almost conspirational fashion as an agent of the criminal control network, this is the effect of his structural position rather than an intentional act of self-interest. In the power structure of the criminal process, the lawyer is just one step above the accused. It is extremely difficult for him to challenge the prosecution's version of truth without running very serious risks (e.g. a higher sentence against his client). On the one hand he needs to disguise his limitations to his client, and on the other hand he must be the agent who functions on behalf of the police, crown attorney, and judge to 'order' (manage) the accused. This is the essence of the ordering of justice: the system allows the accused to be provided with an advocate and then uses this advocate, *trusted* by both accused and prosecution, to order the accused through the court process. As Michael McConville points out,[1]

> The defence lawyer is, like the defendant himself, a prisoner of the system: it is difficult for him to overcome police versions of reality, versions that are legitimated by incorporation into the prosecution file, and the risks of challenging this construction of reality are real ones (e.g. in terms of sentence). In many cases, the result is that the lawyer is structurally impotent to obtain any concession for the defendant in plea discussions. This impotence must of course be disguised – why show the man you are supposed to be helping that you are also shackled by the system? It is in this context that the 'ethics' of the profession are an important backcloth. On the one hand, lawyers need to protect themselves as independent agents acting in the interests of their clients, if they are going to retain any influence with them. On the other hand, police, prosecutorial and judicial power over the defendant is most effective if it flows through an uncontaminated conduit pipe: the defence lawyer, wittingly or unwittingly but anyway inevitably, provides that clinical conducting agency. The defence lawyer is, in short, the open prisoner of the system who is constrained (by police evidence and prosecutorial and judicial power) to compound the difficulties facing the defendant closed prisoner and it is important – but only incidental – that it also serves the lawyer's interest to do so.

In many respects the position of the accused who engages a lawyer is similar to the victim who mobilizes the police. They both subject themselves to a form of ordering that they hope will yield advantage, although the potential for disadvantage is also present (in the victim's case, see Ericson, 1981: chapter 5; Ericson, 1982: chapter 5; see also Christie, 1977). In this chapter we examine the views of the accused on the use of lawyers and consider the question of who controls key defence decisions. This question is addressed further in chapter 4, which focuses upon plea and related transactions involving the lawyer and other criminal control agents, but excluding the accused.

Retaining Counsel

Among the 101 interviewed accused persons, 25 did not retain legal counsel. The majority (17) of these persons, including 2 who initially consulted a lawyer, felt that a lawyer would be of no benefit in influencing the outcome of their case. These persons were typically involved in less serious offences (e.g. causing a disturbance, possession of a small quantity of marijuana, shoplifting, indecent exposure) where there was perceived to be little option but to plead guilty, and/or where the cost involved in hiring a lawyer, and/or going through the application procedure for legal aid, and/or trying to get the attention of a duty counsel on the day of the court appearance were not seen as worthwhile. As Feeley (1979) observes, when relatively minor charges are involved it will typically cost the accused more to invoke his rights, including the retaining of counsel, than to simply plead guilty at the earliest possible juncture.[2]

Many reasoned that a lawyer might have secured some very minor form of amelioration, but that whatever advantage the lawyer could obtain was far outweighed by the disadvantage of the lawyer's fee. For example, an accused who was charged with causing a disturbance after an incident at a tavern pleaded guilty on his first court appearance and was fined $50, although he contended in interview that he was too drunk at the time to have any recollection of the alleged incident. He said he was prepared to accept the police account and just wanted 'to get everything over with as fast as possible.' When asked why he did not obtain a lawyer, he replied that he saw it as unnecessary because he planned to plead guilty and knew the fine would be a small one. He said he was too busy to apply for legal aid. Later in the interview, he said he felt that a lawyer might have secured an even 'lighter' disposition for him, but reasoned, 'Well, even if he got me off with a slap on the wrist, I'd still have to pay him, so it wouldn't have been lighter either way.'

Some unrepresented accused chose a brief discussion with duty counsel after realizing that a regular lawyer would be more of a disadvantage than an advantage. For example, a middle-class 'shoplifter' who pleaded guilty on his first court appearance to three counts of theft under $200, and was fined $100 on each count, said he called the law society about sources of legal representation and was given the name of a lawyer who wanted a $600 fee and who also wanted the accused to undergo a psychiatric assessment. The accused, who felt that this was ridiculous, decided that all private lawyers were probably the same and therefore proceeded on his own except for a brief consultation with a duty counsel on his court hearing date. In retrospect, he stated that he would still not engage a lawyer if he had to do it over again because 'I got fined only $300 and I probably would have to pay more than that for a lawyer.' He added that if one has a lawyer, the judge might think that the defendant can afford a heavier fine. Furthermore, he reasoned that in a case such as his own, the judge might become angry and impose a heavier sentence if the lawyer went 'overboard' in trying to mitigate obvious guilt (e.g. by introducing a psychiatric assessment).

A few people offered other reasons for their decision. One who pleaded not guilty to a charge of shoplifting and was acquitted said he did not need a lawyer 'because I wanted to tell the truth of what happened' and 'I didn't feel that I did anything wrong, you know, to have a lawyer.' He was typical of those who gave up their right to a lawyer because they believe that having a lawyer is tantamount to being guilty or trying to beat the system.

Other accused employed idiosyncratic reasons in deciding not to have a lawyer. One pleaded guilty to possession of stolen property over $200 because he wanted the case transferred to another jurisdiction to be dealt with at the same time as other convictions. He said a lawyer is only useful if one needs to 'deal' with the crown regarding charges and/or sentence. Husband and wife co-accused, charged with offences against the police arising out of a domestic altercation, separately argued that it is strategically advantageous not to have a lawyer because it places the judge in the position of trying to assist the accused, and this in turn gives the judge a sympathetic attitude.

Eleven persons gave as part of their reason for not obtaining a lawyer the inability to afford one. Three were among those who believed a lawyer would be of no real benefit, but indicated that they would have retained one anyway if it was financially possible Two indicated that their cost-benefit analysis was reflected in their decision to plead guilty: it was not worth it to retain a lawyer for an obvious guilty plea case, notwithstanding possible benefits in terms of sentencing representations. Another three said they were refused by legal aid, and one said he knew about legal aid but could not be bothered applying for it.

Among the 25 persons who were not represented by a lawyer, 17 said they were aware of both legal aid and duty counsel, 2 said they were aware of duty counsel only, and 4 said they were unaware of either legal aid or duty counsel. Thus, the decision not to retain counsel could not be linked generally to an ignorance of alternatives that did not entail financial costs.

In general, those who did not obtain legal representation were not disadvantaged by the fact because they faced relatively minor charges, the court outcome of which had been sealed effectively by the police. Pleading guilty on a first shoplifting offence, or possession of a couple of grams of marijuana, or impaired or over 80 mg often amounted in practice to little more than strict liability situations in which the use of a lawyer was seen as an additional financial liability. In some cases a lawyer might have gained a withdrawal, acquittal, or dismissal by generating witnesses and challenging the crown's evidence, but the delay, cost, and triviality of the conviction were seen as making such a defence not worth the effort. Lawyers might have achieved minor mitigation in sentence after guilty pleas had been entered, but again the accused saw the possible gains as minimal.

The 75 persons who engaged a lawyer gave a variety of reasons for doing so.[3] A large majority (54) referred to some strategic advantage in having a lawyer (i.e. he would have means of producing a more lenient outcome than they themselves could achieve on their own). The most common reasons here included an assumption that lawyers are generally useful (i.e. that it is routine to have one), advice from others that it would be strategically advantageous to have a lawyer, and a perception that the charge had important implications for the accused and thus merited the attention of a trained agent. Overall, 24 gave the first reason, 23 the second, and 13 the third.

Most made explicit reference to the strategic advantages; if such advantages were not assumed, it would seem pointless to engage a lawyer. However, it is instructive to examine the variety of strategies which the accused thought to be within the power of lawyers.

One concerns their ability to deal with the police, crown attorney, and judges in out-of-court transactions for concessions on charges and sentences. As we document in chapter 4, this is one area in which the lawyer has almost exclusive access. It is not a matter of the accused being inherently incompetent at negotiating to his own advantage; rather, the organization of criminal control is structured to exclude him from these transactions.

Some lawyers were signified as being especially adept at 'wheeling and dealing' and thus the ones to hire. One lawyer in particular was known as an accomplished out-of-court negotiator. This was partially attributed to the fact that he also worked as a part-time crown attorney and thus had all the 'right' contacts and relationships. One respondent had retained this lawyer on three previous occasions and felt this lawyer was particularly good because of his special access to the other side:

Q: Why did you decide to get a lawyer for this charge?
A: Well, try to keep me out of jail. Like, I knew, I thought I had a chance of beating the whole thing, right? But the way the police made the report up, and everything else, didn't look too good. So, my lawyer made a deal with the Crown to drop the dangerous weapon charge and plead to the public mischief and cause disturbance.
     ...
     [Later, talking about his lawyer's role as a part-time crown attorney]
A: I think it helps, because, like, if he works with the crowns right, I'm sure the crown is going to be a bit lenient.
     ...
     [Later, the accused offers a reason why he would hire the same lawyer again for this case]

A: I would never have been able to make the deals that my lawyer [made] – I can't go to the crown, talk to the crown, and say, 'Hey, I'll plead guilty to this.' He'd just say, 'Hey?!!'

Other respondents referred to the strategic advantages of lawyers in court as well as out of court. One was judged especially adept at 'knowing all the angles,' articulate in court, and the best strategist available to get one off more lightly in what otherwise appeared to be foreclosed matters. This lawyer only accepted private fee arrangements, and he specialized in impaired driving cases. One accused, who had used this lawyer previously, hired him to arrange a settlement on two charges of impaired/ over 80 mg, disobeying a recognizance, failure to appear in court, and breach of probation. After the lawyer arranged a plea and sentence outcome with the crown attorney and the judge,[4] the accused talked favourably of the lawyer, saying he had done his job of getting him 'off the hook' with the lightest outcome possible.

Whether dealing in or out of court, the lawyers were seen as having two main assets which gave them strategic advantage: they were believed to have both superior knowledge and superior credibility in the eyes of the judge and the other law enforcers.

The advantage of the lawyer was seen in terms of both 'recipe' and specialist knowledge. Thus, one accused referred to the advantages of his own lawyer as being that 'He knows the law, and he knows court procedure.' When the interviewer asked him if most lawyers have similar knowledge, the reply suggested that while specialist knowledge is common, 'recipe' knowledge is the necessary added ingredient: 'Yes, [but my lawyer] knows a lot – he knows the judges, he knows the crown attorneys.' Similarly, another accused argued that it is more advantageous to have a local lawyer with a minor reputation and 'recipe' knowledge than an expensive lawyer with a major reputation 'imported' from another jurisdiction: 'I'm saying if I went to [a nearby major city] and I got a big lawyer, he's going to cost me $1500 or $2000 to go and plead a case for me, the crown attorney is going to look at that lawyer differently because ... that crown doesn't know that lawyer as well as he knows the lawyers in [the local] community. Say if I got a lawyer from out of town, that crown attorney doesn't know him and it makes it harder for [the lawyer] to make any pleas, you know, to talk to that JP or that crown attorney because that crown attorney doesn't know him.'

Many accused expressed the feeling that lawyers have special access to a secret knowledge of the law, one that is impossible for them to attain. Thus, an accused said he would not be able to conduct his defence without the special knowledge a lawyer has: 'Oh, for the simple reason if I walked into court without a lawyer they could hit me with anything and I'm, a lot of times I wouldn't understand it. Uh, you need a lawyer, uh, in court to get through a lot of legal red tape, you know, basically. Uh, a lot of times they'd come out with a, you know, things that I just don't understand. That's what your lawyer's there for, eh. So like he knows what's going on in the courtrooms, right.'

The accused is made to feel not only that he doesn't understand the system but also that he is incapable of understanding it. Certainly with information so heavily guarded by the professionals, it is most difficult for accused to get involved.[5] Knowledge is not only secret but secreted. After stating that his lawyer did not explain the court proceedings beforehand, a respondent was asked whether his counsel should have explained them. He replied, 'If it was something that I really, really had to know I think he should have told me. Like I didn't even notice that summarily or integrated or whatever it was. It wouldn't have made any sense to me anyways. Like I just would have been, you know, totally ignorant. Just – know what I have to know.'

The accused also appreciated the strategic advantage of the lawyer's elevated position within the organization's hierarchy of credibility. Part of the strategic advantage in hiring a lawyer is to ride along on the halo effect of his professional status. What the lawyer says and does is treated with organizational respect whereas what the accused says and does is treated as suspect. Thus an accused charged with impersonation reasoned that 'in this society they tend to listen to a lawyer – he's been to college, he's done so many years, and naturally they will listen to him. So I use a lawyer as an instrument knowing that, that's all.' Of course, the fact that the lawyer becomes listened to 'naturally' establishes his place as part of the taken-for-granted order of things. This place is clearly above the accused, as one respondent suggested in describing lawyers as 'the legal part of you, right ... Anybody'll listen to a lawyer before they'll listen to me.'

Twenty-four accused made reference to lawyers generally being needed as part of any criminal defence. For them it was a structural given that lawyers have superior knowledge and credibility; therefore, one should take what the structure gives and hope for the best. Many engaged a lawyer with the view that once that decision was made, all they could do was passively wait for the outcome. Thus an accused charged with driving while disqualified said he hired a lawyer because it 'looks better' and because a lawyer 'can tell you what to do and how to plead.' His lawyer's advice amounted to telling the accused that he should plead guilty and that the fine would be approximately $200. The accused followed his advice, and received a fine of $125 and six months' suspension of his driving licence, in addition to his lawyer's fee. The lawyer later categorized this case as one which the accused could have handled himself: 'I'll get people to come in and they could easily go down [to the court] and do it themselves but they don't. Court is an awesome thing the way we handle it, and it's not friendly at all really, and so they want somebody to hold their hand, you know ... so I do what I have to do and that's about it.'

Some accused went further and stated that they thought it was not only advantageous to retain a lawyer, but mandatory.

Q: Why would you use a lawyer?
A: Well, I always thought that that was procedure.
Q: Do you feel that it's necessary to have a lawyer at all times?
A: Well I, you can't do it yourself.

As previously noted, almost one-third (23 of 75) gave as a reason for engaging a lawyer the fact that they had been advised by someone else to obtain one. It is impossible to say whether they would have engaged a lawyer without this advice. However, this information does indicate that the decision to engage a lawyer was often taken in consultation with others. In this connection we can consider sources of knowledge about legal assistance and the type of lawyer obtained.

The most common source of knowledge used to obtain legal assistance was 'officials' (27), followed by 'friends and relatives' (24). A smaller number (14) said that they had engaged the same lawyer before, while a few (8) said that they had obtained the lawyer in a situation of convenience, e.g. he happened to be in the courthouse on the accused's appearance date and was available for consultation. These figures are comparable to those reported by Bottoms and McClean (1976: 153), who found that most lawyers were selected by 'reputation' (via persons such as officials, and friends and relatives of the accused), and by 'prior contact.'

Those who obtained legal assistance were most likely to use privately retained lawyers (32) or legal aid lawyers (29) rather than duty counsel (12). Privately retained lawyers were most likely to be known about through friends and relatives, followed by officials, previous engagement, and convenience. Legal aid lawyers were most likely to be known about through officials, followed by friends and relatives, previous engagement, and convenience. Duty counsel were most likely to be known about through officials, followed by convenience, and friends and relatives; no duty counsel had been used before.

Over one-third of those who engaged a lawyer said they learned about the legal assistance they obtained through officials. Many were told by a crown attorney that it would be to their advantage to have a lawyer, or by a judge that the case should not proceed without some form of legal advice for the accused. As stated previously (pp 77-8), it is of advantage to the criminal control agents to have the accused represented by a lawyer who knows the court's order of things and will keep the accused in order. However, other situations occurred, including a few cases in which the accused privately retained a lawyer recommended by the police. For example, an accused related that the detective who processed his case initially told him that he did not require a lawyer, but later gave the accused the address and telephone number of his own lawyer after learning of the accused's previous record of related offences.

The decision concerning what type of lawyer to obtain usually included a belief that duty counsel were distinctly inferior, combined with an assessment of whether an application for legal aid would be successful and whether it would be strategically better to have a privately retained lawyer rather than a legal aid lawyer.

Most accused talked negatively of duty counsel, claiming that duty counsel rarely have time to go into the details of a case because they are simultaneously involved in a large number of cases which they have only received on the morning of the court appearance of their clients. Similar findings concerning public defenders in American jurisdictions are reported by Arcuri (1976) and Casper (1978), although it must be noted that in Ontario duty counsel cannot defend a person on a not guilty plea, but only give advice and make sentence representations in court. Duty counsel were described as being 'less interested' in one's case compared with regular lawyers and 'acting on the spur of the moment,' as 'a two-minute thing' in which 'he tells you the same as 25 million other people,' and as similar to a factory worker who does a routine job and acts as if he is not very concerned about it. Many of these perceptions where shared by others who chose not to use a lawyer at all rather than obtain a duty counsel. For example, an accused said he used a duty counsel on a previous occasion but it was of no advantage; he then went on to reason that if duty counsel were as competent as other types of lawyers, there would be no other types of lawyers: 'Why would anyone buy a lawyer if he could get duty counsel to go up and do it for nothing?' In other words, the system was seen as being structurally geared to give out a modicum of assistance, but never so much as to overcome the *value* of paying for it yourself (cf Friedenberg, 1975). Among the twelve people who used duty counsel, four said they felt that a duty counsel could serve their interests as well as any other type of lawyer; two said their charge (one indecent exposure, one 'drive while disqualified') was not serious enough to bother obtaining another type of lawyer; two said they could not afford anything else; and four offered other idiosyncratic reasons.

The basis for choice between legal aid and privately retained lawyers was often viewed in terms similar to the choice between duty counsel and 'regular' lawyers. Many accused believed that legal aid lawyers were second best to privately retained lawyers, being less concerned and less thorough. For example, an accused who hired a private lawyer stated, 'The legal aid lawyer probably does that particular type of work because he is not a very good lawyer ... And you look at [them] like a plant doctor – why is he a plant doctor when doctors make such high fees? He's probably not a very good doctor, and that might be the case with the lawyer.' Another accused who retained a private lawyer questioned both duty counsel and legal aid on the basis of what he saw as a contradiction: 'He's trying to fight the people that are paying him – it just doesn't seem to be a good relationship.' Again, these accused perceived that the system was not going to be structured in any way other than by the *value* that you get what you pay for: as another respondent suggested, 'I think if you pay the lawyer by your own pocket, the lawyer [is] going to do *everything* for you.'

Several lawyers shared this perception. For example, a lawyer stated that he did not usually work as hard on legal aid cases as on cases for which he was privately retained. He represented an accused on legal aid and had him plead guilty to all three charges (impaired, refusal to provide a breath sample, 'drive while disqualified') even though the accused maintained innocence on the refusal to provide a breath sample. The legal aid lawyer for another accused similarly admitted that he would have done a better job of representing his client (on charges of possession of a dangerous weapon and dangerous use of a firearm) if he had been privately retained: '[On legal aid] I couldn't work as hard for him ... because I made so little money on it ... If it had been privately financed, I would have put the blocks to the old crown. It's all money, eh? The whole thing. It's a big game. Whoever has the most money wins ... You see, all legal aid does, as it did in this case, is that it allows for the noises of a defence ... Like, it sort of – it didn't look too bad. If there'd have been people in the audience, they would have thought, oh, I guess he got a fair trial. You know, it sounded like his lawyer was fighting for him.'

In sum, the *value* of the privately retained lawyer was seen as continuous with a central value in our society: what services you can obtain from the private sector, as a result of paying out what you yourself have earned, is far superior to what is obtainable from a government service set up to give the appearance that everyone has equality of opportunity. Several of the accused extended this reasoning to their consideration of how the type of legal representation they chose might influence a judge. For example, an accused charged with property offences, who by all appearances was destitute and an obvious candidate for legal aid, said that he decided to hire a private lawyer, 'Because I wanted to show the judge, that, you know, I give a good impression, like I went out and I worked and I paid for my own lawyer.' One respondent reasoned that a lawyer is necessary because without one 'they'll just think this guy don't care what happens to him,' while another believed a judge 'would probably think you were some sort of a nut, some sort of a fool that would go into a lion's den with no protection.' Given an awareness by accused of the value criteria used by judges to make their sentencing decisions, this reasoning was indeed reasonable.

The question of whether an accused believed having a lawyer would have an effect on the finding and sentencing is another way of understanding reasons for obtaining or not obtaining a lawyer. This question is addressed in Table

TABLE 3.1

Perceptions by the accused of the effect of having a lawyer on case outcomes in general according to whether or not the accused was represented by a lawyer

Effect of having a lawyer on case outcomes	Total		Represented		Unrepresented	
	N	%	N	%	N	%
None	17	17.0	13	17.3	4	16.0
Finding	12	12.0	11	14.8	1	4.0
Sentence	15	15.0	10	13.3	5	20.0
Finding/sentence	38	38.0	28	37.3	10	40.0
Other	3	3.0	1	1.3	2	8.0
Do not know	8	8.0	6	8.0	2	8.0
No information	8	8.0	6	8.0	1	4.0
Totals	100	100.0	75	100.0	25	100.0

3.1, in which we present a cross-tabulation concerning views on whether having a lawyer is likely to affect outcomes according to whether or not the accused was represented by a lawyer. Compared with those who were represented, the unrepresented were as likely to say that a lawyer would make a difference, although they were substantially less likely to say that the difference would be with respect to finding only.

When 16 unrepresented accused who said a lawyer would make a difference were asked why, they referred mainly to the lawyer's superior legal knowledge (8), his superior ability to present every aspect of the case (3), and his superior ability to talk the language of the court (2). One person thought a lawyer would be better because he believed that judges would see an accused as a 'smart alec' or 'hot shot' if he tried to defend himself. Two people gave no reason for why they thought a lawyer would make a difference.

In order to account for the fact that the majority of unrepresented accused felt that a lawyer would have been of some advantage but nevertheless decided not to engage one, we can refer to our earlier discussion about unrepresented accused. As we have learned, most accused who went unrepresented did so because they felt it was not worth the time and financial cost in relation to the triviality of the charges they were facing. While most unrepresented accused believed that a lawyer could potentially do something for them, the advantages of having a lawyer were viewed as too minor to make it worthwhile.

Among the 69 people with legal representation for whom information is available, 13 stated that having a lawyer would make no difference to the finding and sentence outcomes. When asked why they held this view, most gave replies indicating that they believed outcomes depend on facts of the case and not on how a lawyer deals with those facts. Other responses included statements that judges are omnipotent and the lawyer relatively uninfluential when it comes to key decisions regarding findings and sentence, indicating an ideal that a case should be decided on the facts by an impartial, if omnipotent, judge. It is difficult to understand why these thirteen accused did obtain a lawyer in spite of holding these views, especially since nine of them hired private lawyers and thus incurred financial costs. One possible explanation is that they tended to take for granted the acquisition of a lawyer as a normal part of any involvement in the criminal process and believed there was nothing to lose (other than financially) by having a lawyer because he might at least ensure that the outcome was properly arrived at.

Among the 49 represented accused who attested to the advantages of having a lawyer in terms of finding and/or sentence, the largest number (28) believed that a lawyer could potentially influence both finding (e.g. successfully defend not guilty pleas; effect transactions involving withdrawal or reduction of some charges in exchange for guilty pleas on others) and sentence (e.g. secure promises about sentence recommendation from the crown attorney; strategically present character evidence to mitigate sentence). A further 11 saw the main advantage in terms of the finding only, while 10 saw the advantage in terms of the sentence only.

When asked the basis of their perception that lawyers could influence outcomes, 18 referred to a lawyer's superior legal knowledge, 10 mentioned the lawyer's superior ability in talking the language of the court, 10 said they thought a judge would view them as irresponsible if they did not obtain legal assistance, 4 said a judge would see them as a 'smart alec' or 'hot shot' if they tried to defend themselves without a lawyer, 3 referred to the lawyer's superior ability at presenting every aspect of the case, 3 gave idiosyncratic reasons, and 1 gave no reason for his view.

We can receive further instruction about the issues under consideration through an examination of the accused's retrospective views on the work their lawyers did. To this end, we present in Table 3.2 a cross-tabulation on clients' satisfaction with their lawyers' work according to the type of lawyer obtained. Overall, 78 per cent were satisfied with the work of their lawyer, although this varied with the type of lawyer obtained: 83 per cent of those who engaged legal aid lawyers and 81 per cent of those who engaged private lawyers were satisfied, compared with only 59 per cent of those who engaged duty counsel.

Those who were dissatisfied with duty counsel echoed the complaints of those who gave reasons for not engaging duty counsel in the first place; that is, duty counsel were seen as ill prepared and lacking interest in the case. These accused explained this by the volume of cases duty counsel have, and the fact that they do not take on cases until the morning of the accused's court appearance.[6]

The main criteria for evaluating a lawyer's work was in terms of outcome (cf Casper, 1978). Among the 73 persons for whom information is available, 53 per cent judged their lawyer in terms of whether or not the case outcome was seen as lenient, while 30 per cent made their judgment on the basis of

TABLE 3.2

Satisfaction of the accused with lawyer and type of lawyer obtained

	Total		Duty counsel		Legal aid		Private	
Satisfaction – reason	N	%	N	%	N	%	N	%
Satisfied – lenient outcome	33	45.2	4	33.3	16	55.1	13	40.6
Satisfied – lawyer well informed	20	27.4	2	16.8	6	20.7	12	37.5
Satisfied – lawyer tried his best	4	5.5	1	8.3	2	6.9	1	3.1
Not satisfied – outcome not lenient	6	8.2	1	8.3	3	10.3	2	6.3
Not satisfied – lawyer not well informed	2	2.7	1	8.3	1	3.5	0	0.0
Not satisfied – lawyer did not try best	8	11.0	3	25.0	1	3.5	4	12.5
Totals	73*	100.0	12	100.0	29	100.0	32	100.0

*Two cases with missing information were excluded.

whether or not their lawyer appeared to be informed about the case, and only 17 per cent judged in terms of their lawyer's apparent efforts. In other words, most accused judged their lawyers in terms of the finding and sentence, rather than the means the lawyers used to arrive at that result. Their views are well summarized by an accused who claimed ignorance about the details of his lawyer's dealings, but satisfaction with the result of an 'arranged' sentence: 'I don't know how I wanted [my lawyer] to handle it, but he did an excellent job ... [because] he got me just off without going to jail.' Similarly, when asked if he was satisfied with his lawyer's handling of his bail hearing, another accused replied, 'I have to be, I'm out!'

Accused who were negative about their lawyer frequently felt the outcome did not match their expectations. Thus, an accused who was found guilty after a not guilty plea to a charge of obstructing police said he was unable to judge his lawyer's actions except by the outcome: 'I've never really dealt with lawyers before so, for me, to say he did anything, like I really don't know if he did anything or not, you know, but it seemed like he was doing something, but it wasn't enough ... I don't think I'd recommend him because, you know, like I really never got the results I wanted. Like, if he would have won, I would have recommended him, you know, but since I got convicted, you know, it doesn't say too much for my lawyer.'

Similarly, a sentence that was greater than expected was reason for negatively assessing one's lawyer. For example, an accused received 15 months in jail and a one-year term of probation for a series of break, enter and thefts and other property offences; a co-accused received 90 days' intermittent jail and one year of probation for the same offences after being defended by a different lawyer who elected to plead in county court to avoid the provincial court judge. The accused who received the greater punishment expressed reservations about his lawyer's ability and said he would not recommend him to anyone else. When asked why, he replied 'Because I got the fifteen months and I was just wondering if it would be worth it to use him again ... Maybe it's because I wasn't too happy with the results.'

As indicated in Table 3.2, when dissatisfaction was expressed it was also often in terms of apparent lack of effort on the lawyer's part. These persons were negative about the outcome of their case; however, they also pinpointed specific problems with the way their lawyers handled their cases rather than simply saying that the outcome was bad and therefore the lawyer's efforts must have been lacking. Some case examples illustrate the problems perceived by this group.

An accused who hired his lawyer privately after having him recommended by the detective who laid the charge of indecent assault (male) was angry with the fact that his lawyer spent little time discussing strategy with him and that on the morning of the scheduled trial he announced to the accused that a sentence recommendation agreement had been worked out with the crown attorney (suspended sentence plus two years' probation) and that the accused would reciprocate by entering a plea of guilty to indecent assault (male). The accused obliged, apparently in deference to his lawyer's orders and the relatively mild sentence compared with what he believed he might have got if he pleaded not guilty and was found guilty. However, in interview, the accused maintained that he was not guilty of this charge, and he felt that his lawyer had engineered him into it without allowing him adequate opportunity to discuss it and think about it. Added to this were what he perceived as other pro-crown actions by his lawyer, including the introduction of a psychiatric report that the accused believed was detrimental to his case because the report mentioned the accused's excessive drinking and the fact that he was often late for appointments and once missed an appointment. In expressing his resentment about this action by his lawyer, the accused stated, 'I could have added the fact that he was late more than I was for his appointments, but you see he wasn't on report, I was.'

An accused, whose lawyer admitted in interview with a researcher that his client was subject to excessive multiple-charging in a theft case, related that his lawyer went about arranging a settlement to the case without paying heed to the accused's wishes and without properly informing the accused about the possible limits to negotiation.

> Well, I told him [lawyer] I wouldn't plead guilty to more than two because that's all I was guilty of ...
>   Well, he [lawyer] said if I pleaded guilty to two the crown will push on all of them. And there was, I think, eleven or twelve charges. He said he would push on all of them and have me found guilty. And he said it doesn't matter if I'm guilty of two, that I was there and that makes me guilty of all of them. I could be found guilty anyways ...
>   And he talked to the crown, and he came back and he said, 'We'll plead guilty to five.' And that's what I ended up doing.

At a later point in the interview, the accused related that part of the offer also included a prediction about sentence which seemed attractive.

> Mr [lawyer] said, 'Well if you plead, you know, the way the crown wants to go, then you probably won't get any time ...' And then just before I went up for sentence ... I was reading my pre-sentence report, and I said to him, 'Well what do you think is going to happen?' And he says, 'Well I think probation pretty sure.' And then I said, 'OK no problem.' And then we got up there and then, ah, I got three months [prison] and he says, 'Oh, you're lucky you got three months.' I said, 'Thanks a lot, forget it,' and I just walked away from him.

In connection with the sentence, the accused said he was particularly angered because he wanted to have his mother and employer give character testimony, but did not do so because his lawyer argued that it was unnecessary. In combination with other conflicts, this led the accused to state that, in retrospect, 'I'd find a lawyer that's going to work for me ... I feel that through all this mess, Mr [lawyer] had been working against me.'

Another accused was particularly upset because he was sentenced to 14 days in jail intermittent plus 30 months' probation on three break, enter and theft convictions, while his accomplice – who, unlike the accused, had a criminal record – received three years' probation. He imputed the blame for this to his lawyer, who in retrospect appeared to him as not putting forth sufficient effort. The accused constantly criticized his lawyer's 'play it by ear' approach and stated that he was never informed about what was happening: 'I was in there playing it by ear with my lawyer.' He said he trusted his lawyer because he could do little else. 'I trusted him, yes, I had no other thing to do except put my trust in him because I had no legal background or anything.' However, when the lawyer did not make a key sentencing submission regarding the accused's co-operation in returning stolen property, and especially when the sentence was handed down, the accused felt that the trust had been betrayed. He expressed regret at following his lawyer's instructions in a docile manner – at 'just sitting back and hoping for the best' – and he eventually transformed his regret into action by laying a complaint with the provincial law society.[7]

Most accused did not express dissatisfaction with their lawyers. One interpretation of this fact is that they were generally satisfied with the outcome and therefore pleased with their lawyers. Another interpretation is that they were unable to assess the means their lawyers used. Therefore, they were forced to assess them much more in terms of conviction and sentence rather than in terms of any knowledge about specific actions. This argument is elaborated in the next section.

Our assessment of satisfaction with legal representation can be furthered through an examination of responses to questions which asked the accused if they would have engaged a lawyer if they had it to do over again. In reviewing their entire case after it had been disposed of, 15 of 25 unrepresented accused said that if they had to do it over again they would still not engage a lawyer, and a further 3 of 25 said they were uncertain whether or not they would bother to engage one. When asked to give reasons, they offered similar responses to those which they gave for not engaging a lawyer in the first place. The 7 of 25 unrepresented accused who said that in retrospect they would have engaged a lawyer seemed to have concluded in light of their experiences that 'it looks better' to have a lawyer in court and/or developed a belief that a lawyer is more knowledgeable and thus able to perceive advantage in a way the accused cannot. These insights were of course set against the background of the outcomes these persons had received while defending themselves. Overall, the number of unrepresented accused who said they would not use a lawyer if they had it to do over again was almost identical with the number who said they did not obtain a lawyer in the first place because they perceived no benefit in doing so. Those who said that in retrospect they would have benefitted from a lawyer were numbered among those who did not hire one because of financial prohibitions.

When the represented accused were asked to review their case, only 6 of 75 said that if they had it to do over again they would go unrepresented. Three had used a private lawyer and three had used a legal aid lawyer. They were struck by the minimal work undertaken by the lawyer in light of the outcome achieved, rather than totally disillusioned with the legal profession because of the outcome of their case or some particular misdeed on the part of their lawyer. The 69 of 75 who said that in retrospect they would still have engaged a lawyer largely gave the same reasons as they had given for obtaining a lawyer in the first place. The 17 accused in this group who offered different reasons tended to emphasize the value of their lawyer in achieving what the accused perceived as fair and/or lenient results.

To this point we have described decisions by the accused to engage a lawyer or to go without legal representation and considered what the accused said were the reasons for their choice. We have also examined satisfaction with the work of lawyers, noting that the main factor which contributed to satisfaction was whether or not the outcome was seen as lenient. This leads us into other considerations, including aspects of the relationship between client and professional which subordinate the accused to the commands of his lawyer, thereby making what appear to be his decisions in reality decisions by the lawyer.

Legal Dependency

The fact that the accused judged their lawyers largely on the basis of outcomes is not surprising. It is much easier to judge by *visible* outcomes than by the often invisible and usually mysterious means by which their lawyers and criminal control agents achieve them. The accused were almost invariably excluded from out-of-court plea discussions with the police and crown attorney. They were also distanced from the proceedings in court, which from their viewpoint happened in a foreign discourse with rigid rules of taking turns so that often the accused 'switched off,' waiting only to hear the outcome (see chapter 6). In sum, the structure which ensures that the accused has inferior specialist and 'recipe' knowledge, and little access to the out-of-court arenas in which most 'trials' are conducted, thereby ensures that the accused's main evaluation of his lawyer (as well as of everyone and everything else in the criminal process) is in terms of whether or not the outcome is in accordance with his expectations. It is testimony to the order of things that the only thing the accused usually understands is his punishment.

As Blumberg (1967: 112–13) has argued, from the lawyer's perspective this structural arrangement is very enabling. The conditions of 'low visibility' allow him to claim 'secret' 'recipe' knowledge and influence. His knowledge that the accused will assess him in terms of outcome encourages the lawyer to 'prepare' the accused for a favourable view. This can be done, for instance, by exaggerating what the accused can expect to receive and then claiming credit for having obtained charge withdrawals in exchange for guilty pleas on other charges (even though the withdrawn charges would not have withstood evidence tests in court), and for obtaining a lenient sentence (even though the predicted sentence may have been an exaggeration, a possibility facilitated by high maximum penalties in the Criminal Code). Some of the lawyers of accused persons in our sample stated in interview that they engaged in this practice. As far as most accused were concerned, they could only sit back, act on trust, and hope for the best.

The accused we interviewed regularly implied they had no choice but to trust that their lawyer was doing whatever he could to ensure their best interests. To repeat, the reason for having trust is simply that there is no alternative to it. The structural arrangements make the accused incapable of developing an independent assessment of his lawyer's actions that would introduce a measure of distrust before crucial outcomes are accomplished. As an accused expressed it in referring to his trust in his lawyer, 'I thought he knew what he was doing because I didn't know what to do.'

In circumstances where he is unable to observe what his lawyer is doing, or unable to understand it if he does observe it, the accused must fall back on the ideal that his lawyer is doing what he should be doing, putting out every effort to ensure the best interests of the accused. The accused therefore merges the 'is' with the 'ought.' For some of the accused in our sample, trust was something they never questioned until we interviewed them. When they were asked to question it they became somewhat inarticulate, although they nevertheless conveyed the basic message that they had an unquestioning faith that their lawyer was on their side. For example, when an accused was asked if he thought his lawyer was on his side, he replied, 'Yea. Well, he *better be*, you know.' When he was then asked, 'But did you feel he was?,' the accused replied, 'Yea ... because, ah shit, because I, *he's right.*'

The limited comprehension meant that trust of lawyers was often based on characteristics of the lawyer or the situation and not necessarily related to the lawyer's performance:

Q: Did you trust, him?

A: Yeah.

Q: Why?

A: Because I think he's a good lawyer. I like him, he's a nice guy ... If he's going to trust me, if he's going to believe me, I'm going to believe him, right.

The lawyer for the four accused in one case stated that his clients 'would go along with whatever I asked them to do.' He explained later that they knew nothing about the system and that this made it easier for him 'for they trusted me completely.'

As with all relationships between clients and professionals, the element of trust is normally 'one-way' from the client to the professional rather than reciprocal. It is interesting to contrast the trust which the accused expressed in relation to their lawyers with the distrust some lawyers used as a routine component of their relationships with their clients.

Several of the lawyers candidly stated in interview that they developed a policy of distrust and suspicion of their clients' accounts of the trouble they were accused of. In turn, this had obvious implications for the lawyers' willingness to listen to their clients' arguments about particular decisions, such as pleading guilty and accepting settlements arranged through out-of-court transactions. Commonplace were statements such as: 'You can only depend on what your client tells you to a limited extent.' For many lawyers, part of this involves an assumption that the client is guilty until he proves himself otherwise. Of course, the lawyer is no different than the other agents in the system in this respect. All credit police accounts as 'facts.' For example, the lawyer for an accused charged with possession of marijuana said, 'I figured he was a hitchhiker with a joint of marijuana and I thought he was guilty ... I'm going to accept at face value until shown something otherwise.' A lawyer whose client had a shoplifting charge dismissed talked of a presumption of guilt which he shared with criminal control agents: 'I mean, the police don't charge people unless they have reasonable and probable grounds to believe that they've done something.' A lawyer who had his client plead guilty to impaired driving, refusing to provide a breath sample, and driving while disqualified (although his client said in interview he felt not guilty on refusing to give a breath sample) talked of a presumption of guilt: 'Yeah, I have a preconception of guilt. Uh, this is the danger of coming back to the same lawyer ... Because if you've been down the road with somebody three or four times, [especially] on break and enters, you just can't do a good job for them on the fifth time. You believe they're more guilty than the police do.'

Several lawyers said the assumption of distrust leads them to do routine checks on the credibility of their clients. Indeed, some lawyers seemed more likely to do credibility checks on their clients than on the police construction of the case against their clients. The main standard of assessment in these checks was the official record or accounts of the police and crown attorney. For example, the lawyer for an accused charged with weapon dangerous, causing a disturbance, and mischief viewed the charge of causing a distur- bance as the only legitimate one and eventually transacted a guilty plea agreement to this charge in exchange for the withdrawal of the others. The lawyer remarked that his normal procedure is to obtain the 'objective facts' from the crown attorney and sometimes the victim, rather than believe his client's account, the implication being that only the accused slants his account: 'It's always better to get the objective version of the facts as soon as possible, find out whether or not you should enter a plea or whether or not the evidence is there to warrant a conviction.'

The lawyer went on to remark that in this particular case his client had been more 'objective' than usual because his account was similar to the official version: '[The accused] was much more candid and objective in his version of the facts than most of my clients are. Usually when you interview a man who's charged with a criminal offence they tend to slant the facts obviously to their advantage. A lot of times they will not tell you the truth as [it] actually occurred. Usually you have to get a better picture of the offence through your reading of the crown brief, through discussing the matter with the person who is the victim and the crown. In this case, [the accused's] version of the facts almost correlated exactly with the version as it occurred.'

There were other indications that the trust of lawyers was directed toward law enforcement agents and their order. One said that he generally tried to avoid an ongoing relationship with a client because familiarity might lead him to 'cater' to the client in opposition to his own ethical stance. Of course, this lawyer's ethics did not similarly lead him to sever his ties with the agents of criminal control; on the contrary, he also worked as a part-time crown attorney and actively cultivated ties and ongoing relationships with these agents. This inevitably gave him a pro-law enforcement orientation. Some details of his client's case further the point.

The lawyer's client pleaded guilty to 17 counts of property offences after his lawyer had arranged a sentence recommendation (90 days in jail intermit- tent plus 18 months' probation) with the crown in exchange for guilty pleas. The accused related in interview that he was unsure if he was guilty to all counts as read in court, but felt that it was of little consequence because he would still end up with the same prearranged sentence. The lawyer, who had routinely made the plea arrangement with the police and crown attorney, stressed the ethics of not having an ongoing relationship with accused persons: '[As] a lawyer once told me, if you're going to do criminal work the only way to do it is that you assume that each client you'll never see that client again. And the reason is, that's so you can, you know, you don't cater to the client, you cater to your own concept of ethics, OK.' Earlier in the interview he said that with first offenders such as his client, it is advisable not to give the impression that the lawyer will do everything in his power to get his client the most lenient outcome possible because the client will derive a distorted conception of right and wrong. The lawyer then revealed his conception of his role by concluding, 'So, I'm part of the deterrent factor.'

Among the lawyers interviewed, a prevailing view was that it is necessary for the lawyer to make key decisions (e.g. regarding submissions concerning election, plea, and sentence) because the accused simply does not understand the process. A revealing example is provided in the case of an accused who complained of being rushed into a guilty plea to indecent assault (male) without being properly informed by his lawyer about the nature of the arrangement for sentence recommendation that had been made with the crown attorney. He said his lawyer made all the decisions without explanation and without paying attention to the accused's argument that he had not actually indecently assaulted the victim. In interview, the lawyer said that in this case, and in general, he paid little attention to his client's wishes and did not bother to keep him informed because he 'wouldn't understand.' For example, in discussing the election decision the lawyer stated,

L: I basically made the decision for him.
Q: And he didn't put up any –
L: No, I really have a tendency to decide myself which is better for the client and I don't say, well, these are the avenues, because I don't think they understand enough of what I'm talking about. I don't think they're capable of me explaining everything to them because it took me a long time to learn what the different avenues meant too.

When subsequently asked if he would offer greater information to a client who was particularly knowledgeable and sophisticated about the criminal process, the lawyer said he would still control the decisions but he might spend time giving his client reasons for his decisions. 'If they seemed to grasp what I was talking about I'd explain to them why I was taking it to such and such a court.' In this case one is left wondering what level of knowledge and sophistication would be required, since the accused was a person with an extensive criminal record going back a number of years. Lawyers with this approach place the onus on the accused to comprehend, rather than attempting to make themselves comprehensible; either way decisions are still taken according to their orders.

The accused can only be depicted as unknowledgeable and unsophisticated within the criminal process because he is structurally precluded from becoming anything else. His problem is structural, not a personal one. Contrary to those who argue that the recidivist becomes more sophisticated and thus able to win advantage (e.g. Newman, 1966; Skolnick, 1966; Chambliss and Seidman, 1971; Conklin, 1972; Galanter, 1974) we argue that previous experience in the criminal process has quite a different effect. The more experience the accused has in the criminal process, the more likely he is to accept passively the fact that he is structurally precluded from informed participation in the negotiated outcome of his case, and the more likely he has had experience with lawyers who encourage 'legal dependency' in their clients. The lawyer becomes the accused's agent of order, keeping him in place through the various stages of the court process. For the accused, the court process becomes a spectator sport, at least until the time he has to pay for his admission.

In stating that experienced clients are more accepting of the system, one lawyer compared the 'rounder' with the novice 'white-collar criminal': 'You have to explain everything to him. You have to explain about committal for trial. You have to explain about pre-trials. Someone who has been through the system before is aware that almost, you know virtually if you don't get committed for trial they are going to indict you anyway and they understand that. Well, at least accept it if they don't understand it. A white collar person who is discharged at a preliminary hearing thinks the matter is over and then when he is indicted he is outraged, perhaps rightly so.'

Another lawyer, representing a client who was a first offender facing three counts of robbery, said that his client's previous inexperience in the process made him less accepting of the procedures and therefore in need of more ordering from the lawyer than is usual with experienced offenders:

L: I think I had to control him a little more than I would other clients who knew what was going on – you know, other people who know more about it. He was the type who would sort of suddenly look frightened and trapped, and need an explanation right there.

Q: In court?

L: Yeah, if he wasn't going to blurt out something. You know.

Q: So you had to kind of keep an eye on him?

L: Oh yeah, one eye on him and the other on the judge [laughing] ... [We had] no real disagreements. He got excited, and wanted to pull back from it, but I straightened that out right away by showing him the [contempt of court] section [of the Criminal Code].

What is interesting to note in the above examples is not whether experienced or inexperienced accused were better clients but rather that what made either of them, according to each lawyer's taste, better was the ease with

which they could be controlled and dictated to. Those lawyers totally accepting the fact that any relationship between professional and client is also a
controlling relationship would undoubtedly see their upper hand in decision-
making as entirely proper. Propriety is not at issue, only the fact that
engaging a lawyer usually means an accused is ordered in a way not dissimilar
from the ordering experienced with the police and other agents of legal order.

As someone who is expected by other agents of the criminal process to
keep the accused in order, the lawyer becomes committed to producing a
passive, a co-operative client. It is viewed as being in everyone's interests to
have the accused processed efficiently and effectively within the prevailing
order of things (Blumberg, 1967; Hostika, 1979; to the contrary, see Heumann, 1978). Thus, it is not surprising when a lawyer states approval of his
client in the following terms: '[The accused] is a very intelligent fellow. He, uh
recognizes his position immediately, and, he maximizes himself, gets the best
result by almost blending completely with his lawyer.'

The lawyer prepares his client for accepting the results of the out-of-court
transactions the lawyer engages in. For the in-court transactions, he prepares
a docile client who appears to be committed to the order of things. Indeed,
some of the lawyers interviewed in the study of defence counsel established as
the ground rule of their relationship with their client the fact that they would
be in total command at every point. One lawyer repeatedly stated in separate
interviews involving different cases that a condition of his agreement to
represent someone was *total* control. For example, regarding one of his
clients the lawyer stated:

> [At the bail hearing I told the accused] to keep his mouth shut and let me do the
> talking...
>
> Any lawyer who's worth his salt tells his client how to dress, how to have
> his hair cut, how to have it combed, how to behave, how to answer questions...
>
> I don't allow my clients to have reservations [about me], they either follow
> my advice or find another lawyer.

The same lawyer was asked if he had any disagreement with another
client. He replied, 'No,' and then went on to describe his view of his own role
as a lawyer:

Q: Were there any disagreements between yourself and your client about the con-
     duct of the case?
L: No. I'll tell you why. I tell every client of mine that when it comes to the
     courtroom, I am the boss and if they're not ready to accept that, find them-
     selves another lawyer. I tell every client when they walk into my office, how
     there's only one lawyer in this room. I am noted for being nasty that way. I
     don't take advice from clients and clients don't tell me how to handle a case.
Q: Did that also hold for the whole question of plea?
L: Yes.

Q: Okay. is your client satisfied with your representation of him?

L: I rather think so ...

Q: What role do you think your client saw you as performing for him in this case?

L: Godfather. I think that describes it. They come in and they put their hands out with complete trust in you. And that is what is unfortunate that there are so many young lawyers coming out that are getting this trust that don't deserve it – who do more harm to their clients than do good. Because I'm willing to bet you that 98 per cent of the clients who come in, come in with complete faith and trust in you.

Q: How about the so called rounders ... ?

L: I like them, because I'll tell you, the rounders or the confirmed criminals are the ones who will come in and be the most honest with you. They really will. They'll walk in and lay all the cards on the table because they've dealt with lawyers before. And I will tell every client, the greatest enemy of any defence lawyer is surprise, so I've got to know everything. And the professional criminal will walk in, and he is a delight to defend, because he'll just lay it all on the line and say the ball's in your court.

Q: Okay. What role did you see yourself as having in this case?

L: I wish I could say as the advocate. I was commercial. I was out to make a buck. He was paying me $750 and I saw him as $750.

The fact that the charges of impaired/over 80 mg were dismissed made the accused in this case particularly accepting of his lawyer's orders. When asked if he was satisfied with his lawyer's handling of the case, the accused replied, 'Yes, he got me off.' When asked if he trusted that his lawyer was on his side, he replied, 'For seven hundred bucks I hope he's on my side.' The accused's only concrete basis for trusting his lawyer's knowledge was also expressed in terms of the outcome: 'Well he got me off, I think he knows what he's doing.'

The 'godfather' quality of the lawyer's role is particularly in evidence when it comes to making key decisions, because the lawyer often formulates the 'choices' available to the accused in 'an offer you can't refuse' terms. While we were unable to observe these formulations directly by sitting in on discussions (however, see Macfarlane, 1982, for observational evidence) we did learn from the accused that matters were often put to them in ways which meant they had no choice but to follow what their lawyer had prearranged with the police and/or crown attorney. This was usually the case with plea settlements transacted by the lawyer. The lawyer would return to tell the accused that if he did not accept the settlement, the risks would be extremely high in terms of more convictions and/or stiffer penalties and/or more delay. Similarly, the accused talked of bail decisions formulated by their lawyers in terms which could only produce one result. For example, an accused described the work of his duty counsel at his bail hearing as involving discussions with the crown regarding what conditions would secure release. He was not privy to these discussions, but simply nodded agreement to whatever the duty counsel said the crown counsel would agree to: 'He says, 'I can get you out on one condition ... that you quit driving and that you quit drinking totally.' So I agreed to that and then he started talking and they talked and then he came back over and he said, 'One other condition will *have to be* that you are in the house every night by ten-thirty. Do you agree to that?' So I said, 'Yes,' and then he said that he'd do this and then that got me out.'

As we document in chapter 4, in some cases lawyers' efforts were decidedly in the best interests of their clients and in other cases they were not. Regardless, the accused had very little say in the matter. The effect is that the accused's wishes and decisions are usually no more than a reflection of his lawyer's commands. Similar to the situation with the police, the accused realizes that he is not really making 'decisions' as such but just going along with the lawyer's order of things:

Q: [Your lawyer] handled the case?

A: Yeah ... I had my decisions to make too but they were, they were nothing, you know.

Q: What were your decisions?

A: He just said, he just advised me what would be better, let's put it that way. I didn't, like, they weren't really decisions. They were more his advice, what would happen and that.

Q: Okay. Now, was the decision ultimately yours then, is that what you're saying?

A: Well, if I had wanted it, it would have been. But like I said, I went along with the lawyer, and what he thought was best.

In sum, the accused could do little more than have blind trust that things would unfold *just* as they should. His lawyer was relatively free from client control because he knew that his client was structurally bound to the dependency of blind trust.[8] From where the accused sat, literally, justice was blinded.

The Election Decision

We can consider influences on defence decision-making through views on how key decisions were made. In this section we consider the decision on election for trial, while in the next section we examine the decision to appeal.[9]

Among 101 interviewed accused, only 36 had charges which enabled an election choice between the lower and higher courts of the province. Among these 36, 30 elected to have the case heard in provincial court; 1 elected county court judge sitting alone; 3 elected county court judge and jury; 1 initially elected county court judge and jury and then elected down to the provincial court after an agreement for a guilty plea and charge withdrawal had been worked out between his lawyer and the crown; and 1 elected supreme court judge and jury.

The accused said they themselves made the election choice in 15 instances and their lawyers made the choice in 21 instances (34 of 36 accused with an election choice had a lawyer). When the accused said they made the choice, it was invariably to stay at the provincial court level and most often because they wanted to get the matter over with (10 of 15) or because they were happy with the provincial court judge who was scheduled to hear their case (3 of 15). When the lawyer was said to have made the choice, it included five decisions to elect up and one decision to elect up and then down. The reasons for the decision when the lawyer controlled it were greatly varied, and they were much more likely to include a strategic element.

When the accused claimed that they had input into the election choice, it was most often combined with a wish to expedite their case. Many saw county court election only in terms of the delay it would bring, and thus elected provincial court without further consideration. Furthermore, the accused's desire to get a case over with was *the* reason for ignoring or refusing to take the lawyer's advice on election. While this situation did not appear frequently, we have indications from accounts of both accused and lawyers that it did happen. For example, an accused said he was going to plead guilty to a mischief charge until he was advised by a duty counsel to plead not guilty and take it to trial. He said he was then faced with the prospect of election, but he was ignorant of what the choice entailed and decided solely on the basis of getting the matter over with immediately:

A: I didn't know what they were talking about, 'cause they named all these – do you want to go to judge and jury, da, da, da, da. I didn't know what was happening. So ... after I went and says [to the duty counsel], 'What have you been talking about?' And he says, 'Well, I just want you to know [your options]. And I says, 'I just wanted to get it over with today, okay, tell him [judge] that.' So that's what I did.

     ...

Q: When they read the mischief charge, did you understand that?

A: Not really.

Q: Okay.

A: I didn't understand anything. I just wanted to get it over with, and get out of there.

The lawyers for two accused in different cases stated in interview that their clients ignored their suggestions for electing up because they wished to avoid delay. The lawyer for one accused said he had worked out with the crown an agreement for a guilty plea and charge withdrawal regarding the multiple charges against his client and advised his client that they should 'judge shop' in order to obtain a suitable judge for sentencing. The lawyer stated that when they were unable to obtain one of two favourable judges at the provincial court level, he advised his client to elect up but his client refused because he wanted to get it over with. The lawyer for the other accused said that he suggested a county court election to his client as a strategy for obtaining a bail review so the accused might be released from custody while awaiting trial. The accused apparently refused his advice, saying he would prefer to get the matter over with by electing provincial court trial, even if it meant awaiting trial in custody.

Several accused were essentially ignorant about the existence of the election choice, and once they learned about it when it came up in conversation with their lawyer or in open court, they could not grasp the meanings and implications involved. Nine of the accused with an election choice said they were not at all aware of it before it came up in court.[10] Some did not pay attention to it even at the court stage. Included in this group was an accused who was unaware that an election choice was part of the proceedings and who retrospectively defined provincial court as the criminal court and county court as 'divorces and things like that.'

Among the 27 accused who said they were aware of the election choice beforehand, 17 said they learned of it from their lawyer while 10 said their knowledge came from previous experiences in the court process. However, many of these persons revealed in interviews that they did not grasp the full meaning of the election choice, or the strategic elements involved. For example, an accused said that while his lawyer did not discuss the election choice with him, he knew about it because 'I've been through it before.' However, his knowledge was obviously limited and the lawyer had clearly controlled the decision to stay in provincial court for reasons unknown to the accused. When asked why he elected provincial court, the accused replied that he wanted to get it over with and planned to plead guilty at that level even though he believed that at county court he would have had a better chance of being found not guilty:

Q: Did [your lawyer] talk to you about the election at all?
A: No.
Q: He didn't say anything?
A: Not that I recall.
Q: So I mean, when you went into court that day, how were you going to decide when they asked you what kind of court you wanted to go to?
A: Well [my lawyer] was standing beside the box, yeah, he did ask me.
Q: And what did you say?
A: Wanted to get it over with that day.
Q: Did he give you any advice as to whether or not you should go to a higher court?
A: No.

Q: No? Why didn't you consider going to a higher court?

A: Would have took a longer time. Would have sat in jail for maybe a couple of months instead of a weekend. I guess it got it over with faster.

Q: So you chose the provincial court just to get it over with?

A: Yeah.

Q: Were there any other reasons why you chose it?

A: No.

Q: If you had chosen a higher court would your plea have been different?

A: Yes.

Q: How would you have pleaded?

A: Not guilty.

Q: To all of them?

A: Yes.

Q: Why?

A: Because in high court you can't bring up all these papers that you can in low court.

Q: What papers?

A: Like, ah, [police] statements, you can't use that as evidence, so they wouldn't have had no evidence on us.

Similarly, another accused said he knew about the election choice prior to the court appearance because of previous experiences with the court process. He admitted that these experiences had not enlightened him, and he therefore decided to seek the instruction of his lawyer. However, the instruction came not in the form of knowledge but in the form of an order: 'I don't understand any of that [about elections], right, so I mention that to [my lawyer]. He says, "Just sit down and don't say nothing, he says, and I'll say it all for you."' The accused then went on to say that provincial court was elected to avoid the inevitable delay caused by electing up.

If the accused was aware of strategic advantages in the election choice, it was usually in cases where the lawyer was said to have made the choice. Several accused mentioned a belief that there was likely to be more scrutiny of a case if it went to a higher court. Some believed that this scrutiny included a more legalistic approach in the higher court, an impression that may have been reinforced by the greater degree of formality in the higher court. For example, an accused charged with threatening his wife's life over the telephone and planning to plead not guilty said that on his lawyer's advice he was going to elect a county court judge and jury trial. However, the charge was withdrawn by the crown before the election choice had to be made. The accused thought that electing up was advantageous because there would be more detailed legal scrutiny of the complainant and her allegations adding, 'They're more law [in county court], they go more by the books than the provincial judge does.'

In relation to eight accused, the election choice was said to revolve around the question of whether a provincial court judge would be leniently disposed. In five instances, it was decided to stay at the provincial court level, including three in which the accused said he himself made the choice in consideration of the particular judge hearing the case. In three instances the accused said their lawyers elected the county court level in order to avoid having a provincial court judge hear the case.

When lawyers were controlling the election choice in terms of 'judge shopping,' it was not always with reference to a specific judge or judges, but more in consideration of what some judges at each level were likely to be amenable to. For example, an accused charged with weapons dangerous said he elected county court on his lawyer's advice to avoid a provincial court judge and to go into the evidence in more detail. In his account, the lawyer said he elected up to obtain disclosure through an examination of witnesses at a preliminary hearing, and because it would 'give us a better opportunity to negotiate a plea if one was required.' At the county court level, the lawyer said he held a discussion in the judge's chambers with the judge and crown attorney and agreed to a guilty plea in exchange for a non-custodial sentence.

Several accused who were involved in cases that were clearly foreclosed said that they elected provincial court in the belief that they would receive a more lenient sentence because they would not be wasting the court's time by electing up. For example, an accused stated that 'if you are found guilty of the same offence in high court as in low court you get a longer sentence ... because of the amount of money you are costing them, the government.' Indeed, this was sometimes an element used by lawyers to encourage their clients to elect provincial court. For example, a lawyer said he formulated the election choice to his client by informing her that the higher you go, the harsher the sentence. An accused who planned to plead guilty on one count of break, enter and theft said his lawyer advised him not to elect county court on the grounds that it would be perceived as a waste of the court's time and might therefore result in a harsher sentence. The accused translated this into a belief that it is sometimes better not to subject yourself to the greater scrutiny that is perceived to be characteristic of the higher courts: '[The provincial court judge is] just sitting there waiting to get rid of you ... I think he probably, just to get rid of you, [says], "OK, kid. Thirty days. Get out of here." You know, meanwhile the kid probably deserves three months.'

In light of their experiences, the 36 accused with an election choice were asked if, in retrospect, they would have elected differently. Over one-third (13 of 36) said they would have elected up if they had it to do over again.

Seven accused who had their cases dealt with in provincial court said that if they had it to do over again they would elect county court with the judge sitting alone. Three of these persons said they made the original election choice to get the matter over with. The remaining four said their lawyer made the original election choice: two were involved in elections forming part of a guilty plea arrangement with the crown attorney, and two were involved in cases where the lawyers believed that the provincial court judge would be relatively lenient in sentencing after guilty pleas. In general, it appears that these accused would have changed their election in light of what they perceived to be harsh sentences received at the hands of provincial court judges.

Six accused said if they had it to do over again they would elect county court judge and jury. Five of these persons had their cases heard before a provincial court judge and one had his case heard before a county court judge. Two persons originally elected provincial court to get the matter over with, accompanied by some urging from their lawyers: one wanted to avoid 'dead time' awaiting trial and was upset at receiving 22 months in prison for guilty pleas to three robbery charges, and the other was upset that his accomplice on a series of break and enters received a short jail term and probation after going to county court, while he himself received 15 months in prison plus probation at the provincial court level. Another pair originally elected provincial court because of specific judges who were believed to be 'soft,' but they turned out to be not so soft. These persons believed they could have obtained a fairer (equals more lenient) hearing from a judge and jury.

In sum, the majority of the accused with an election choice did not make the choice themselves. They frequently had a poor understanding of what the choice entailed and what strategic advantage it might bring. Whether or not they were upset with the decision that had been taken depended largely upon their expectations. They were satisfied with the election if it yielded the outcome they expected, or if they persisted in believing that the alternative choice (e.g. wasting the higher court's time; proceeding before an unfavourable provincial court judge) might have had even worse consequences.

The Decision to Appeal

Appeals as we know them have been allowed in Canada since 1923 (Salhany, 1978). By statute a defendant is allowed to appeal against his conviction and/or sentence on either indictable or summary conviction offences. Similarly, the crown has the right to appeal against an acquittal/dismissal and/or sentence.

On the whole, appeals were unappealing to the accused. Only four stated that they planned to appeal their sentence and two planned an appeal on their conviction and sentence. All six had been sentenced in magistrates' court. One of the two who appealed both conviction and sentence was a person convicted and sentenced for attempting to cause a disturbance. The accused was charged as a result of his involvement in allegedly impeding traffic as a member of a union picket line. The accused's lawyer had been hired by the union and the appeal was instigated by the union. There was more at stake here than the accused's conviction. 'It's just ah, if they don't appeal it the law goes down into the books as a, okay, that you are convicted of attempting to impede traffic. So whenever there is a strike anywhere in Canada the police could use this as a means of force, to force people not to participate in a strike. They can just come by and say well, "you are attempting to cause a distur-bance, come along with me" and they keep going every day [of the strike].' In this case the accused said he made use of his rights, including the right to silence at the police station, pleading not guilty, and, finally, appealing the conviction. However, he was part of an organization and the power of that organization was backing him.

The other appeal on conviction and sentence was initiated by the lawyer for a person convicted of refusal to take a breathalyser test. The appeal was to be based on the argument that the accused had been advised by a lawyer (not the one retained for the trial) not to take the breathalyser test, and therefore he should not be held responsible for the act.

Four accused said they planned to appeal the sentence they received. One was sentenced to maximum consecutive terms adding up to one year in prison after he entered guilty pleas on two counts of breach of probation. The lawyer for this person said he would argue that the guilty plea should mitigate the sentence, especially in light of the fact that avoiding a trial saved child witnesses from having to testify. The lawyer said he would also argue that the month the accused spent in custody awaiting trial should also have been taken into account in the sentence. The accused whose case we outlined in chapter 1 planned to appeal his sentence of four years' imprisonment, a penalty which both he and his lawyer viewed as too harsh. Another person said he would appeal his sentence of two years less a day definite plus two years less a day indefinite in a provincial reformatory, in the hope that he would be given a longer sentence which would be served in a penitentiary. He believed that he would be paroled earlier from penitentiary than from the provincial reformatory. Another accused said he contemplated an appeal on his sentence of $300 in fines and suspension of his driving licence for his convictions for refusing to take a breathalyser test and impaired driving. The accused said his main motive for the appeal was his wish to avoid immediate suspension of his driver's licence.

In all six cases in which an appeal was contemplated, it was the lawyer who took the initiative in suggesting the appeal.

Among the remaining 78 accused for whom the question of appeal was applicable, 28 said they were not appealing because they were satisfied with the outcome, 21 said an appeal was not worth the trouble, 14 feared a worse outcome if they appealed, 3 felt an appeal would not be successful, 3 gave other reasons, and no information was available for 9. Many who said they were not appealing because they were satisfied with the outcome, or because an appeal was not worth the effort, expressed a desire to put their involve-ment with the criminal process behind them. Thus, one accused stated, 'I was thinking of appealing it but, I don't know I want to get it over and done with so I can get the heck out, you know, and have no more hassles, so I'll get my time done and get out.'

Time and cost were other reasons given by the accused for appeals not being worthwhile. For those in custody, appeals against sentence may be of little consequence since the sentence may already have been served by the time the case is heard in appellate court. For example, the appeal of the case of one accused had still not been heard seven months after his one-year prison sentence was given. Another accused said he did not consider appealing his sentence because on a previous occasion it took '12 to 14' months for the appeal to go through. Another respondent felt that an appeal was not worth the time and money:

Q: Okay. I just want to ask you a brief question about your appeal. What is it that you're not sure about in terms of appealing the case.

A: Well, like the point is, like, I can appeal it, okay, but, meanwhile all this is going to cost me more money, right. And really at the end, the most I can get out of it, is get maybe, my mug shots or my fingerprints burned or something like that, but I figure, really they're not going to get burned, cause they're going to keep them, you know, it's going to make a point that I'm right and he's wrong, but, really what's it's going to do to him, eh. That's what I figure, you know, like, I'd like to prove that I'm not guilty, right to everybody in my family, my mother and father, all my friends, you know, show that I'm not guilty, right, but, you know, in the end is it going to do me any good?

These reasons are based upon non-legal issues. In a system where the end rather than the process is the most intelligible part for the accused, one could hardly expect them to prolong the process in the knowledge that they still would have no control over the end result.

Fourteen of the 17 who felt an appeal would be unsuccessful expressed the fear that they could receive a more severe sentence. This is possible in the Canadian judicial system (see Ruby, 1976: 277–9):

Q: Okay now. I was asking if you plan to appeal your sentence?

A: No.

Q: Why not?

A: I can't win so why fight.

Q: Why can't you win?

A: I well, if I appeal I can get, maybe they'd ah, the higher ups would give me more time. You never know, see.

As we have seen repeatedly, the accused's fear of some potential worse consequence if he does not co-operate is an intrinsic threat throughout every stage of the process. The accused person is sometimes threatened with more charges, being held in custody, and/or a more severe sentence if he does not sign a statement. He is threatened with the possibility of a more severe sentence if he does not plead guilty. After conviction and sentence, there is an implicit threat of a harsher sentence if he appeals.

It is, of course, possible and even probable that an appeal in most cases would have been unsuccessful and that the accused's counsel is aware of this. The fact that only 20 accused even spoke to their counsel about appeals is tantamount to saying that the appeal decision was actually made by the lawyer. Some accused felt the decision about appeal was the lawyer's alone. For example, an accused who pleaded guilty to break, enter and theft and was sentenced to 60 days' intermittent plus two years' probation, had this to say about an appeal:

Q: Do you plan to appeal your sentence?
A: No.
Q: Did you talk with [lawyer] about appeal at all?
A: No.
Q: Why don't you plan to appeal?
A: I have no – I just – I just can't see appealing it.
Q: Well, why?
A: Like, okay – the only thing that come up was the breach of trust. Like, it might get me thirty days off, or something. But, uh, when you get down to, uh, going back through courts again –
Q: Uh-huh.
A: Uh, lawyers cost, and everything – for thirty days – I don't think it would be worth it. You know – unless he suggests it, eh? If he – you know, if he thought the judge was unfair –
Q: Uh-huh.
A: – then he would have suggested it. But I guess he figures everything was pretty good.

As in many other stages of processing, the accused is usually either not informed or misinformed. One of the reasons for there beng no discussion between the accused and his lawyer about appeals is that once the accused is sentenced everyone's involvement except his ceases. It is not surprising, therefore, that the accused also feels that after sentencing it is the end of the line. A number of accused commented in the interview that they had little or no interaction with their lawyer after their case was disposed of:

Q: Have you talked about an appeal with your lawyer at all?
A: No, I haven't said nothing to my lawyer at all since that [sentencing] happened. He hasn't even, he said, the only thing he said to me was, 'the judge said 90 days, 3 months on each count.' And he said, my lawyer looked at me and said, 'You're lucky that's what you got,' and he walked away. And then a lady officer took me away and I haven't seen him since.

The lack of interest in the accused shown by his counsel after sentencing is not completely surprising. Forty-two of the accused interviewed were represented by lawyers under the legal aid plan; twelve of these were duty counsel. When the accused is granted legal aid, the certificate covers only the lawyer's activities up to and including sentencing. If an appeal is to be launched, he must apply for a new certificate. The law society makes a judgment on the potential success of the appeal before a certificate is issued. Since they are only being paid up until the accused is sentenced, most legal aid lawyers do not bother even discussing appeals with their client.

Among the six who were appealing, four were represented by counsel retained privately. The other two were on legal aid certificates and one of these two accused stated that he was paying his lawyer a sum above and beyond the amount assigned by legal aid. Of the 32 interviewed accused who had retained a lawyer privately, 10 (31 per cent) discussed an appeal with their lawyer. Of the 42 interviewed accused who were represented by a lawyer retained on legal aid or by duty counsel, 9 (21 per cent) discussed an appeal with them.[11] In a world where you get only what you pay for, the accused in criminal court must pay for what he does not want, and he must pay more to get less of the unwanted service.

In this chapter we have considered the autonomy of the accused in decision-making in relation to their lawyers. The accused has some apparent autonomy in deciding whether or not to engage a lawyer. However, he is likely to engage a lawyer because a lawyer has institutionalized privileges not available to the accused acting alone. The lawyer has access to out-of-court arenas and information not open to the accused, is deemed to have superior ability in interpreting and using information, and is seen as having power within the 'hierarchy of credibility' based upon his professional status. Therefore, there is a strong tendency to engage a lawyer. Moreover, there is a propensity to engage a lawyer as a taken-for-granted part of the process.

If a lawyer is engaged the accused tends to defer to the lawyer to the point where what are ostensibly his own decisions are in reality the lawyer's decisions; that is, the lawyer 'orders' the decisions and then leaves it up to the accused to follow them. Similar to what we discovered in examining transactions between the police and the accused, 'ordering' does not usually have to take the form of a stern command because there are enough other enabling resources available to accomplish the task. Instead, the 'ordering' consists of a formulation of the choices so that there is in reality only one alternative, namely that which is in accordance with the lawyer's orders and the wider ordering of justice. The accused accepts on trust the formulation and the 'obvious' choice that follows from it because he has no independent resources to challenge it.

An appreciation of the dependent position of the accused in the criminal process must go beyond the boundaries the accused is aware of. While accounts of the accused provide our primary data, we must also consider decisions taken by others which clearly circumscribe his or her choices and actions. In the case of lawyers representing the accused, the focal point for inquiry is out-of-court plea discussions with the police, crown attorney, and judges. It is in this context that many 'trials' are conducted. Since the accused is not usually present at these 'trials,' he is forced to make his decisions based upon how and what his lawyer tells him about what happened and what are the limits to the possible. In the next chapter we enquire into how these limits are generated, and what this entails for the accused's dependent position in the criminal process.

4

Order out of Court I:
The Process of Plea Transaction

There's no better way of exercising the imagination than the study of law. No poet ever interpreted nature as freely as a lawyer interprets the truth.
   Jean Giraudoux, *Tiger at the Gates* (1935)

There is no such thing as justice in the abstract; it is merely a compact between men.
   Epicurus, 'Principal Doctrines,' in *Letters, Principal Doctrines and Vatican Sayings* (3rd century BC)

The Process of Plea Transaction in Perspective

Researchers and commentators on the criminal process stress the pivotal nature of the guilty plea decision, because it involves the simultaneous consideration of past, present, and future aspects of the case.[1] This decision is arrived at as part of a process which transpires outside the courtroom. There is an order out of court which 'frames' this decision so that it becomes a routine matter for organizational participants and routinely accepted by the accused. In what follows we consider the constitution of this order and its implications for the position of the accused within the criminal process.

In Anglo-American legal systems the determination of guilt or innocence is most often dealt with not in the context of open scrutiny in the court, but in various 'low visibility' contexts out of court. Charge alterations, possibilities for evidence submission, and ranges of sentencing are discussed in a variety of locales, e.g. in the courthouse corridors and offices, in the judge's chambers, at a lunch counter, and over the telephone. These discussions are directed at making an arrangement satisfactory to all parties whereby the accused can be convinced to plead guilty. This process has been variously referred to as plea dealing, bargaining, discussion, transaction, and negotiation. As Cousineau and Verdun-Jones (1979, 1979a) point out, the literature is full of conceptual ambiguity and some bias which has confused discussion of the topic.

The main body of legal commentary and academic research on the topic of plea discussions has emanated from American sources. In the past century, the Americans have moved from a judicial position that such a practice is a 'moral outrage'[2] to a judicial and legislative legitimation of the practice via a series of US Supreme Court decisions and amendments to the Federal Rules of Criminal Procedure.[3] Regardless of the judicial position, guilty pleas have always characterized the disposition of cases in American criminal courts. Heumann (1978) documents that for successive periods going back to the last century, nine-tenths of cases in selected Connecticut jurisdictions have been disposed of by guilty pleas. There is now a large volume of American empirical research on the topic of plea transactions. This literature documents the institutionalized pervasiveness of the practice. For example, a study in New York City conducted by the Vera Institute (1977: 133) reports on 'a system dominated by plea bargaining, in which only 2.6% of the cases ended in trial' (for other examples, see Newman, 1966; Blumberg, 1967; Church, 1976; Heumann, 1978; Law Enforcement Assistance Administration, 1978; Utz, 1978; Feeley, 1979).

In the United Kingdom there has been relatively less attention given to the phenomenon of plea discussions. The main impetus to some public awareness and debate came about as a result of a judicial ruling in *R. v Turner* (1970) 2 ALL ER 281. This case limited judicial involvement in the process of plea discussion to making general statements regarding sentence. For example, a judge can say that he has a non-custodial sentence in mind, but not state the specific sentence, as a guide to counsel weighing up the plea decision. Turner also reiterated the fact that a guilty plea could be a mitigating factor in sentencing.[4]

On the research side, there have been few efforts made to document the practices involved in plea discussions and the extent of these practices. In a document study, McCabe and Purves (1972) found that among 112 defendants who pleaded guilty after a last-minute change of mind, 64 had 'an arrangement of pleas accepted by the court' which involved some discussion among the defence counsel and the prosecuting counsel and/or the judge. Bottoms and McClean (1976: 126) report that from an interview sample of 293 accused, only 3 were involved in 'plea bargaining,' defined as 'the defendant agrees to plead guilty to at least one charge in return for some concession by the prosecution.' In contrast, Baldwin and McConville (1977: especially 28–32) report that in a sample of 121 interviewed accused who were 'late plea changers' at the crown court level, 19 were involved in plea 'bargains' related to sentence (9 of which the researchers judged to be in violation of the *Turner* rule), and 3 were involved in plea 'bargains' related to charge reductions. A further 16 accused reported that their lawyer had probably struck a 'bargain' on their behalf but they were unaware of the details.

Probably because it is rooted more in British than in American traditions, the Canadian legal system has given little attention to the role of plea discussions, and academic researchers have been similarly inattentive. Where there has been recent judicial comment on the practice, it has been to denounce it.[5] Denunciation has also been forthcoming from the federal Law Reform Commission (1974–5: 14) and Ontario Law Reform Commission (1973: Part II). However, there is little specific detail on what is being denounced because there has been little specific data collected on the practices involved. Apart from preliminary work on the role of prosecutors in Canadian jurisdictions by Grosman (1969) and Wilkins (1976), the small document-based study by Hartnagel and Wynne (1975), and the prisoner interview study by Klein (1976), there has been no empirical research on the topic. Academics have explored some of the issues (Ferguson, 1972; Ferguson and Roberts, 1974; Cousineau and Verdun-Jones, 1979, 1979a), but similar to the commentators from law reform commissions they have little Canadian data upon which to base their arguments. Cousineau and Verdun-Jones (1979: 305) do note that the main research need is for a study that 'traces the flow of accused persons through each phase of the criminal justice process ... [and which] would necessarily include *direct observation* of the plea bargaining process itself.' This can be taken as a prescription for the research we are reporting in this volume.

There can be little doubt that plea discussions, aimed at an agreement by the defence to plead guilty in exchange for some perceived benefit, are an integral part of the criminal process in Anglo-American jurisdictions. There are many structural reasons for this being the case. Indeed, comparable forms of discussion, negotiation, manipulation, coercion, and bargaining are characteristic of legal frameworks outside the criminal law, and organizational frameworks outside the legal institution (cf Strauss, 1978). For example, Ross (1970) analyses the civil law process involved in insurance claims, and documents that 90 per cent of all insurance claims are settled out of court. The claimant's position is in many respects similar to that of the accused. He is involved in a common stake with the other side (to settle as quickly as possible in the easiest way possible) as well as a mutually exclusive stake (one party's gain is the other's loss). He is a 'one-shot' player while his legal agent and those on the other side are repeat participants (Galanter, 1974), making the matter routine for them but not for him. The option exists to 'go it alone,' although the belief that the inexperienced and unrepresented usually receive less benefit creates a strong propensity to engage a lawyer. The option exists to have a trial and settle in court – something which can be used to advantage by either side – although there are enough drawbacks in doing so that it is usually used more as a threat than taken up. The balance of power is unequal, favouring the prosecution, with the defence lawyer structurally constrained to do little more than keep the case, and his client, orderly as the matter proceeds through the court (see pp 77–8).

While the phenomenon of dealing for advantage is widespread in all forms of organizational life, it undoubtedly varies in both quality and quantity according to the particular structural arrangements within which it is framed. Even within the organization of criminal law enforcement, there is likely to be significant variation according to the structure of formal rules and how these interact with the particular community and court organization in which they are implemented. Thus, we would expect to find variation among American, British, and Canadian jurisdictions, as well as within particular jurisdictions in each of these countries.

In any particular jurisdiction in which data are collected, the researcher must consider the limits which frame what it is possible to make an agreement about. Some of these limits are obvious to any experienced participant in the organization. The law itself frames the nature of the transaction. For example, in Canada if a person is charged with impaired driving and refusal to provide a breath sample, he can be convicted on both counts. A defence lawyer might attempt to obtain withdrawal on one count in exchange for a guilty plea on the other, in which case he is seeking a possible concession. However, if a person is charged with impaired driving and excess blood alcohol level (over 80 mg), he can only be legally convicted on one charge *or* the other.[6] Consequently, discussions will centre upon which of the two might be the subject of a guilty plea (assuming the evidence is there) rather than whether or not there will be a withdrawal of one charge. Statutory minimum sentences for repeated impaired convictions also control what the crown might be able to offer in terms of recommendations for leniency in either case.

American literature informs us about the impact of charges on plea transactions. Church (1976) studied an attempt to ban charge-reduction practices in drug cases. The practice had been for the prosecution and defence to agree to a reduced charge in exchange for a guilty plea. A ban on this practice produced new forms of plea arrangements in which judges were brought into the discussions, and the dealing focused upon sentences rather than charges. Moreover, after the ban, prosecutors were much more likely to reject police-laid charges because of the seriousness of the charges (maximum 25-year prison sentence) without the possibility of charge reductions.

The impact can also filter through to the punishment segment of the criminal process, as indicated by the changes in sentencing law in California (cf Alschuler, 1978; Puglia, 1979). Under the Adult Authority system, substantial discretionary power was taken away from the prosecutor. He could do little dealing over sentence because the sentence length and conditions were largely within the hands of the Adult Authority rather than the judge. Moreover, the prosecutor knew that charges not processed were still on the accused's record and would be taken into account by the Adult Authority in the parole decisions even if they were not registered as convictions. There could not be an easier way to penalize an accused, since the prosecutor did not have to prove the charges and yet he knew they would have an impact upon sentence. Under the new fixed and presumptive sentencing law, power is brought into the hands of the prosecutor because he can agree with the defence to withhold or introduce aggravating or mitigating factors according to whether or not the accused complies by pleading guilty. The new law gives the prosecutor a greater ability to influence the duration of the sentence, and thus a greater power in plea discussions with the defence lawyer.

Canadian commentators (e.g. Grosman, 1969; Klein, 1974) have argued that the legal structure in Canada makes it more important to negotiate with respect to sentence rather than charges. A conviction on a reduced charge may still bring the same sentence as a conviction on the original charge. Moreover, to the extent that judges are known to give concurrent rather than consecutive sentences on multiple counts, negotiating for a reduction in counts is less likely to make a difference in the sentencing outcome.

In addition to the limits framed by the penalty structure, and by sentencing practices of judges, there are substantial influences coming from other sources. Chief among these is the charging practices of the police, which frame what the other parties have to discuss once the case reaches the court stage. Commentators have frequently referred to the importance of police charging practices in influencing the negotiation process. Thus, Alschuler (1968) states, 'The charge is the asking price in plea bargaining, and the drafting of accusations is therefore an integral part of the negotiating process.' However, until recently there has been very little research attention to the way in which the police lay charges in anticipation of influencing the framework of negotiations at the court stage.[7] For example, our observation of the police in constructing cases against our accused respondents (Ericson, 1981, 1982) led us to conclude that an established practice was to charge every accused in a case with everything possible as a means of creating a maximal starting position for plea discussions. This was undertaken even on some occasions when the police explicitly stated that some of the charges against some of the accused would clearly not be upheld in court. Moreover, detectives frequently participated in plea discussions and were often acknowledged by the defence lawyer and crown attorney to be the key participant because they had the most intimate official knowledge of the case and thus were deemed to be in the best position to decide the limits of negotiation.

Another important consideration in understanding limits to plea discussions is that they often remain at a covert level. As Morgan (1975) points out, there is a 'covert implicit substratum of negotiation' in any bureaucratic organization. Often 'silent bargains' (Strauss, 1978: 227) are struck which have a profound impact on decision-making and which fundamentally influence social relations within the organization. For example, the crown attorney may have an agreement with the police that while dual charges arising from the same incident (e.g. theft/possession of stolen property) can legitimately be laid in some instances and result in convictions on both counts – *Côté* v *The Queen* (1974) 18 CCC (2d) 321 – the crown attorney will routinely withdraw one count in exchange for a guilty plea on the other count. Thereafter, whenever these circumstances arise all parties know the limits to negotiation and will routinely accept a guilty plea to one count in exchange for withdrawal of the other count even though it is legally possible to seek convictions on both counts. In cases of this type there is not likely to be much, if any, discussion about a charge 'deal' because 'everybody knows' in advance what the 'deal' is and is not. In this type of case there is no 'deal' at all, only an acceptance of the existing practice for how normal cases of this type are normally handled (Sudnow, 1965).

In light of such practices as police 'overlaying' higher and multiple charges, and routinized agreements for withdrawal of dual charges arising from the same incident, it is extremely difficult to ascertain what a 'deal' or 'bargain' consists of. As we document in the following sections, there were cases in which a reduction in charge appeared more related to problems of evidence on the higher charge than to any concession from the crown; cases in which the withdrawn charges had no evidence on which to proceed and thus provided no concession from the crown; and cases in which the withdrawn charges were so trivial in comparison with the charges to which the accused pleaded guilty, that again there was no concession from the crown. Furthermore, given the greater number of elements which go into judicial determinations of guilt or innocence, and sentence, it is also difficult to say whether someone in any particular case might have 'got off more lightly' by pleading not guilty than by agreeing to a guilty plea arrangement, or vice versa.

It is possible to state that plea *discussions* took place, and whether or not these discussions resulted in a plea *agreement*. It is much more difficult to say that these discussions involved a *deal* or *bargain* for either side.[8] In the aggregate, what lawyers obtain for their clients from plea transactions cannot routinely deviate from the tariff or going rate they themselves set along with the criminal control agents (Feeley, 1979). Indeed, when an especially advantageous deal is obtained by either the defence or the prosecution, the process is operating in a capricious and erratic manner compared with what normally happens.

The question of whether a 'deal' or 'bargain' is obtained must be answered ultimately in terms of the perceptions of the various actors. Defence lawyers, crown attorneys, and police officers can judge an agreement based upon their 'recipe' knowledge of the local court and its tariff structure as they *use* it in any particular case. The accused, without this 'recipe' knowledge, and without even a peek at the plea transaction process, is forced to make his assessment of the agreement from a distance. To the extent that the criminal control agents reach an agreement that merely reflects the going rate (as we document later in this chapter), and to the extent the accused is nevertheless made to believe that he got a bargain (as we document in chapter 5), the term 'plea bargaining' can be seen as another source of mystification for keeping the accused in order.

In the remainder of this chapter we examine lawyers' accounts of the volume and nature of plea transactions. We then consider the manner in which these transactions are conducted, and how particular settlements are reached. In the next chapter we compare the lawyers' accounts with accounts by the accused as a means of ascertaining the extent to which the accused understand the out-of-court 'trials' conducted on their behalf by the lawyers. We then examine the plea decisions of the accused in terms of the various influences coming from the order out of court.

In what follows, we view plea *discussions* as being initiated to reach an *agreement* whereby the defence will plead guilty in return for a promise of some benefit from the crown. Plea discussions can be characterized by coercion, manipulation, or negotiation (Strauss, 1978). Plea discussions can take place without an agreement being reached, an obvious point which has been largely ignored by other researchers.[9] When agreement is not achieved, steps taken during negotiations can become irretrievable and still influence the outcome. Plea agreements can be reached which are seen as bargains by the lawyer but not his client, by the client but not his lawyer, or by both of them. This is a refinement on the Law Reform Commission of Canada (1975a: 45) definition of plea 'bargaining' as 'any agreement by the accused to plead guilty in return for the promise of some benefit' because it recognizes that the accused sometimes does not make the decision, but has it made for him by his lawyer. This is a broader definition than that provided by researchers who include only sentence concessions in their definition (e.g. Baldwin and McConville, 1977: 19) and who thereby ignore other commodities (charges, protection from investigation, submission of evidence) that are trafficked in by the police and crown attorneys and sometimes purchased by the defence.

Lawyers' Accounts of Plea Transactions

Lawyers do not always have discussions with the police or crown attorney prior to the appearance in court. In cases where there is nothing to seek a concession on in terms of a plea agreement, the lawyer may talk with the police or crown attorney only about their evidence for the case. If the evidence is treated routinely or as 'obvious' by the lawyer, he may not even bother to talk with the police or crown attorney for discovery purposes. Among the interviewed lawyers for 80 accused persons, lawyers for 57 accused said they had plea discussions, and lawyers for 15 accused said that they had discovery discussions only without entering into plea discussions.

As Lynch (1979) observes, it is difficult to distinguish between discussions for discovery and discussions for the purpose of seeking a plea agreement since one entails the other. For the purposes of our study, we relied on lawyers' accounts as to the nature of the discussions. Among the 15 discovery discussions, 9 involved the police alone, 5 involved the crown attorney alone, and 1 involved both the police and crown attorney. Among the plea discussions, 4 involved the police alone, 26 involved the crown attorney alone, and 27 involved both the police and the crown attorney. The lawyers for three accused said that the plea discussions also included the judge.

Among the 23 accused whose lawyers said they did not engage in any plea discussions, 17 had a single charge against them. In comparison, among the 57 accused whose lawyers said they did participate in plea discussions, only 9 had single charges against them. A major reason why the lawyers for the 17 of 23 accused who had a single charge against them did not partake in plea discussions was that they were precluded from the most frequently occurring topic of plea discussion, namely that dealing with the withdrawal of some charge(s) in exchange for guilty pleas to others.

When accused were facing single charges, one of three general categories was typically involved. First, in some instances the offence was a relatively minor one and the entire matter was effectively foreclosed at the police stage. These cases were similar to those described by Bottoms and McClean (1976: 230): 'the final, formal decision as to plea was little more than an official acknowledgement of processes that had already been accomplished in police-suspect transactions' (see also Feeley, 1979). For example, an accused was charged with one count of driving while disqualified and pleaded guilty. His lawyer said there was no need for plea discussions because it was a 'simple matter' of pleading guilty: 'Once your client tells you he did it that's the end of it really ... *Obviously* there was no question but that he was going to plead guilty in his mind ... I advised him that was the only course he could take.' Second, in some cases the charge apparently was not backed up by substantial evidence and the crown attorney made the decision to withdraw it without attempting to pursue the matter further. For example an accused was charged with indecent assault (female), but the charge was withdrawn on the trial date because the complainant was unavailable (having moved to another province) and the crown attorney had no other substantial evidence to support the charge. Third, a charge was sometimes laid for which there was sufficient evidence from the crown attorney's standpoint and a substantial defence from the lawyer's viewpoint, leading both parties to a trial in court. For example, an accused pleaded not guilty and was acquitted after arguing that the umbrella he had allegedly shoplifted was taken out of a store 'absent-mindedly.' Among the group whose lawyers said there were no plea discussions, nine entered guilty pleas, four had their charge withdrawn, and ten pleaded not guilty and went to trial.

Most often it was the lawyer who initiated plea discussion (Macfarlane, 1982). The lawyer's decision to engage in plea discussions was most often preceded by a decision that his client was going to plead guilty to something. It was much less often preceded by a decision to keep the matter of plea open until an adversarial out-of-court 'trial' had been conducted with the police and crown attorney (Utz, 1978). The lawyer typically entered the discussion with the idea of gaining leniency, or at least the appearance of leniency, to satisfy his client that some concession had been won from the other side. As we shall proceed to document, most often it was only the appearance of leniency that was gained from these discussions, since most of the 'concessions' were in the form of withdrawn and reduced charges which were dubious or of secondary importance in any case. Thus, most of the plea discussions involved sorting out charges to suit the police and crown attorney's wish to gain a conviction on something and the lawyer's wish to 'cool out' (Goffman, 1962) his client by showing that the charges had been reduced in number and/or in severity.

Among the lawyers who said they had plea discussions with crown attorneys, the most prevalent topic of discussion was the withdrawal of charges. The lawyers for 20 accused said they had a discussion on this topic alone, and in all 20 instances an agreement was reached whereby the crown attorney actually withdrew one or more charges in exchange for a guilty plea on another charge or charges. For example, a lawyer related that he and his client arrived in court on the trial date with the intention of pleading not guilty on all three counts – taking a vehicle without the owner's consent, careless driving (Highway Traffic Act sec 83), and failure to report an accident (Highway Traffic Act sec 39). The lawyer said he told the crown attorney on the morning of the trial date that not guilty pleas on all counts were planned, and he talked with the police about a plea arrangement although nothing specific was decided. Later in the afternoon the crown attorney approached the lawyer and asked him if his client would accept a guilty plea to careless driving under the Highway Traffic Act in exchange for a withdrawal of the other two charges. The lawyer said his client agreed to this arrangement, and a guilty plea was entered. The lawyer did not view the two withdrawn charges as legitimate, and he described the careless driving charge as dubious, so that the final arrangement was seen at best as a compromise rather than as a bargain.

The lawyers for a further six accused persons said they entered into plea discussions regarding charge withdrawals as well as sentence recommendations. Three of these apparently resulted in an agreement being reached while three resulted in only partial agreement. The partial agreements involved the agreement to a withdrawal *or* sentence considerations, but not both. For example, the first lawyer for one accused said that after the case had been stood down twice, the crown attorney offered a plea agreement involving the withdrawal of four counts – mischief, liquor available (Liquor Licence Act sec 48[1]), possession of marijuana, and failure to appear in court – in exchange for guilty pleas to two counts (theft under $200, failure to appear in court). After the lawyer accepted the arrangement the accused hired a second lawyer for sentencing purposes. The lawyer said he tried to negotiate a lenient sentence recommendation with the crown attorney. The crown attorney reportedly refused to co-operate, saying he would seek a custodial sentence. The lawyer said that he then asked the crown attorney to specify the range of the prison sentence he was seeking, but the crown attorney refused this request.

The lawyers for an additional five accused persons said they were involved in plea discussions with a crown attorney which included both charge withdrawals and charge reductions in exchange for a guilty plea. It should be noted that four of these five accused were involved in one case and were represented by the same lawyer. This lawyer arranged a 'package' whereby all four accused would plead guilty to two counts of theft over $200 and one count of possession of stolen property under $200 in exchange for a withdrawal of three counts of theft under $200 and a reduction from possession of stolen property over $200. The lawyer worked out the details of the 'package' with the investigating detective and then secured confirmation of the agreement with the crown attorney (for a more detailed description, see Ericson, 1981: 171–2).

Lawyers for another four accused said that their plea discussions focused on sentencing recommendations only; all resulted in guilty plea agreements. For example, a lawyer said he agreed with the investigating detective and crown attorney to plead his client guilty to one count of indecent assault (male); in exchange, the crown attorney agreed not to mention the accused's record (which he adhered to even though he later discovered that the accused had a related record for sexual offences) and not to make a specific sentencing recommendation.

The lawyers for two accused said they took part in plea discussions which involved both charge withdrawal and charge selection. Both discussions resulted in guilty plea agreements. These were both cases in which the lawyer successfully negotiated the charge on which the guilty plea would be entered as well as the withdrawal of a charge (e.g. plea of guilty to refusal to provide a breath sample; withdrawal of impaired driving).

The lawyers for another two accused said the plea discussions centred on charge reductions alone. Both accused were involved in the same case. The lawyer for one accused said he tried to have a break, enter and theft charge reduced, but the crown attorney would not agree. The lawyer for the other accused discussed the reduction of two attempt robbery charges to attempt theft, and this reduction was later carried out. The accused pleaded guilty to these two counts and to one count of break, enter and theft even though both the accused and his lawyer questioned the legitimacy of these charges.

The lawyers for a further two accused said their plea discussions with the crown attorney centred upon charge selection along with sentence recommendations. In one case the lawyer entered into a discussion with the judge and the crown attorney which resulted in a plea to over 80 mg rather than impaired driving, no reading in of the accused's previous impaired conviction, and an indication from the judge that a conditional discharge with probation would be regarded as an appropriate sentence.

Lawyers for the remaining 12 accused each stated that their plea discussions involved idiosyncratic elements, including such things as charge reduction and sentence considerations, charge withdrawal against a co-accused, charge substitutions alone, and charge withdrawal and evidence submission considerations. Some of these also involved concessions from the lawyer in addition to a guilty plea, such as waiving a preliminary hearing and not electing up. Among these twelve, six were said to have resulted in agreement, four in partial agreement, and two in no agreement.

As previously noted, all but four discussions with the police also involved a crown attorney at some point. In these four instances, the lawyers said that they worked out the entire agreement with the police and that the police then went to obtain confirmation from the crown attorney, without any direct plea discussions between the lawyer and crown attorney. In three of these four instances the crown attorney agreed with the arrangement worked out between the lawyer and police.

Among the 31 instances of police involvement in plea discussions with lawyers, 16 involved charge withdrawal considerations alone, 5 involved charge withdrawals plus charge reductions, 2 involved substitute charges, 2 involved charge reduction and sentence recommendations, 2 involved charge reductions, and 4 involved other considerations. In only two instances were agreements not reached. In one case the lawyer said he tried to have an 'assault police' charge changed to common assault but the charge was not altered.[10]

These data clearly point to the frequent involvement of police officers in the plea discussion process. Approximately 39 per cent of the accused whose lawyers were interviewed had some plea discussions between the police and the lawyer in their case.[11]

The accounts of lawyers allow us to conclude that plea discussions were a widespread and integral part of the order out of court. In the next section we present an analysis of some cases in order to document the *process* involved in reaching a plea agreement out of court.

The Process of Plea Transaction

The disposition of many cases was settled in the course of out-of-court plea discussions among the defence counsel, crown counsel, and police officers. Each of these parties entered into discussions in order to make the outcome more *predictable* in terms of what they felt was just and justifiable under the circumstances. They used the various options at their disposal – especially charge reductions and withdrawals, elections, selective use of evidence, and sentence recommendations – to coerce, manipulate, and/or negotiate the outcome they had in mind.

The police sought a guilty plea outcome for a number of reasons (Ericson, 1981: chapter 6; Ericson, 1982: chapter 6). It saved them the extra work required in preparing a case for trial (e.g. preparing a more extensive brief for the crown attorney, taking statements from witnesses and subpoenaing them, preparing exhibits of evidence for court). It allowed them to sidestep the possibility of a judicial questioning in court of the process by which they constructed their charges and secured the conviction. Indeed, it allowed them to gain public verification and credit for their work, since a court-registered conviction serves to confirm their earlier decisions. Furthermore, a conviction resulting from a withdrawal of some charges in exchange for guilty pleas to others allowed them to perpetrate their multiple-charging practices regardless of the legitimacy of these practices. These practices swell police statistics, which have a function both for the officer seeking personal recognition and for the police organization seeking public recognition.

The crown attorney works toward conviction and sentence outcomes that are just – and justifiable in court. Similar to the police, he works to secure a plea agreement not just for the sake of efficiency, but also for the sake of conviction (cf McBarnet, 1981). The crown attorney considers the police accounts and/or the opinions of the police and defence lawyer in deciding upon the limits to negotiation. In most cases the limits arrived at are acceptable to all parties. Of course, in the process of setting the limits each party predicts what the other is likely to accept, so that a reasonable agreement is likely. On the rare occasions when they cannot agree, the case goes to trial, and the trial becomes an 'appeal' from what took place in the out-of-court transactions.

The defence attorney seeks conviction and sentence outcomes that are both just and justifiable to his client. The appearance of a concession is important as a means of inducing the client to accept the guilty plea agreement. At the same time the lawyer has to consider his own interests, including the most lucrative options available to him, his ongoing relations with the police and crown attorneys, and his reputation as a lawyer for prospective clients.

In sum, police, crown attorneys, and lawyers collaborate in collectively achieving an outcome that serves their respective interests. The manner in which they routinely accomplish this is best appreciated through a description of typical cases. In the remainder of this section we consider cases involving charge reductions, charge withdrawals, and sentence recommendations, as well as cases in which there were 'plea disagreements' leading to a trial in court. This adds qualitative flavour to the quantified types of plea discussions we enumerate in other sections of this chapter.

An example of agreeing to a guilty plea in exchange for a charge reduction is provided in the case of an accused who was arrested and interrogated after a complaint from a seven-year-old female victim that the suspect had lifted her skirt as he was passing her on an apartment stairwell. According to the researcher observing the investigating detectives (Ericson, 1981: 168–70), the detectives admitted to each other that, at the most, they had evidence for a common assault. They also considered the problem of having a child victim and wanted to avoid a trial at which the victim might be called upon to testify. In this context, the detectives decided to 'charge up' to the higher category of indecent assault (female) in the hope of 'levering' a guilty plea to common assault. In doing this, the detectives used the great interpretive latitude available to them. In his written statement, the accused did not admit to touching the girl's private parts: 'I just reached out and flipped her skirt and I don't know if my hand touched her or not.' In the occurrence report of the patrol officer who first responded to the complaint, the most serious recorded allegation was that, 'Apparently the suspect then lifted the victim's short skirt and exposed her undergarments.' However, in constructing the 'facts' to justify the indecent assault (female) charge, the detectives wrote. 'As the accused passed the victim, he reached out with his hand, lifted the child's skirt and touched her buttocks. The victim yelled to the accused, who turned and faced her, and then the accused continued down to the main floor, where he exited the building.'

The lawyer said he telephoned the detectives 'three or four times' to learn about their facts and to discuss a plea agreement. He said that this was his usual practice because detectives play an instrumental role in arriving at case outcomes while crown attorneys are typically ill prepared. The lawyer said the detectives agreed to a guilty plea to common assault along with a non-custodial sentence recommendation.

On the morning of the trial the detectives outlined the agreement to the crown attorney. The crown attorney agreed that it would be difficult to obtain a conviction on the indecent assault (female) charge because the accused did not admit to an indecent assault in his statement of confession, and because of unsworn evidence from a child witness. The crown attorney readily confirmed the common assault plea agreement, but he held the indecent assault (female) charge out as a threat to the lawyer as their negotiations proceeded.

The lawyer approached the crown attorney on the morning of the trial to ensure that he would accept the plea agreement. In addition, the lawyer wanted the crown attorney to recommend a conditional discharge along with psychiatric treatment conditions. The lawyer began by giving psychiatric explanations for his client's actions, then introduced the coercive threat of electing a trial at the county court level:

L: I'm sure you are aware that even if you went on an indecent assault, I'd take it upstairs, he's *not* going to get a jail sentence. And just recent clippings in the newspaper – have you seen them all – the conditional discharge, and where the guy got punched after court.

CA: He got what?

L: Punched. And the other one was a suspended sentence. What I want to do is prevent him from having a criminal record.

...

[After the threat to elect up, the lawyer switched back into mitigating arguments in terms of the accused's character and facts of the case]

L: You know, he has a girlfriend who doesn't know anything about it – she became devoutly religious after her pilgrimage to —— . So what we're faced with is a young kid, he's no danger, even in the incident in question. He says that he wasn't exposed. Whether he hit the girl's rear end or not, he told me he wasn't sure. He did flip up her dress. Whether, in passing, he touched her rear end, is not sure.

CA: I'd take a plea to common assault.

L: OK.

CA: I'm not going to support you for a discharge, although I'm not going to argue strenuously for anything, but I'm not going to support you when you ask for a discharge.

At this juncture, the parties had verbally agreed that the prosecution of the case had been desirable and that a conviction was in order. However, when it came to deciding upon what sentence was appropriate, the crown attorney laid down very definite limits backed up by his own coercive threats. The lawyer persistently asked for a conditional discharge with out-patient psychiatric treatment conditions but the crown attorney persistently refused. The lawyer then asked if they could hold a plea discussion that included the judge:

L: I'm just wondering whether, you know, like, now you see usually in [nearby city] sometimes, you just have a conference with the judge. I'm not sure that, you know, even if this merits it.

CA: They're [judges in this jurisdiction] not so keen on having you come in to talk to them, having, I don't mean you, but having counsel come in to talk to them, from what I've seen.

Apparently accepting this limitation as described by the crown attorney, the lawyer again asked why the crown attorney would not support a recommendation for a conditional discharge.

CA: Just the nature, it *is* an indecent assault and means there are problems because we have a child complainant etc. One of the reasons that I'd reduce it to common assault. But the nature of the incident is still sexual and on that basis alone, if the judge wants to give you a discharge he can do it.

In this reply, the crown attorney entered a new justification that he had not previously entered in discussing the charge reduction. He stated at this point that the offence '*is* an indecent assault' and that the problem of child testimony has led him to reduce it to common assault in exchange for a guilty plea. This is certainly a rationale for accepting a guilty plea to a reduced charge, but not the only one the crown attorney and detectives originally used to accept the reduction (admitted poor evidence; wishing to avoid the election up and trial threatened by the lawyer). The lawyer then decided to enquire into the judge's sentencing habits, and was told by the crown attorney that the presiding judge was 'generally a very light sentencer.' The lawyer then asked once more for a conditional discharge recommendation, and the Crown attorney finally silenced him:

L: You wouldn't anticipate a jail sentence.
CA: No. OK!?
L: OK. So there's no way I can get you to move for a conditional discharge?
CA: No!
L: But there's no way that you're going to oppose it, you'll just leave it up to his discretion?
CA: Well, I'm going to oppose it by not saying anything, but I'm not going to support you.
L: But there are more strenuous ways of opposing it by saying, you know, it is, could be indecent assault because the young lady here –
CA: I'll go to the Court of Appeal. I told you what I said that's what I'll do! Just, the facts are there, and Judge — can do what he wants with it.

Upon pleading guilty to common assault, the accused was sentenced to a conditional discharge plus one year of probation, along with psychiatric treatment at an out-patient clinic. The accused said he was aware of his lawyer's discussions with the detectives and crown attorney and that a week before the trial date his lawyer convinced him of the advantages of pleading guilty to common assault. At this point six months had passed since the charge was laid, and the accused was very anxious to have the matter finalized:

> [The lawyer said] if I pleaded guilty to common assault it would be easier to get off, that sort of thing ... [He said] they didn't have a really strong case against indecent assault and it would cost a lot of money and a long time for such a minor offence and so it would be better to plead guilty to a lower offence and then probably get off fairly lightly ... I thought it would be the only thing, the best thing to do. I wanted to get it over with as quickly as possible ... If they wouldn't accept anything he wanted to go for a trial by judge and jury and drag it out and drag it out as long as he could.

The accused later stated that the sentence was fair, adding that 'it was the lightest that they could sort of possibly give.'

When an accused was subject to more than one charge, the most common type of plea agreement, namely withdrawal on some charge(s) in exchange for a guilty plea on other charge(s), became a possibility. In cases in which the charges arose out of the same 'fact situation,' a withdrawal was legally required, e.g. *Kienapple* v *The Queen* (1974) 15 CCC (2d) 524. For example, while it was legitimate for the police to charge both impaired driving and over 80 mg, a conviction could be sustained on only one of these counts. In cases of this type, the discussion centred upon which charge would be withdrawn, with the defence preferring a withdrawal of the 'impaired' because it is seen as more serious. Two case examples illustrate that the outcome arrived at in cases of this type was not just a matter of objective criteria such as the level of the breathalyser test reading. Rather, it was a matter of what justifiable excuses the parties gave in the circumstances, and what justifications were accepted by them in reaching what they saw as a just conclusion.

One accused was charged with impaired driving and over 80 mg after the police recorded a blood alcohol level of 200 mg. On the trial date, the lawyer contacted the patrol officer and crown attorney in the crown attorney's office. The lawyer wanted to have the impaired charge withdrawn in exchange for a guilty plea to over 80 mg because it 'looks better' in terms of the accused's record. The crown attorney insisted on a guilty plea to impaired and withdrawal of the over 80 mg, using the justification that the breathalyser reading was too high to allow a withdrawal of the impaired charge. The crown attorney then offered to speak in court about the accused's co-operation with the police and good driving record as a means of possibly influencing the judge's sentence. The lawyer immediately accepted this, and the entire transaction was over in a few seconds:

> [Lawyer enters crown attorney's office]
>
> L: Hi [names accused] ... would you take a plea to the excess.

CA: I can't ...
L: On the basis of the driving that he did. All he did was weave within the lane apparently, there was nothing else that really ...
CA: Hum, I, I, I can't to this extent – first thing, it doesn't matter, you know that ...
L: I know, I know ...
CA: My rationale is that, ah, you know, it's sort of ah, the ah ... I, I can't in good conscience. The only reason I can't is that the reading is, you know, it's 70, it's almost 80 above what the normal rate is, and I, like, there's no other rationale, ah, than. But, ah, you know, are you the officer on this case?
PO: Yah.
CA: Oh, I would presume that ah, on, you know, on a plea to impaired that you know, I'd indicate you know that he was co-operative and
L: I understand he was, he was co-operative, he seemed to be holding, eh.
PO: He definitely was, or he did most of the things he was asked.
CA: So, what I'm saying to you is, I'm not asking (unintelligible), I'd indicate that I'll, I'll say this that, if you want me to for the high reading –
L: Uh-huh.
CA: Ah, his driving was somewhat better than could be expected.

The accused, who had no prior record of convictions, was fined $250 and given a three-month suspension of his driving licence. In interview, he said that he took a fatalistic approach to the outcome of his case because his lawyer indicated that the chances of 'beating' the charge were 'about the same chances as winning the Olympic lottery.' In this light, the accused said he accepted his lawyer's advice to plead guilty to the impaired driving charge and to 'throw yourself on the mercy of the court.' He believed that the crown attorney had shown some leniency in withdrawing the over 80 mg charge, although he saw this as a 'normal' practice in exchange for a guilty plea. He perceived multiple charging as a means by which the prosecution could ensure conviction on something: 'One charge may fall through, like and they have always got the other one to charge you, counter charge you with. If you could beat one charge, they have still got you on the other one.'

In comparison, the accused in the second case, charged with impaired driving and over 80 mg after the police recorded a breathalyser test reading of 240 mg, was able to plead guilty to the over 80 mg charge in exchange for sentencing concessions and a withdrawal of the impaired driving charge. The accused, himself a lawyer, hired a lawyer with an excellent reputation for handling 'impaired' cases in the jurisdiction. The lawyer, who in interview said his client was 'guilty as hell,' initially secured the crown attorney's collaboration in proposed plea and sentence arrangements. The lawyer and crown attorney then held a conference with the judge on the case. The lawyer said he argued that the accused was not impaired, and that this argument was accepted by the crown attorney and judge (compare with the accused in the first case, who had a lower breathalyser reading). The lawyer said he also argued successfully that the accused's prior conviction for impaired driving should not be taken into account because it had occurred more than five years earlier. The lawyer then offered his other arguments to mitigate sentence. In interview, the lawyer said the accused had 'a thousand and one mitigating circumstances whereby he shouldn't be convicted because he was a member of the profession and because he was on hard times.' The judge stated that the most lenient sentence possible, a conditional discharge, was reasonable. In court, this sentence was duly pronounced, along with a one-year term of probation that included treatment and reporting conditoins. In interview, the accused said he knew about the plea discussions arranged by his lawyer, but he refused to elaborate on the nature of the discussions. When asked why the impaired driving charge was withdrawn, he said that there was insufficient evidence on driving to sustain that charge.

It was routine practice for the police to charge every person possible with every offence possible in a case, except for the occasional minor charge that was not laid in exchange for information (Ericson, 1981, 1982). This maximized the prosecution's starting position for negotiations regarding plea settlements and ensured that at the point of disposition there was something in it for everybody.

An extended case example can be used to illustrate this practice, and the type of plea discussions and settlements that followed from it. Four accused were arrested by patrol officers after complaints from the owner and the manager of a dance hall that they had a fight with the accused while trying to evict them for drinking beer on unlicensed premises. The complainants alleged that the accused initially left the premises, but then two of them returned with a baseball bat and hockey stick to engage in a further scuffle with the owner and the manager. The accused also reportedly broke a window at the dance hall. The accused were returned to the divisional police station and held overnight for interrogation by detectives the following morning. The detectives obtained written statements from each of the accused, and then charged each of them with 'causing a disturbance,' 'mischief,' and 'possession of a weapon dangerous to the public peace.'

Each of the four accused retained a different lawyer. The lawyers viewed the case as typical of police 'overcharging' practices. For example, the lawyer for one accused said, 'I do not think he should have been charged with three offences. There is a policy now with, as a result of increased plea bargaining, of ... police officers overcharging... It's my experience in these matters that usually if there are four co-accused who are involved in a certain action that they usually charge all four with the same offences even though maybe two or three of them are more responsible than the others.' The lawyer for another accused observed that this practice was not only functional for the police, but useful for lawyers in giving their clients the appearance of a concession in conjunction with a recommendation for a guilty plea: 'The police I think believe that most lawyers like to have an overlaying of charges because it gives them an ability to deal with their client and makes them look good, and also negotiate the charges.'

The lawyers were most interested in having the weapons dangerous withdrawal of the weapons dangerous and mischief charges. The other detective in advance of the trial date and received the detective's verbal agreement on a guilty plea to causing a disturbance in exchange for a withdrawal of the weapons dangerous and mischief charges. The other lawyers also obtained the detective's agreement to withdraw the weapons dangerous charge, partly based on the argument that the accused were acting in self-defence after the complainants had threatened them with baseball bats. On the morning of the trial date, the detective (D) indicated to the crown attorney that there was room for negotiation over the weapons charges, and he explicitly admitted overcharging on this offence:

CA: They [lawyers] wanted to deal? I don't know anything about it. I was told by [first name of the lawyer for one of the accused], he's crown attorney in court-room number one and he couldn't come over 'till that was finished, so I haven't even touched the thing, I know nothing about it. I've got all kinds of things to do here.

D: What it is basically [crown attorney's first name] – won't be two seconds on it. Ah ... they went in drinking into this disco, a disturbance arose, a window was broken, and a bit of pushing arose as well, and ah ... they went out and got a baseball bat and hockey stick, and then the police arrived and charged with cause a disturbance, mischief and possession of weapon dangerous. They are willing to deal if we drop the weapon dangerous ...

CA: Are they all parties to the weapon dangerous? four of them?

D: No, just two of them. Two never knew what was going on in regards to the baseball bat.

It was routine practice for the lawyers to contact the police about the possibilities of a plea settlement prior to discussions with the crown attorney. The police had more information about the details of the case and how it was constructed. Crown attorneys were assigned to a court rather than to a case, so that lawyers could not accurately predict who the crown attorney would be on the trial date. In the case under consideration, the trial date was set four and one-half months before, yet the crown attorney still had not familiarized himself with the case by the time he was approached about a plea settlement on the morning of the trial. As crown attorneys repeatedly stated,[12] they were in a dependent position in relation to what the police and lawyers had worked out in advance:

CA: What do you want to do now [lawyer's first name]?

L: Well, it has been offered a plea.

CA: Who offered?

L: A police officer, senior police officers rank with crown attorneys.

CA: I'm sure they rank ahead of me.

Lawyers know that to increase the predictability of the outcome in terms acceptable to themselves, and in terms that can be made acceptable to their clients, they can benefit from initial discussions with the police officers involved.

On the trial date a number of developments influenced the course of the plea transactions. Some crown witnesses unexpectedly arrived, which led at least one lawyer to change from his original plan of pleading not guilty. This lawyer became active in plea transactions, along with the lawyer for another accused. Both of these lawyers were well known to the detectives and crown attorney prosecuting the case. Both lawyers were active in the same jurisdiction as part-time crown attorneys. Indeed, one of them was serving on the same day as both a defence lawyer and crown attorney in different courtrooms. The fact that this lawyer was engaged in another courtroom as a crown attorney was a reason why the case was moved back on the docket until the afternoon, facilitating time for sporadic plea discussions on the case as the day progressed.

This lawyer, keen to have the weapons dangerous charge withdrawn, decided to approach the crown witnesses to ensure that they had nothing to say that would implicate his client on this charge. He also said he engineered their accounts to accord with the outcome he thought his client deserved. He then approached the crown attorney and told him what his client would plead to based upon what the crown witnesses were going to testify:

> I'd grabbed the witnesses ... without the crown's permission. The crown was not to give that. I found out the story, then I went to the crown and said, I understand that this is your evidence. And he said, oh? And I said, why don't you check it out with your witnesses? He said, okay, and he did, and confirmed what had happened. And of course, see, what happens on that is that you agree that [the accused] did this, or didn't do this. And you know, you socialize with them in a very nice sort of way, and by this time their – the incident is long gone. Plus it's [the witnesses' dance hall, the reputation of which they might want to maintain by not having the publicity of a trial] a public place. They don't want to ruin their image ... Their wording towards my client was not as severe as if I hadn't talked to them and they'd taken the stand in a trial. As a result that by the time the Crown talked to them, they had already pinned themselves down to statements that were somewhat helpful.

The lawyer agreed with the crown attorney that his client would 'take' the mischief charge along with the causing a disturbance charge in exchange for a withdrawal of the weapons charge. The lawyer said the co-accused were blaming his client for breaking the window and for the weapons; therefore he felt that it was pragmatic for his client to plead guilty on the mischief count. The lawyer's next task was to convince his client – who had wanted to plead not guilty on all counts – to accept the wisdom of the plea settlement. The lawyer said he talked his client into the agreement by arguing that it was a matter of the accused's credibility versus the credibility of the witnesses, and suggesting that it was the accused who stood lower in the hierarchy of credibility. The lawyer also suggested to his client that he would likely receive a more severe penalty if he pleaded not guilty and was found guilty than if he entered guilty pleas. The lawyer discussed how he formulated the matter to his client in 'an offer you can't refuse' terms:

> I told him that the witnesses are going to say what the police have told me they're going to say. Then it becomes a credibility issue. You versus the witnesses. You have a record, they don't. You're going to have to take the stand to deny it. Uh, what's going to happen is, because most of these matters are summary matters, to be dealt with in a provincial court, Judge —— who's seen you maybe before, who knows about you – your chance of getting acquitted is pretty negligible ... I'm simply saying you may be telling me the truth, but I'm telling you it's not a question of what the truth is, it's a question of who the judge believes ... But I'm telling you also the judge thinks you're lying, you're adding time onto yourself ...
>
> I was telling him ... if you plea, the very worst thing, even with the weapons charge, maybe you're looking at an extra thirty days [in jail] ... I said if you don't plead, and you take the stand, I said, you're looking maybe – you're looking at three to six months on that charge alone. So that's the prediction I made ...
>
> He decided to plead [guilty] ... I never recommend, I try not to. I simply say, these are the factors. But I suppose I'm putting the factors together in such a way that there's a strong inference – that it amounts to recommendation.

This lawyer's client 'wisely' accepted the offer he could not refuse. He said he paid particular reference and deference to the lawyer's sentence predictions in accepting the plea arrangement.

A: [My lawyer advised a guilty plea because] if I pleaded not guilty, and was found guilty, I could, uh, I'd go end up [in prison] ... I'd get a heavier sentence ... Maybe the judge figures, well, you've wasted all this court time, and, you know, paid for it, and everything else. And you're guilty, so uh, you know. Or he figures you're trying to beat – cheat him out of justice, or whatever, right?
    ...
    [My lawyer said] if I was found guilty, I would be looking at about six months or so ... Between three and six.

Q: Okay, now, did that affect how – your decision on how to plead?

A: Sure did!

Q: So you decided to plead guilty as a result?

A: [My lawyer] even said when, if I pleaded guilty to the mischief and the cause disturbance, I would get about 30 days, 30 to 60 days, eh? That's what my lawyer thought.

The accused said he was very pleased when he was sentenced to a $150 fine or 30 days in prison for causing a disturbance by fighting and $100 restitution plus 60 days' probation for mischief. He believed that his lawyer had skilfully negotiated and 'got me off,' without any incarceration. The accused said in retrospect that he would obtain a lawyer and plead the same way.

The lawyer for a co-accused sought a withdrawal of the charges of weapons dangerous and mischief against his client. Although he had the detective's agreement to this arrangement, the crown attorney initially baulked at it and said he would only withdraw the weapons dangerous charge. However, when they appeared in court the crown attorney agreed to go along with the guilty plea to causing a disturbance only. The accused was given a conditional discharge, one year of probation, plus $75 court costs on this conviction. The lawyer saw this as a bargain, stating in interview that although he did not think his client was guilty of causing a disturbance, he was guilty of mischief and there was a '50-50' chance that he was guilty of weapons dangerous. The lawyer attributed the plea agreement to the influence of the detective, to the crown attorney's desire to avoid a trial because of a heavy schedule, and to the crown attorney's satisfaction with having obtained a conviction on something plus restitution for the mischief occurrence from another accused:

L: I went back to the crown, and I said, [detective's first and last names] is willing to take the plea of cause disturbance. And he said, 'I'm not willing to take that. I want the two charges.' And, so, I said, well, I'd like to talk to you further about it. And, so I went back – first of all, the case was put over to the afternoon, it had been indicated that it would be resolved. So I went back to [detective's first and last names] and I told him that the crown wasn't prepared to do the two ... [Detective's first name] then indicated, alright, lets put it over 'till the afternoon, see what we can work out. I'll talk to them. When we came back in the afternoon, the crown was tied up on another matter, and I couldn't get in to talk to him. I waited outside; finally, he just went into court and called the case. And, oh, called up my client, and at the front of the court, said now, we're taking a plea as to the mischief and the cause disturbance. And, I said, no, we're not, we're just doing the cause disturbance.

Q: This was –

L: This was in court.

Q: So that everyone can hear, or –

L: No, it was in whispers, the judge was there. And, I said, I just want to do the cause disturbance. My impression was that it was such an overwhelming day, I mean he had so much other stuff going, he had all the pleas arranged from the other two accused, that he just said, 'Okay, fine.' And that was the way it went.

Q: OK. Uh, you say that you know Detective —— . Do you think the fact that you have established a certain rapport with him and have dealt with him before had any effect on the ultimate outcome?

L: Oh, there's no doubt. I felt with Detective —— that if I told him my impression of this boy, and I told him that that youngster reacted badly, that he really wasn't of a criminal nature, otherwise a good reputation in school – that he would give the boy a break. [Detective's first name] indicated that he would.

The other defence lawyer, who was a part-time crown attorney with close contacts among the police and prosecutors, attributed the ease of the plea settlement to these contacts:

L: Another advantage in that case. [Names lawyer for second accused] was one of the co-counsels for one of the four accused ... and he has, with certain officers, a rapport. And that helped, because he couldn't demand from my client any more than he could demand from [the lawyer for second accused].
    ...

Q: And you'd dealt with these particular investigating officers before?

L: Right, right.

Q: And did this affect – have any affect on the outcome of the case? The fact that you dealt with them on previous occasions?

L: Again, it's this trust situation. That, you know, they know that information they would give me would [be held in confidence] – if it's off the record, it's off the record, and if it's on the record, it's on the record.

The lawyer for a third accused secured a withdrawal of the weapons dangerous and mischief charges in exchange for a guilty plea to causing a disturbance. While stating that the police had clearly overcharged his client, he also stressed how co-operative they were in withdrawing the two charges. He believed that the causing a disturbance charge was a 'catch all' by which the police ensured at least one conviction against his client. The lawyer perceived no bargain from the agreement, although he believed that his client perceived a bargain because he would have pleaded guilty to all three counts without the assistance of counsel. In speaking about how his client saw the lawyer's role, the lawyer stated, 'Well I represented him in court, and he didn't have the capacity obviously to speak to the crown attorney on his own and to the police officers and articulate his defence and I filled that role I hope.'

The lawyer for the fourth accused, who apparently had a similar level of involvement in the incident as the third accused, also arranged a plea settlement whereby he would plead his client guilty to causing a disturbance in exchange for a withdrawal of the other two charges. However, in apparent violation of the trust emphasized so much by the other lawyers, the lawyer for the fourth accused reneged on the agreement just as the case was about to begin in court. The crown attorney – who according to two other lawyers was anxious to avoid a trial and who had secured what he wanted from the incident – withdrew all the charges against the fourth accused. Assuming the legitimacy of at least the 'catch-all' charge of causing a disturbance against the fourth accused, he received the best bargain of all. This apparently resulted from his lawyer strategically 'reading' the crown attorney's situation with the case, and capitalizing on this situation at the appropriate moment.

In some cases involving multiple charges, the plea discussion centred upon the sentencing outcome with little concern for the withdrawal of charges. All parties agreed that the accused was guilty to some number of offences, and effort was directed at making the sentencing outcome within a predictable range agreeable to all parties. This type of plea transaction is illustrated in the following case.

The accused was apprehended by patrol officers after the victim of a residential break, enter and theft reported a suspect fleeing from the scene. After spending the night in a cell at a divisional police station, the suspect was turned over to detectives for interrogation. The detectives charged the accused for the one break, enter and theft occurrence and then canvassed the neighbourhood to ascertain whether there had been other occurrences. This was followed by a search of the accused's apartment. These investigations led the detectives to lay a total of 11 charges, including break, enter and theft (3), break and enter (3), attempt theft (3), possession of stolen property (1), and possession of narcotics (marijuana) (1).

The accused was released after a bail hearing, and he returned to his parent's home in another jurisdiction. The detectives continued their investigation of the accused and eventually executed a search warrant at his parent's home and arrested him once again. The accused confessed to more offences, and was charged with 10 more counts, including break, enter and theft (3), theft under $200 (4), attempted theft (2), and possession of stolen property (1).

The accused retained a private lawyer who had considerable experience in the jurisdiction as both a defence counsel and crown counsel. This lawyer first contacted the investigating detectives in order to obtain disclosure and to explore possibilities for plea agreement. He commented in interview that this was a routine practice and described it as the most practical thing to do and as something which both crown attorneys and the police accept with 'credible counsel,' i.e. counsel who will not 'abuse the information' by using it in court to embarrass the police or crown attorney. In other words, as long as the lawyer is predictably reliable in not upsetting the order in court, he is allowed to participate in the constitution of the order out of court.

The lawyer subsequently arranged to meet with a crown attorney, then with the detective, the crown attorney, and other crown attorneys. The lawyer discussed his reasoning on the case and what he was looking for from the prosecution side.

> After speaking to the officer ... I came to a sort of decision about the case. Simply, that, look, there's no doubt that the police will have no problem of getting convictions on some of the matters and when you have those many charges there's always a natural argument that, well they can't convict him on all because they'll never be able to get all their witnesses together to do all of the, I mean, there would be problems with identification. But they're going to get convictions for some of them and a judge is going to be cognizant of the total number of charges. At some point, he's going to get aware of it, you know, even though they can't prove their case and because of that, that will carry more impact during a trial, so if you go through a trial and he's acquitted of some and convicted of some, he doesn't get the same penalty [as when he pleads guilty on a pre-arranged agreement]. In fact, there's a double danger that the judge can then say, they're separate dates, separate locations and I will now legally consider consecutive sentencing. And that's quite appropriate. There's a mild argument that I can make that because he was somewhat on drugs at the time that I could argue that these were concurrent. That he had a continuing state of mind. But a judge doesn't have to accept that and he wouldn't accept if I sort of screwed up the system [by going to trial]. So, you know, sort of saying that to yourself you're saying, well, if I go to the crown and start hassling numbers, that takes it away from what we're really talking about as to time and sentence. So I don't take that approach of going to the crown and, I know that crown's office won't do it out here. So I won't go to them and hassle with numbers. So I simply walked into their office, picked a crown, talked to a crown, said look there's this guy charged with various number of things. He's basically a good kid, he's got a lot of things going for him. This is what he's all about and what are you looking for in the way of sentencing and what do you think you can get convictions on and just leave it to the crown to sort of honestly make his decision. Again I have trust for the crown. The crown made his evaluation. He agreed to the extent that as far as the kid was concerned that the fellow shouldn't get jail as far as he, as the accused is concerned, but there was a deterrent factor, okay. A general deterrent. And I said, okay, let's have a meeting ... I told him I'd see him in a couple of weeks and I phoned [detective's first and last names] and I said, [detective's first name], I got to be at the crown's office on such and such a date. I was discussing [a murder case]. I said why don't you drop in. I mean that's how these are set up and [detective's first name]

said okay. And I said I'll be up there between ten and twelve and [detective's first name] dropped in and the crown was there and there were a couple of crowns there and another defence counsel dropped in at that time and we were just chatting. And [detective's first name] said he had no particular point of view and that, everyone, the kid was good, the family was good. They had taken steps to take care of the kid and wasn't really asking for anything as far as the police officer is concerned ... The crowns meet once a month to determine policy as to the increase in the B and E's in the area and as a result of that they said, look, okay leave it with us. I think two of them decided and said there should be jail and one said that, no, he thought no jail and they said leave it with us and we'll come out with a policy decision. I said, well first deal with my client and then deal with your policy decision ... I put my case to them [as I would] put to the judge.

In proceeding this way the lawyer ensured that there would be collaboration on the agreement in the crown attorney's office. He hoped thereby to commit the particular crown attorney who handled the case on the day of the trial. The lawyer secured an agreement that the accused should be allowed to continue his schooling, and therefore what was called for was an intermittent jail sentence to be served on weekends. Since intermittent sentences could only be given for periods up to 90 days, this established the maximum limit. The crown attorney agreed to make this sentence recommendation. He also withdrew two counts of possession of stolen property and one count of attempted theft because he saw them as overlapping back-up charges covered by other charges. In court, the crown attorney could not find the information for one of the break and enter charges, and he withdrew that charge. The lawyer talked with a federal crown attorney about withdrawing the possession of marijuana charge in light of all the other charges against the accused, and the federal crown attorney agreed to do so.[13]

In reviewing the case in the research interview, the lawyer said that the accused deserved a jail sentence. He said he regarded it as part of his role to impress upon the accused the seriousness of the matter and to collaborate with the prosecution in being part of the 'deterrent factor.' However, he indicated he also believed that his client had received a bargain under the circumstances. He repeatedly stated his belief that if the case had proceeded to trial the judge 'would just be getting mad at the kid,' and this would result in a longer sentence. 'So you know, you could rationalize with this kid, nine months to a year on those offences,' versus the crown attorney's recommendation for 90 days' jail intermittent.

In the end, the defence entered guilty pleas on 16 counts, the crown attorney made his sentence recommendation, the defence counsel presented sentencing submissions and testimony on the accused's behalf, and the judge sentenced him to 90 days' jail intermittent plus 18 months' probation.

The accused said that he left the plea discussions and other aspects of settling the case to his lawyer. 'He was doing a great job and I left that up to him. He's the lawyer, I really didn't worry about it.' He stressed the importance of the lawyer having a good relationship with the crown in working out a deal and felt that in his case this may have been facilitated by the fact that his lawyer was also a part-time crown attorney. The accused also perceived the crucial importance of plea transactions and sentence recommendation agreements because, in his view, the judge routinely accepts the crown attorney's recommendations: 'They are sort of one, the crown and the judge are sort of one person or one being ... [The crown attorney] makes all the suggestions and the judge goes along with it and says, "Okay, that's fine with me," and there's no more said.'

The accused said he planned to plead guilty all along, 'Because I was guilty, I told the police everything and that's all there was to it.' In this light, and in conjunction with his lawyer's work in making a plea settlement, the accused remained passive throughout. 'I knew I was pleading guilty. I knew the charges were going to be read and I knew there was going to be a sentence. And that's all I knew ... All the legal stuff, I don't know what happened and it doesn't really bother me to know or not to know.'

The accused's sense of guilt, in keeping with his lawyer's approach, was that he had done some illegal things and therefore he should receive some just consequence. He was generally guilty of something, but when it came to the specifics there was a considerable discrepancy between what he said he did and what he was convicted of doing. He said that when the charges were read out in court, he only recognized 'half of them anyway':

Q: Some of them you didn't recognize?

A: Not in court. I recognized most of the things I stole. Then, like they said, they said a lot of things, that a lot of the ones were. He went through it, left it, and didn't steal nothing, you know, I couldn't be sure that I did that.

Q: Okay, why did you plead guilty to it?

A: I don't know, I guess I imagine I could have done it. That's the only reason I can think of.

Q: But don't you think –

A: 'Cause my lawyer said to me plead guilty to them. He said if I tell you to plead guilty, plead guilty, so I did.

The accused also complained that some charges were unfair in the context of the incidents. For example, break, enter and theft charges were laid for incidents where he had allegedly entered garages attached to houses and taken things from cars. He claimed some of these cars were not in garages.

The accused stated that in retrospect he would not have confessed to the police. He also stated that he would have pleaded not guilty to some of the charges although he also believed that this would make little difference in the context of the overall plea 'package' and sentencing outcome. In keeping with his lawyer's opinion, the accused knew that the police did not have adequate evidence on many of the charges, but he also believed that it was better to bet safely and seek a plea package with sentence recommendations than to play the numbers game of charge alterations:

A: Knowing what I know [now] I'd plead not guilty to some of the charges.

Q: Which ones?

A: The ones, like he [crown attorney] said, 'He went into this car, went through the glove box, nothing was stolen and left.' Like that I wouldn't plead guilty to again.

Q: Why?

A: Because how would they know if I did it or not, you know? When it came to the time, when if I said, 'Not guilty,' and they said, 'Well we think you did it,' they couldn't prove – couldn't prove I did it.

Q: Why did you plead guilty to those ones?

A: I don't know, just because it could have been, if it was up to 17 it could have been 1700, it wouldn't have made much difference.

Q: What do you mean, it could have been up to 1700?

A: Well, like I had 17 counts against me, it could have been 50 counts against me. And you know one more doesn't make all that much difference when it gets up to that many.

As holidaymakers, restaurant-goers, and other consumers recognize, package deals are easier and cheaper than going à la carte. However, in buying into them the consumer gives up a degree of individuality and independence. Moreover, in throwing everything together the proprietors can usually get away with cutting corners, and this takes the edge off the bargain.

Academic research and commentary on the topic of plea bargaining concentrates upon completed guilty plea agreements and has ignored plea discussions that do not result in guilty plea agreements. This is a peculiar omission in the literature, since it is important to know conditions leading to a failure in negotiations in order to obtain a fuller understanding of both the limits to negotiations and the conditions leading to successful agreements (Strauss, 1978).

Defence lawyers, crown attorneys, and the police sometimes enter into plea discussions only to discover that the other party is demanding too much. In these circumstances there may be some minor offers made in an attempt to adjust particular aspects of the case, but the main issue can be resolved only by taking the matter to the final step, the trial. Moreover, when the final step is taken the earlier steps of a failed negotiation are often irretrievable and bear on the outcome.

An accused was arrested by uniformed patrol officers after a complaint from his mother and grandmother that he was threatening them with a knife and with a loaded shotgun. The accused was charged with possession of a dangerous weapon in relation to the knife, and with dangerous use of a firearm in relation to the shotgun.

The lawyer for the accused decided he would argue that the accused could not form intent because on the night of the incident the accused claimed to have been drinking alcoholic beverages, smoking marijuana, and to have taken three LSD tablets. On the day of the trial, the lawyer entered the crown attorney's office and immediately indicated that he was prepared to go to trial on both charges:

L: [Crown attorney's first name], what are you going to do with [the accused] on the pointing firearm, are you going to proceed by way of indictment and combine that with the preliminary hearing on the other one, er?[14]

CA: I don't know, you obviously want to go to trial on it.

L: Yeah. I'd like to have a preliminary on it anyway to find out what, what the story is.

CA: He's got a record, not a substantial record, the gun was loaded, that's the really worrysome part of it. Ah ... let me think about it.

During a recess from another case in court, the crown attorney returned to his office and greeted a police officer involved in the case. Just as he was about to discuss strategy with this officer, the lawyer appeared and established that he was going to trial even though the crown attorney offered to withdraw the dangerous weapon charge.

CA: I think [lawyer's first name] is talking about ah ... going on a prelim. If I can help it, I'll avoid that.

PO: Good day.

L: Hi.

CA: Ah ... we've got the two weapons, one is a knife and one is the firearm ... I would ah ... my preference is to go on the firearm charge, it all relates substantially to the same incident.

L: And drop the other one?

CA: Yeah, I'd drop the other one.

L: And go summarily?

CA: Yeah, I'd like to keep it down here, I don't think it's a case that should go upstairs.

L: It was loaded.

CA: Yeah it was loaded but

L: Cocked finger on the trigger

CA: You know, is the guy likely to get more than six months on it?

L: He's likely to get probation, 'cause he has no record, and he's young.

CA: He's absolutely clean on his record is he?

L: Yip. He may not be clean *after* that, he's clean before I think.

CA: Hm. May I ask what the issue is on trial?

L: I don't really know yet until I hear what the witnesses say. A couple of little points here and there.

CA: OK, well that's what I'm going to do.

L: Gonna withdraw the other?

CA: Depending on what happens I would say. Assuming that we'll get a conviction out of it. I'll put it this way, I would be very ah ... distressed if I, if I didn't get the case proved on the pointing the firearm, and, you know, presumably if we didn't get that, then we'll go on the other one. I would say on the basis, if we get a finding of guilt on the dangerous use of firearm, then we'll drop, withdraw the other one.

L: OK.

The lawyer said he was willing to elect up to a county court trial by judge and jury. He felt that the crown attorney wanted to avoid this because of the time and cost involved and was content to secure a conviction with some reasonable penalty (short-term incarceration) attached, a goal that was achievable via a summary conviction trial. The lawyer felt the indictable dangerous weapon charge was withdrawn because the defence has the option of electing up on the charge and that the crown chose to proceed summarily on the charge of dangerous use of a firearm to prevent the defence from having a full trial before judge and jury.

The accused, who took the stand in his own defence, was found guilty. Referring to the accused's age, first conviction status, and favourable pre-sentence report, the judge sentenced him to a suspended sentence with 18 months' probation. The lawyer felt that the conviction was fair because the defence did not develop sufficient evidence. He referred to a civilian witness and an expert witness (medical doctor) who could have been mobilized to strengthen the defence of the accused. He then went on to state that if he had been retained privately rather than on a legal aid certificate, he could have shown other forms of resourcefulness in strengthening the defence of his client in a case he had prejudged from the beginning as appropriate for trial.

> If it had been privately financed, I would have – I would have put the blocks to the old crown. it's all money, eh? The whole thing. It's a big game. Whoever has the most money wins ... They got resources. They've got the whole police force at their disposal.[15] Those crowns, they can phone any police officer, anywhere in Ontario, at any time of the day or night, and say, I want you to go and sniff around in those woods up there and find me something ... You see, all legal aid does, as it did in this case, is it allows for the noises of a defence ... It didn't look too bad [in court]. If there'd have been people in the audience, they would have

thought, ah, I guess he got a fair trail. You know, it sounded like his lawyer was fighting for him. But most of the real work in a trial is done before. That's where you win or lose, in the preparation.

Of course, lawyers vary in the degree of clout they have among the police and crown attorneys. A lawyer with a good reputation as a trial lawyer can arrange settlements without trial based upon his reputation. However, he can also demand too much and be forced to trial, in which case he must also back up his reputation by going to trial, and possibly beyond.

An accused privately retained an expensive lawyer who had an excellent reputation. The lawyer was especially noted for his skill in defending clients charged with the offences facing this accused, namely impaired driving and refusal to provide a breath sample. The lawyer planned to have his client plead not guilty on both counts. On the impaired driving charge, the argument was based upon insufficient evidence about driving: the police approached the driver after a collision with another vehicle, and the accident was apparently caused by a tire failure. On the charge of refusal to provide a breath sample, the lawyer contended that another lawyer who was at the scene of the accident advised the accused not to provide a breath sample; the defence lawyer planned to argue that his client should not be convicted because he was simply following the professional advice of someone he believed to be an authoritative legal expert.

On the morning of the trial the crown attorney attempted to negotiate a plea settlement. The lawyer refused to yield on either count, and the case proceeded to trial:

CA: If a lawyer says to a fellow, 'Don't take the test' do you think that's reasonable excuse given we can satisfy the court that the lawyer is wrong in saying that.

Second CA: I think it depends on the facts, and if there is absolutely no reason in law ...

CA: You see, if it wasn't [first and last name of lawyer] making the submission we'd have a chance.

L: [Crown attorney's first name], this is my position. Maybe the lawyer is wrong in his advice but is it wrong for a person to rely upon the advice of his lawyer? We are supposed to be gentlemen learned in the law whether we are or not and surely the public has a right to rely on his lawyer and when his lawyer says no, don't do it ...

Second CA: I think it depends on the context, [lawyer's first name].

CA: What, you're forcing the lawyer to prosecute somebody for counselling the commission of an indictable offence. If you succeed in that defence.

L: They had it out west. I'll make a bigger fee defending him, one dollar, professional courtesy.

CA: I'm not concerned with your fees but if you succeed in that defence then we've got to make it clear to the public that they can't just accept the advice of a lawyer.

L: Alright, that's fine, when you make that clear to the public, but surely to God an individual charged with a criminal offence has the right to rely on the advice of a lawyer. If he doesn't have the right to rely on the lawyer, why do we give him the right to telephone a lawyer, why do we say that a defense is that he was not allowed to telephone his lawyer?

CA: Ah ... you're very compelling today.

L: And you've got all kinds of cases to back me up on that. Now, if he has got the right and we say you cannot convict him if you refuse him the right to phone his lawyer, how in the hell can you say that he's guilty of an offence because you let him phone the lawyer and he followed the advice of the lawyer? Now really, [CA's first name].

CA: What do you want me to do? Do you want to plead guilty to the impaired?

L: Take parking on the side of the road.

CA: You plead to the impaired and we'll withdraw the refusal, [L's first name].

L: No way, no way, no way.

CA: We may well go summarily and we may appeal it just as a matter of interest to see what happens in county court.

L: Oh, I'd love that, my client is rich. No, my client has got money, I can afford to go all the way to the Supreme Court of Canada on this one, no bullshit.

CA: Have you got our civilian witnesses here?

Police officer: Ah, Have you got the sheet there?

CA: Yeah, I do, there are two of them, you can carry that one around and look for our civilian witnesses.

L: And as I said, for the first time I found an honest cop, he saw the flat tire and knew it caused the swerve.

CA: We have got an expert report in there that seems to suggest that the vehicle was working properly until the accident.

L: You have not.

CA: I do too.

L: You little bugger, you haven't.

CA: I didn't show that to you [L's first name], I just wanted you to get out and make that submission. I wanted you to cross examine our witnesses along those lines and then our last witness is going to shoot it all down [states name].

PO: He's the licensed mechanic.

CA: Is he here today?

PO: He's available.

L: Brake peddle movement has nothing to do ...

CA: Still offer you the impaired [first name of L].

L: No way, youngster, you've got a loser.

CA: I think I probably do any time that you stand up in court out here don't I?

L: No, no, every once in awhile the judges are foolish.

CA: I'm looking forward to the day [first name of L] when you tell me that I've got a loser and by some quirk of fate it walks out and I'm a winner.

At trial, the accused was found not guilty of impaired driving and found guilty of refusal to provide a breath sample. The lawyer appealed the conviction and a trial de novo was held. The conviction was affirmed and the sentence of $200 fine or 14 days' jail plus 30 days' licence suspension remained the same.

While we have depicted the process of plea transaction, we have not addressed systematically the question of what was gained from it. The usual assumption in any negotiation is that there is something in it for everybody. The outcome is a compromise, bringing some relative advantage to every side and not absolute advantage to any side. We now enquire into the advantages perceived by lawyers in guilty plea settlements, whether they thought there were any bargains to be had, and what these bargains consisted of.

Lawyers' Perceptions of Plea Bargains

In Table 4.1 we enumerate lawyers' assessments of plea 'bargains' for each of the 57 accused whose lawyers were interviewed and said they took part in plea discussions. These assessments were extracted from all sections of the lawyer interviews dealing with plea discussions and from the lawyers' assessments of the legitimacy of the charges against their clients. These categorizations are admittedly 'loose' because subtle elements of each case are inevitably lost in the process of categorization. Moreover, while lawyers and law enforcement agents routinely do their work by making predictions about whether or not a charge would stand tests of evidence in a trial, the accuracy of their predictions are questionable. As Baldwin and McConville (1977: 108) state, there is an assumption within the ordering of plea agreements 'that lawyers can readily identify those cases that are hopeless and can therefore advise their clients of the risks of fighting the case in court. It seems to us that there are great dangers in this assumption.' In constructing Table 4.1 and using the data therein, we assume that lawyers know a bargain when they see one. This assumption is necessary for our present purposes, although we shall have occasion to question it.

From the viewpoint of lawyers there were most often no bargains to be had by entering into plea discussions. Lawyers for only 14 of 57 accused said they were involved in plea discussions yielding an agreement which amounted to a 'bargain.' Among the remaining 43, the lawyers for 5 said they did not reach an agreement and the lawyers for 38 related that the agreement reached brought no advantage.

Among the lawyers who felt they had achieved a 'bargain,' the most frequently mentioned bargain was in the form of a sentence concession (9 of 14). These were sometimes relatively minor concessions after the lawyer had made concessions to the crown attorney. For example, a lawyer said that he pleaded his client guilty to all three counts (impaired driving, refusal to

TABLE 4.1

Assessment by lawyer of each accused's case concerning whether plea discussions resulted in plea 'bargains'

Whether plea discussion resulted in plea 'bargain'	Number	Percentage
Yes – plea 'bargain'		
Sentence-related concession	9	15.8
Charge-related concession	3	5.3
Sentence- and charge-related concession	2	3.5
No – no plea 'bargain'		
Withdrawn/reduced charges not a concession because they represent questionable/illegitimate overcharging	23	40.4
Withdrawn charges not a concession because they represent 'kicker' charges	8	14.0
Withdrawn charges not a concession because they were an insignificant part of a 'package' arrangement	7	12.3
Plea discussion did not result in a plea agreement	5	8.7
Totals	57	100.0

provide a breath sample, driving while disqualified) because he felt there was little chance of having the crown attorney withdraw any one of them. He parlayed this co-operation into an attempt at securing a sentence concession. Since this was the accused's third conviction for impaired driving, he was facing a mandatory jail term of three months. Using the reasons that the accused was steadily employed, and had a wife and two children to support, the lawyer asked the crown attorney if he would agree that the jail term be served on an intermittent basis. Since intermittent jail sentences were only possible on terms of 90 days or less and not three months, the crown attorney agreed to state in court that he was not opposed to a term of 90 days. The lawyer was then to enter his argument that the sentence should be served intermittently to continue the stability of the accused's occupational and domestic circumstance.

A further three lawyers said they had achieved charge concessions. For example, a lawyer agreed to a plea settlement whereby his client would plead guilty to one count of willful damage in exchange for the withdrawal of one count of theft under $200, one count of possession of stolen property, and two counts of failure to appear in court. The lawyer felt that although they were legally legitimate, the theft/possession charges represented 'double-barrelling' and the mischief charge was very questionable and petty. He agreed to the guilty plea arrangement because of the major concessions involved in withdrawing the 'solid' charges of failure to appear as well as the theft/possession charges. It is important to note that the lawyer said he originally planned pleas of guilty to both the charges of theft and failure to appear, and he believed the major concession was only forthcoming because his client was serving as a police informant. In light of his own questioning of police charging practices, as well as our extensive documentation on the lawyers' perceptions of illegitimate and questionable charging practices by the police, it is also noteworthy that this lawyer viewed any charge withdrawals as a concession. 'You have to be realistic about the thing because if the guy wasn't guilty or shouldn't be involved, generally he wouldn't be charged.'

The remaining two lawyers who perceived a bargain talked about concessions in the form of both charges and sentences. For example, a lawyer had extensive discussions with the detective, and some with the crown attorney, resulting in the reduction of what the lawyer regarded as two legitimate robbery charges to one charge of theft over $200 and one charge of theft under $200, along with the crown attorney's promise not to oppose a recommendation of a lenient sentence (short jail term). This was perceived as a major bargain by both the lawyer and the accused and clearly resulted from the persistent efforts of the lawyer (for greater detail on this case, see Ericson, 1981: 193–8).

Among the lawyers who related that the guilty plea agreement represented no bargain, over half (representing 23 accused) indicated that withdrawn and/or reduced charges were not a concession because they were part of questionable and/or illegitimate overcharging by the police. The attribution of illegitimacy does not mean that the lawyers saw these charges as legally improper; rather, they generally saw them as excessive in the circumstances, representing more the organizational production requirements of the police bureaucracy than what would stand up under the scrutiny of the courts.

We have had occasion to discuss some of these cases before in remarking upon police practices of charging every person possible with every offence possible, and charging to a higher category than the evidence seemed to merit. In some cases even the detectives and crown attorneys admitted to each other that there was questionable evidence to sustain the charge(s) originally laid. In sum, plea discussions were inevitable in these cases and it was almost as inevitable that the agreement reached contained no major concessions from the crown.

While most of the cases in this category were settled in a routine manner, a few involved unique factors calling for a unique settlement. Among these is the case of an accused charged with three counts of 'break and enter with intent to commit an indictable offence' after allegedly breaking into a house, and allegedly breaking into a school on several occasions. The accused admitted these entries, and to actions of a sexual nature connected with them (leaving obscene notes at the school; masturbating into the victim's underclothes in the house). Apparently because he wanted to avoid embarrassing testimony that would likely be revealed at trial, he was willing to plead guilty to all three counts.

The defence lawyer challenged the legitimacy of the charges because the accused arguably had no intent to commit an indictable offence once in the premises. The lawyer talked with one crown attorney and they agreed to the withdrawal of the charges in exchange for a guilty plea to the substituted charge of being unlawfully in a dwelling house. However, another crown attorney believed that it was inappropriate to do this and felt that the accused should stand trial on the three original counts and seek acquittal. The crown attorneys held a conference at which it was agreed that it was inappropriate for the accused to plead guilty to the 'break and enter with intent' charges. The task was to find a solution that would not involve a trial and thus take into account the accused's desire to avoid embarrassment. As one crown attorney remarked to a research fieldworker: 'It isn't too often you find an accused willing to plead guilty and the Crown not wanting to accept it.'

The solution was to have the accused plead guilty to three counts of petty trespass under a provincial statute. In accepting this arrangement, the lawyer agreed to have his client convicted on minor charges and receive the sentencing consequences even though he was invited to have the original charges go to trial with a good probability of acquittal. In order to avoid any judicial inference that the lawyer had inappropriately accepted a 'deal' to plead guilty to lesser charges rather than go to trial on the original charges, the lawyer arranged for new informations to be laid on each of the trespass charges.[16] When asked in interview about this settlement, the lawyer stated, '[To] me, all that happened was a planning of the truth ... [The] best way to describe it is, it's a judicial decision outside the courtroom. It's saying, we all sit down and say, "That's the same decision a judge would make."'

Returning to Table 4.1 we find that a further eight persons were judged by their lawyers not to have received a bargain because the withdrawn charges, while legitimate, were originally charged as 'kickers' to maximize the chances of getting a conviction on something. Included here are the four accused persons in one case of 'shoplifting' who were all represented by the same lawyer. The four accused were each charged with two counts of theft over $200, three counts of theft under $200, and possession of stolen property over $200. After laying the charges and releasing the accused, the investigating detective telephoned the lawyer and they arranged a plea agreement whereby each accused would plead guilty to two counts of theft over $200 and one count of possession of stolen property *under* $200; the three charges of theft under $200 against each accused were to be withdrawn. The crown attorney accepted this agreement, as did all four accused. The lawyer stated in interview that the plea agreement was no bargain except as a mutually beneficial means of expediting the disposition of the case: 'Well, it's not really making a deal. They just wanted to expedite matters ... I got nothing. I got nothing in terms of concessions because it didn't really matter.'

A further seven accused were subject to plea agreements which were not viewed by their lawyers as 'bargains' because the withdrawn charges were an insignificant part of an overall 'package' worked out with the crown. For example, an accused pleaded guilty to possession of a stolen automobile, dangerous use of a firearm, theft under $200, and failure to appear in court after charges of possession of stolen property, possession of a restricted weapon, and dangerous driving were withdrawn. The lawyer saw the withdrawals as no concession because the withdrawn charge of possession of stolen property was covered by the 'theft under' guilty plea, the withdrawn charge of possession of a restricted weapon was covered by the 'dangerous use of a firearm' guilty plea, and the withdrawn dangerous driving charge was related to the police pursuit incident to the alleged dangerous use of a firearm. The lawyer said he wanted concessions via withdrawal of the charges of failure to appear and theft (which he felt might have led to a more lenient sentence) but the crown attorney refused. He felt that the crown attorney had secured convictions on all three charges that would influence sentence. When asked in interview if the dangerous driving withdrawal was not an important concession, the lawyer replied that it was insignificant beside the charge of dangerous use of a firearm: 'Once you're convicted of murder, why indict a man for dandruff?' The lawyer went on to state that he 'got nothing out of it' and that he told his client 'You've really got nothing and if you want to try and get something, we're just going to have to monkey around ... to try and keep remanding the case 'till we can get it up in front of a judge who I have a little more confidence in.' The accused, who was being detained in custody awaiting trial, accepted the agreement while agreeing it was no bargain.

Obviously there is some degree of overlap among these three categories of cases in which a guilty plea agreement was not perceived as a bargain. All of these cases had the appearance of crown concessions via the withdrawal and/or reduction of charges, but a closer analysis of lawyers' views reveals that the charges being discarded were insubstantial, questionable, or insignificant in the context of the total case against the accused.

As indicated in Table 4.1, there were also no 'bargains' for five accused whose lawyers were unable to reach a plea agreement. Their cases involved plea discussions in which the lawyers sought charge withdrawals or reductions but were denied these by the police and/or crown attorney. In two instances the decision was taken to go to trial, while in the other three instances the lawyers accepted the limitations imposed by the crown and had their clients plead guilty as originally charged.

Another way of assessing whether any plea 'bargains' were struck is to consider the outcome of each charge laid in terms of whether or not the lawyer viewed the charge as legitimate, questionable, or illegitimate. In chapter 2 we discussed the lawyers' perceptions of the legitimacy of their client's charges on a case basis. Here we wish to discuss their perceptions on a charge-by-charge basis. The reason for doing this is that in assessing whether any 'bargains' had been reached, according to the lawyer, we must look at the perceived legitimacy of each charge compared with the outcome of each charge in the context of the overall negotiation. Data addressing this relationship are presented in Table 4.2, in which we cross-tabulate the lawyer's assessment of each original (police-laid) charge and the outcome of each charge for the 80 accused whose lawyers were interviewed.

As indicated in Table 4.2, 96.2 per cent of the 132 original charges which resulted in a guilty plea were deemed by the lawyers concerned to be legitimate, while 2.3 per cent were seen as questionable and 1.5 per cent as illegitimate. These data clearly indicate that, as far as lawyers were concerned, they rarely had clients plead guilty to charges which they did not think were legitimate. The questionable charges which were pleaded guilty to included a break, enter and theft which the lawyer felt was a 'cheap' charge because the accused argued that the dwelling involved belonged to a friend who on other occasions had given him permission to use it, and because there were already enough more substantial charges against he accused; a willful damage charge which the lawyer viewed as very petty, but which he accepted for a guilty plea because it was part of a package deal involving substantial charge withdrawals in exchange for the accused's co-operation as an informant; and a break, enter and theft for which the accused protested innocence and his lawyer did not disbelieve him. The illegitimate charges which were the subject of guilty pleas included one count of possession of marijuana in a case where the other two (illegitimate) counts (possession of stolen property) were withdrawn; and causing a disturbance, where the lawyer believed the police had unnecessarily constructed the charge against his client as an 'order maintenance' measure following a dispute at a tavern.

A total of 18 charges were the subject of guilty pleas after charge reductions (or equivalent charge substitutions), including 11 in which the original charges were seen as legitimate, 2 where the original charges were seen as questionable, and 5 where the original charges were seen as illegitimate. On the surface, this makes it appear that 11 reductions clearly favoured the accused because the original charges were judged by their lawyers to be legitimate. However, closer scrutiny of these cases reveals that in the eyes of the lawyers concerned some of them had inadequate evidence to sustain the original charges and others involved reductions which were part of an overall package arrangement which was not a concession. The two reductions from questionable original charges ('attempt theft' from 'attempt robbery') were both in the case of one accused who maintained innocence but pleaded guilty against the initial advice of his lawyer. The five reductions from illegitimate charges included the three 'petty trespass' charges substituted for the 'break and enter' charges as described previously (pp 145–6).

A total of 10 charges were subject to not guilty pleas but resulted in a finding of guilt, including 5 deemed by lawyers to be legitimate, and 5 which were seen as illegitimate. Another 11 charges were also the subject of not

TABLE 4.2

Assessment by lawyer of each charge and its outcome

| | Total | | Outcome of each charge | | | | | | | | | |
| | | | Guilty as charged | | Guilty to reduced charge | | Not guilty plea – found guilty | | Not guilty plea – acquitted/ dismissed | | Charge withdrawn | |
Lawyer's assessment	N	%	N	%	N	%	N	%	N	%	N	%
Legitimate	201	72.3	127	96.2	11	61.1	5	50.0	5	45.4	53	49.5
Questionable	39	14.0	3	2.3	2	11.1	0	0.0	3	27.3	31	29.0
Illegitimate	38	13.7	2	1.5	5	27.8	5	50.0	3	27.3	23	21.5
Totals	278	100.0	132	100.0	18	100.0	10	100.0	11	100.0	107	100.0

guilty pleas, but these did not result in findings of guilt. Among this group were 5 charges seen by lawyers as legitimate, all of which were dismissed after not guilty pleas were entered. Three of these dismissals were in cases in which the accused pleaded not guilty to other charges and were found guilty.

The remaining 107 charges were withdrawn, including 49.5 per cent which were judged as legitimate, 29 per cent as questionable, and 21.5 per cent as illegitimate. On the surface, the withdrawal of 53 charges seen by lawyers as legitimate appears to represent substantial concessions, especially if we consider that these charges involved 27 different accused persons. However, concessions were only forthcoming in a few situations; for example, where the crown withdrew because he was not ready to proceed, or because the defence had something extra to offer such as the accused's value as an informant. As documented on a case basis, withdrawn charges were typically minor 'throw away' charges in light of the main charges to which the accused pleaded guilty, 'kicker' charges laid by the police to induce a guilty plea to the main charge, or dual charges where one was routinely withdrawn after a guilty plea agreement was reached regarding the other.

The withdrawal of questionable and illegitimate charges was seen as no big deal. Among the 31 withdrawn questionable charges, 24 were against 4 accused in one case whose lawyers described the matter as a 'numbers game' played for the charge credit of the police bureaucracy. The 23 withdrawn illegitimate charges mainly involved very poor evidence from the crown's perspective coupled with the availability of other charges with which to secure a conviction. In sum, the substantial withdrawal rate (38.5 per cent of 278 charges) was a reflection of police overcharging practices and the corrective this brought at the pre-trial stage, rather than an exercise in leniency on the part of the crown.

If we examine the data in Table 4.2 in the other direction, we can provide additional insight into the matter of concessions from the crown. There were 38 original charges against 26 different accused that were deemed by their lawyers to be illegitimate. Among these, only 5.2 per cent were the subject of guilty pleas as originally charged, while an additional 13.2 per cent were the subject of guilty pleas after a charge reduction. A further 21.1 per cent were the subject of not guilty pleas (including 13.2 per cent which resulted in conviction and 7.9 per cent which did not). The majority (60.5 per cent) of the charges deemed illegitimate were withdrawn by the crown attorney, apparently based on the prediction that they would result in dismissals if taken to court, and/or on the fact that there were other charges against the accused which would be the subject of guilty pleas.

There were 39 original charges against 16 different accused which were assessed as questionable by their lawyer. Within this group of charges, 7.7 per cent were the subject of guilty pleas to the original charges and 5.2 per cent were the subject of guilty pleas to reduced charges. Only 7.7 per cent of the charges were challenged with not guilty pleas, and all 3 of these resulted in an acquittal. The vast majority (79.5 per cent) of questionable charges were withdrawn by the crown attorney; they were multiple charges which could be withdrawn while still ensuring the conviction of the accused concerned on other charges.

There were a total of 201 original charges perceived by the lawyers as legitimate. The majority were the subject of guilty pleas, either as originally charged (63.1 per cent) or after a reduction (5.5 per cent). A further 5 per cent were the subject of not guilty pleas; half of these cases were dismissed and half resulted in convictions. The remaining 26.3 per cent of the charges considered legitimate were withdrawn, mainly because they were 'throw away,' 'kicker,' or 'dual' charges which were routinely withdrawn in lieu of guilty plea agreements to the main charge(s) against the accused.

To this point we have considered the pre-trial order out of court as participated in by the lawyer, police, and crown attorney. We have described and analysed plea discussions in terms of the resources which each party brought to bear on these discussions to overcome the limits created by the others and concomitantly to erect their own limits. We have considered also the question of whether, from the defence lawyer's viewpoint, the agreements arising from these discussions constituted a bargain beyond the obvious advantage of expediting the conclusion of the case via guilty pleas. Employing both case-based and charge-based data from the group of interviewed lawyers representing the accused in our study, we have shown there were few bargains to be had.

Lawyers were simply participants in, and recipients of, existing practices for the ordering of justice out of court. Participating as knowledgeable consumers of the system, lawyers were able to have some influence on the asking price. However, their efforts could be directed only at securing the going rate, not at achieving a deal that would upset the ordering of justice and the interests it protects. Thus, lawyers contributed to the system by helping to put the case and their client in order for court appearances. We now turn to a consideration of the accused's place within this order, gaining further appreciation of how the accused comes to give legitimacy to a process within which he is so dependent.

5

Order out of Court II:
The Position of the Accused
and the Plea Decision

The weak are always forced to decide between alternatives they have not chosen themselves.

Dietrich Bonhoeffer, 'Miscellaneous Thoughts,' *Letters and Papers from Prison* (1953)

It is always thus, impelled by a state of mind which is destined not to last, that we make our irrevocable decisions.

Marcel Proust, *Remembrance of Things Past: Within a Budding Grove* (1918)

The Views of the Accused on Plea Transactions

The accused is excluded from the process of plea transaction. Therefore, his perceptions of this process are at a distance from the phenomenon and must be based upon what his lawyer relates to him and the outcome produced in court.

While accused persons who engaged lawyers did so because they thought it would bring some advantage, they rarely mentioned having the lawyer participate in out-of-court plea transactions as a reason for engaging the lawyer. Among the 75 interviewed accused who engaged a lawyer, only 9 said that they retained the lawyer for purposes of out-of-court plea transaction, and 5 of these 9 also stated other reasons for having a lawyer. Furthermore, when talking about the functions of having a lawyer, only 15 made any mention of plea transactions. Four accused said that one function of the lawyer is to conduct plea discussions with the prosecution for concessions, 6 said that the lawyer should conduct plea discussions only if it is in the accused's best interests, and 5 explicitly stated that plea discussions should *not* be one of the lawyer's functions.

In sum, the accused did not typically think of their lawyer's work in terms of out-of-court plea transactions. This may be due to the fact that these transactions were not open to the accused for direct participation, or even observation. Moreover, if the lawyer provided the accused with an account of the transaction, he gave little knowledge and no insight. Thus, when an accused was asked how his lawyer was able to arrange for the withdrawal of two charges, he replied, 'That's what puzzles me. I asked him and he said, "Don't worry about it. It has been taken care of." '

Interestingly, while the accused rarely discussed lawyer participation in plea transactions as a reason for engaging a lawyer, or as a significant component of the lawyer's role, they were often aware of what their lawyers had transacted out of court in their own cases. Among the 61 accused for whom we have both lawyer interviews and accused interviews, there was a high degree of agreement (approximately 80 per cent) concerning whether or not a plea transaction took place. In 15 instances the lawyer and accused both stated no plea transaction took place. In 3 instances the accused believed a plea transaction took place but the lawyer said there was none. In the 43 instances in which the lawyer said that a plea transaction took place, all but 9 accused said they were aware of it. Furthermore, in the 34 instances in which the lawyer and accused concurred that there was a plea transaction, there was no disagreement about the nature of the transaction in 21 instances, partial disagreement in 11 instances, and total disagreement in only 2 instances. These data, when compared with the accounts of their lawyers, indicate that the accused were usually informed that transactions took place, and frequently informed about the general topics discussed.

A scrutiny of the cases involved in this comparison provides further insight. In 1 case where the accused did not mention a plea transaction while the lawyer said there was one leading to charge and sentencing concessions, the accused was a lawyer who refused comment on the matter but was probably aware of what took place. In all 3 cases in which the lawyer did not mention a discussion but the accused thought one had taken place, the accused believed, in light of the sentences received, that their lawyers had bargained for sentencing concessions. As we document in chapter 6, many accused saw their lawyer's work, and most other aspects of the criminal process, in terms of the observable order in court and the outcomes that were announced (rather than decided) in that context. In the 2 instances where there was total disagreement on the nature of the discussion, the confusion was over whether the plea agreement had been for a charge reduction or a charge withdrawal. Among the 11 cases where there were only partial agreements as to the nature of the discussion, 6 involved the lawyer saying there had been a sentence concession as well as charge reductions or withdrawals, while the accused were unaware of the sentence concession.

In all but two cases the accused believed that their lawyers had initiated the plea discussions with the police and/or crown attorney. Since lawyers and not law enforcement agents were seen as the initiators of plea discussions, the accused were thereby encouraged to believe that plea discussions held out the promise of advantage they would otherwise have been unlikely to receive. It also fostered the view that lawyers were working in the best interests of their clients.

The question of who initiated the discussion was usually of little importance; all parties agreed a discussion was necessary, and the limits to the arrangement were not a function of who initiated it. The point we are making is that the accused believed his lawyer had taken the initiative to enter into these discussions and that he would do so only in the search for some advantage to the accused. This contrasts with the experiences of the accused in 'dealing' with the police which, in 38 of 39 instances reported by the accused, were initiated by the police and most often seen as initiated for the purpose of bringing relative advantage to the police (see chapter 2).

As Polstein (1962: 41) states in his 'practical guide' for lawyers entitled, 'How to "Settle" a Criminal Case,' after the 'deal' has been struck 'the client still has to be sold the idea he is getting a bargain.' Since there were usually no substantial bargains to be gained from plea discussion, this selling job required some skilful impression management on the part of the lawyers. The lawyer's task was to formulate the matter so that the accused saw concessions and therefore went along with the agreement for a guilty plea.

The accused are interested in ends, not means.[1] As an accused said when he was asked about his lawyer's involvement in plea discussions, 'I wasn't really interested in that, how *he got* charges dropped or anything. I was just interested what he was going to do but I didn't care how he did it.' Similarly, another accused was content with the plea discussions his lawyer engaged in, whatever they were:

A: Everything was taken care of beforehand, which is all right.
Q: Okay. Now, do you have any idea what he talked about with the crown attorney?
A: No idea, that's, you know, that's his job.
     ...
A: [My lawyer] made the decision and then he came up and said, 'Okay, plead guilty to careless and he'll drop the other ones.' 'Fine' – that's what I said, 'Fine with me.'
Q: You mostly took advice from him?
A: Oh yeah, I let him do everything, yeah I didn't say anything, whatever he says is fine with me.
Q: Now why did you do that, why did you let him do the thinking?
A: That's what he's paid for.

In most cases this reasoning was reasonable. The accused knew that they were excluded from plea discussions, and that even if they were included they would have had difficulty understanding all the ramifications. They knew also that tinkering with the details was of no benefit in itself, and that it could only be measured by the end product. From the lawyer's viewpoint the task was to convince the accused that the end product was more than just a by-product, that it was only possible because of the lawyer's efforts. This task was greatly facilitated by the dependent position of the accused in having to rely upon what his lawyer said about the transactions.

Apart from the hope that the sentence outcome would match or better the expectations of the accused and thereby cast a favourable light on the lawyer's efforts, the lawyer could use certain elements of the plea agreement to impress upon his client that some leniency was being exercised. For example, even though charge withdrawals represented no real concessions from the crown, the lawyer could present them to his client as if they did. A good illustration of this is the case of an accused who was originally charged with 12 property offences and who eventually pleaded guilty to 5 of them after a plea agreement between his lawyer and the crown. By all accounts of the lawyer for this accused and the lawyers for three co-accused, the police had overcharged in this case. In relation to this accused, charges of mischief and possession of stolen property over $200 had been laid which were admitted to by the co-accused and for which he was not responsible. These charges were among those withdrawn, but according to the lawyer this was no bargain. Moreover, 10 theft under $200 charges all arose out of the same incident and could have been covered by 1 charge. The evidence was deemed poor on several of these theft counts, especially since the detective returned most of the stolen property to the victims after anticipating that there would be a guilty plea agreement. The lawyer viewed the entire plea discussion as 'meaningless' because it corrected only the overcharging: 'In retrospect, the negotiation was only as to the extent of the number of counts that he was to plead guilty to. I think that I made it clear [to the crown attorney and detective] that it was really only 1 count. So it was meaningless. It was just a play of numbers or words.'

The lawyer also stated, 'I knew it wouldn't make any difference in the sentence anyways, but the accused might think it's great.' However, the accused apparently did not think it was great and told his lawyer he wanted to plead guilty on two counts only. According to the accused, the lawyer told him that if he did not plead guilty to the five counts, the crown attorney would proceed to trial on all the original charges; moreover, the lawyer gave him a prediction that the crown attorney would be able to secure convictions on all twelve. When this prediction was contrasted with the prediction that guilty pleas to the five counts would likely result in a non-custodial sentence, the accused complied: 'I figured well, that's the way *they* want it, go ahead with it. I'll get it over with and I won't have anything to worry about after that.'

These examples indicate that one of the influences on the accused in pleading guilty was a plea agreement worked out by the lawyer and urged upon the accused. Plea settlements arranged by lawyers were potentially a significant factor influencing the plea decision of the accused, but there were many other influences that had also to be taken into account by the accused. We now turn to a consideration of plea decisions by the accused and examine the role of plea agreements among other elements.

The Plea Decision

The plea decision encapsulates the criminal process. In deciding on plea, the accused potentially takes into account what has taken place before – e.g. transactions with the police, including whether a statement was given, and transactions with a lawyer, including whether the lawyer came up with a plea agreement – and what will happen afterwards, including predictions about what would happen if there is a trial and what the sentence outcome is likely to be. In what follows we present the plea and finding outcomes for each interviewed accused person; consider whether particular pleas were entered because the accused were commited to them, or for some other reason; enumerate the reasons of the accused for entering the pleas they did; and ascertain whether in retrospect the accused saw problems with the pleas they entered which might have led them to a different course of action if they had it to do over again.

As enumerated in Table 5.1, 70 of 101 accused entered guilty pleas and received that finding for at least some of the charges they were facing.[2] Another 13 accused entered not guilty pleas on the charge(s) they were facing, but were convicted on at least some of them. An additional 6 accused entered not guilty pleas for the charge(s) they were facing, and 4 had their charge(s) dismissed while 2 had the charge(s) acquitted. One accused pleaded guilty to some charges and not guilty to others and received convictions after a withdrawal of some charges. Finally, 11 of 101 accused had their charge(s) withdrawn by the crown prior to a finding being reached in their case.

If from the law enforcers' perspective we take as the criterion of 'success' conviction on something from the original charges, then there is a very high 'success' rate.[3] Among the 101 accused, 84 were convicted on something. Among those who were not convicted, only 6 of 17 successfully defended their position in court after entering not guilty pleas, while the remainder avoided the court's disposition because the crown attorney withdrew the charge(s). Thus, 93 per cent (84 of 90) of accused who had their case go to the point of disposition in court were convicted.

TABLE 5.1

Plea and finding for each interviewed accused person

Plea and finding	Number
Guilty of 1+ charge(s) after withdrawal of 1+ charge(s)	32
Guilty of 1 charge as originally charged	24
Guilty of 2+ charges as originally charged	7
Guilty of 1 charge after a charge reduction	3
Guilty of 2+ charges after a charge reduction	2
Guilty after a reduction and withdrawal of some charges	2
Guilty of some, not guilty of others – conviction for some, withdrawal of some	1
Not guilty – convicted	7
Not guilty – dismissed	4
Not guilty – acquitted for some/convicted of others	3
Not guilty – acquitted	2
Not guilty – acquitted for some/convicted of some/some withdrawn	1
Not guilty – convicted of some/some withdrawn	1
Not guilty – convicted on reduced category	1
Charge(s) withdrawn	11
Total	101

This finding suggests that the agents of law enforcement put together a criminal case in a way that usually ensured a conviction outcome. Moreover, since a large majority of accused entered guilty pleas, it suggests that the matter of conviction was usually determined out of court. What we wish to understand is why the large majority of accused conceded to 'the other side' when they had a legal right not to, and how their reasons reflected their position within the order of things. We agree with Cousineau and Verdun-Jones (1979: especially 296) that the rate of guilty pleas is a crude and imprecise measure of out-of-court settlements, although it has been used by many researchers and commentators on the topic of plea transactions. What we are arguing is that the case is constructed ('framed') in such a way that by the time he comes to the plea decision the accused more often than not has no real decision to take. This construction is of course largely an accomplishment of the police and the resources at their disposal, although it is often solidified through the plea transactions among the police, crown attorney, and defence lawyer.

Pleading Guilty while Maintaining Innocence

In Table 5.2 we consider the plea decisions taken by the accused according to whether or not they admitted guilt to the research interviewer. Of course, an admission of guilt in a research interview does not take into account conceptions of legal guilt that might stand up in the courtroom, but it does give an

TABLE 5.2

Admission of guilt by the accused in research interview, plea, and finding of court

	Number
Admission of guilt in research interview	
Guilty plea(s) and finding(s)	54
Not guilty plea(s) – found not guilty on some or all	4
Not guilty plea(s) – found guilty on all	2
All charges withdrawn	5
Total	65
No admission of guilt in research interview	
Guilty plea(s) and finding(s)	16
Not guilty plea(s) – found guilty	8
Not guilty plea(s) – found not guilty on some or all	6
All charges withdrawn	6
Total	36

indication of whether or not the accused felt they were innocent. The vast majority (54 of 65) of accused who admitted to their offence(s) in interview pleaded guilty. Among the six who admitted to their offence(s) in interview and pleaded not guilty in court, four obtained dismissals or acquittals on at least some charges and two were found guilty as charged.

Among the 36 persons who did not admit to their offences in research interviews, 16 nevertheless pleaded guilty as charged. By way of comparison, Baldwin and McConville (1977: 62) found, in an interview sample of 121 persons who changed their pleas to guilty after initially deciding to plead not guilty, that 33 (27.3 per cent) claimed innocence on all charges, 12 (9.9 per cent) claimed innocence on some charges, 13 (10.7 per cent) made a 'token claim' of innocence, and 12 (9.9 per cent) were uncertain about their innocence. In an interview study of 118 young incarcerated offenders, Arcuri (1976: 184) reports that less than 10 per cent claimed innocence. Bottoms and McClean (1976: 120) said that 18 per cent of their interviewed accused retrospectively claimed innocence after pleading guilty.

One reason for pleading guilty while still feeling innocent was the perceived risk of facing worse consequences if a not guilty plea was entered and the person was found guilty.[4] This was usually considered in the context of a lawyer-arranged plea settlement with the crown that was formulated to the accused in an 'offer you can't refuse' manner. For example, an accused charged with 'wounding' maintained both to the police and in interview that he had been arbitrarily selected out as the culprit, and that the 'victim' was more the aggressor as evidenced by the more serious cuts and bruises on the accused: 'I didn't assault, I was being assaulted that night, and I just can't figure things out.' The accused related in interview that he had argued with his lawyer about the decision. He said he wanted to plead not guilty, 'But my lawyer [said]... you should plead guilty because if you plead not guilty and they find you guilty then they might look at you a little more stiffly when they sentence you.' In interview, the lawyer confirmed that his client wanted to plead not guilty and added that he 'was unrealistic about his position.' In order to introduce a sense of 'realism' into his client, the lawyer said, 'I told him that if he got convicted of wounding he might get a penitentiary term.' The lawyer arranged an agreement with the detective and crown attorney to have his client plead guilty to the lesser included offence of 'assault occasioning bodily harm' (not requiring the specific element of intention necessary in the wounding charge), even though he admitted in interview that 'there's some little question here whether the actual bodily harm took place... the crown didn't prove that very well.' Suggesting that a guilty plea to the reduced charge would bring a lower range of sentence, the lawyer convinced his client of the wisdom of a guilty plea. The accused was sentenced to six months' imprisonment.

A woman charged with obstructing police when she allegedly interfered with officers arresting her husband during a domestic dispute felt pressured into a guilty plea by her lawyer's arguments that to do otherwise would bring more serious consequences. The police later added a charge of assaulting police, which was then used by the crown attorney as a lever in plea discussions with the lawyer. The crown attorney offered the withdrawal of the charge of assaulting police and no specific sentence recommendation in exchange for a guilty plea to the charge of obstructing police. The accused said that the lawyer tried to convince her to plead guilty by telling her the facts were against her; for example, '[He said] you don't have to really be physical with them for them to consider it assault.' The lawyer added in interview that part of the persuasion was in terms of the consequences of not guilty pleas: 'Well I believe she was a bit taken aback [by the suggestion of a guilty plea]... but I persuaded her that it might be in her interest to do so because here, you see, you're taking a chance, you plead not guilty then the evidence is laid, she might be convicted of both counts.' The lawyer related that he felt quite proper in urging the accused to plead guilty because, '[I must] consider what is in the best interest of the client... It's not what the client says, you know, it's what comes out in court.'

The lawyer very clearly asserted that he was pleading his client guilty even though she perceived herself to be innocent. He also believed he had convinced her of the strategic wisdom of this decision, even if she was not personally convinced. The accused said that she believed there might have been more serious consequences if she pleaded not guilty, and that at this stage – nine months after the original charge – she was mainly concerned with getting the matter over with:

It's one of the reasons why I pleaded guilty because ... it was going on for nearly a year, you know, and it really bothered me mentally to have this sort of thing hanging over my head. You know, you just wanted to get it over and done with, whatever happened ... it was going to be that day ...

I know I didn't do anything ... but ... the law is set up in a way that, I mean, if I didn't plead guilty, what if they found me guilty, you know? ... I'm not that versed with the law, what is what, what they could come up with, you know. I figure well if this is the way to get over with it I'll just get over with it ... In a way I felt, you know, cheated, I've cheated on myself, I shouldn't have said it [guilty plea], but I said it because I wanted to get rid of it, I wanted to get it over and done with, something dragging on for a year.

The situation of this accused reflects two features present in the case of other accused who pleaded guilty while maintaining innocence. First, it was a matter of deferring to the lawyer's judgment because the accused had no other source of knowledge and opinion to rely upon. Indeed, accused who felt not guilty sometimes conceded to the lawyer's suggestion of a guilty plea even though there were no arrangements with the crown which the lawyer could use to urge the accused into a guilty plea. Second, it reflects the pressure which some accused felt to plead guilty simply to get over the delays awaiting trial.

In the case of one accused, avoiding delay was more important than convictions for three offences he claimed he did not commit. He was charged with being unlawfully at large (which he admitted to), two counts of attempt robbery, and one count of break, enter and theft (all of which he did not admit to). As recorded in chapter 2, this accused said he was told by the detective that if he did not confess to these offences he would be charged with attempt robbery rather than attempt theft. The accused decided not to confess to something he persistently claimed he did not do. However, after a period of awaiting trial in custody he became willing to say he was guilty to expedite the conclusion of the case.

In interview, the accused said he had been falsely accused in the statement of his co-accused. He believed that in the face of this evidence he might have difficulty proving his innocence. However, his main concern was to have the matter settled in order to avoid months of 'dead time' in custody awaiting trial, and he said he pleaded guilty for this reason. His lawyer obtained a reduction of the two attempt robbery charges to attempt theft, apparently because a co-accused was being charged only with attempt theft, but this did not seem to be a factor in the accused's decision to plead guilty:

Q: Were you satisfied with that kind of 'deal'?

A: Well, I guess I had to be, you know.

Q: Well, what kind of deal would you have liked?

A: Drop them all ... except for the one I'm guilty of ... unlawfully at large.

...

Q: When did you first decide you were going to plead guilty to them?

A: Well, I had no choice ... I read the statements [of co-accused] against me – three statements against me. So I was –

Q: And you decided then you were going to plead [guilty]?

A: Yeah, well, I had no choice right?

Q: Did you ever consider pleading not guilty?

A: Oh, yeah. But then I figured maybe they'd find me guilty, you know.

Q: Because of the statements?

A: Yeah, and then I'd be doing a longer time ... all that dead time ... six months, seven months dead time.

The lawyer for the accused stated in interview that he felt that some charges were highly suspect, but he decided to accept his client's wish to plead guilty to get it over with. In particular, the lawyer questioned the break, enter and theft charge:

> Well, the way I dealt with [my client] was that I was in court that day on other matters. I got a message from the cells, or the gentleman from the Salvation Army, that [my client] wanted to see me. I went and talked to him, he informed me of the charges, he informed me as to what he'd like to do. I told him that it was in his interest that the matter go over for consideration so I could evaluate the charges and the evidence. he said, 'No,' he wished to have the matters dealt with today regardless. He then advised me that, as to certain charges that he was not guilty of but – at least the break and enter he said – he gave me a defence, a possible defence to the break and enter to which he said he wasn't guilty or didn't do, he gave me a possible defence. I told him from what he told me he had a valid defence and he still insisted he wanted to plead guilty because he knew he was going to go down on something and he sort of has a sense of knowledge that whatever he goes down on is going to have the same effect. I got him to sign a written instruction saying that, notwithstanding I told him he has a good defence, he intends to plead guilty to certain charges.

The lawyer was less certain about the possible innocence of his client on the attempt robbery charges. The lawyer's solution to the situation came from a lunchtime meeting with the crown attorney, the lawyer for a co-accused, and the police. The lawyer, noticing a discrepancy in accounts between his client and the police, decided that the police account was justifiable, and therefore went for a guilty plea 'package.' In doing this, the lawyer seemed to accept what he had previously stated was his client's view, that he was 'going to go down for something [and] ... whatever he goes down on is going to have the same effect':

> [At the meeting] there was sort of a feeling that the matter should be all wrapped up together ... I spoke with the officer ... [and] I found out that what my client had told me and what the officer had told me was somewhat in

conflict. However, if my client was to be believed he still had a valid defence. The accused's record was substantial and the crown offered at that time to take a plea to two counts of attempt theft rather than the two counts of attempt robbery which were the purse snatchings. I felt that quite legally – the accused never gave me a defence to the purse snatchings although he indicated that the people who the purses came from might have had problems identifying him (they never gave any statements to the police) – I felt that they were actually robberies subject to the issue of identification and in view of that I suppose because of what the officer had told me, I felt a little bit more at ease taking the plea in the sense that I felt that the crown had a valid case to put before the jury and my client's chances were somewhat reduced as to success on a not guilty plea ... On the break and enter charge, there was no statement but the officer informed me that he was informed that there was fingerprint evidence. Now the officer very fairly said he understands there were fingerprints and it implicates my client but he also said he's not swearing to that because he'd have to talk to the identification officer, OK. Knowing the particular officer and knowing what my accused, my client had told me, I felt I suppose more at ease of accepting my client's instructions and consequently, because of the reduction of the charges from a robbery to an attempt theft, the attempt theft under, you know, I don't think he could, he couldn't have done better than that, you know, even on trial.

The accused's strategy of pleading guilty to avoid 'dead time' awaiting trial was very successful, as he only spent three weeks in jail from the time of arrest to the time of conviction, and another two weeks before he was sentenced to 18 months definite and 18 months indefinite, concurrent on all charges.

One of three co-suspects who implicated this accused in 'purse snatching' offences said that although he himself was not guilty of two 'purse snatchings' he nevertheless was willing to plead guilty to them to protect his friends who were the culprits. He believed that guilty pleas on these two offences would likely make little difference on his overall sentence since he was facing five other charges. He said that his lawyer advised him to plead not guilty on these two offences, but he ignored his lawyer's advice. The lawyer related in interview that he believed his client was innocent of the two 'purse snatching' charges. The lawyer also expressed suspicion about why one of the four co-suspects was never charged and suggested that this person may have been granted leniency as an informant against the others.[5] Nevertheless, the lawyer apparently made no inquiries with the police along these lines. He accepted the wish of the accused to plead guilty to these two offences along with five others, although he eventually arranged a plea settlement whereby three counts (including one of the two 'purse snatchings') were withdrawn in exchange for guilty pleas to four counts.

Among the idiosyncratic reasons for pleading guilty while maintaining innocence was an accused's explanation that she became very nervous in court and pleaded guilty to a charge she was planning to plead not guilty on. She was arrested and charged for theft under $200 (shoplifting), and when a search revealed that she was in possession of allegedly stolen identification she was also charged with possession of stolen property. She maintained in interview that the identification was not stolen, but when she appeared in court without a lawyer she found it difficult to understand the proceedings and entered guilty pleas to both charges.

Another unrepresented accused had problems of understanding as well as a strategic reason for entering a guilty plea even though he maintained innocence. He was charged with possession of stolen property over $200 after he was caught driving a vehicle the police believed to have been stolen. He maintained he borrowed the vehicle from someone to whom he thought it belonged, and he maintained innocence from the time he dealt with the police through to the retrospective interview with our researcher. At three different points during the interview he said one reason for pleading guilty was his belief that once a person is found with stolen property it is a strict liability situation.[6] For example, at one point he stated, 'I was innocent, I didn't know the car was stolen' but then went on to say, 'There is no way around it as long as you've got it in your hand, or if you are sitting in a [allegedly stolen] car, that's it.' When the accused was asked why he did not explain to the judge that he did not know the borrowed vehicle was stolen, he replied, 'Doesn't make any difference. You've got to plead guilty to it so even if you're innocent beyond a shadow of doubt, you're guilty.'

The accused related another reason for entering a guilty plea. He said he was charged with two other offences in another jurisdiction, and that he was pleading guilty to them. As a parolee, he predicted he was going back to the penitentiary on these convictions; therefore, he wanted to expedite the process rather than face the 'dead time' awaiting trial on the possession charge, which in any case he felt would not have much influence on his sentence. By pleading guilty to the possession charge he could have it transferred to the other jurisdiction for sentencing on all three and thereby speed up his re-entry to the pentitentiary to begin serving his time there.

In the main, people who pleaded guilty while maintaining innocence decided to plead guilty because they saw no other option, because they thought it would not have a significant impact on their overall sentence in connection with other convictions they were facing at the same time, and/or because they perceived some personal advantage in pleading guilty (e.g. expediting the disposition or protecting a friend). Some of these elements entered also into the decisions of people who admitted in interview to their offences and who decided to plead guilty rather than contest the matter.

Reasons for Pleading Guilty

Among the 71 people who entered a plea of guilty to one or more charges, the most frequently mentioned reason was 'I was guilty.' Among the 31 (44 per cent) people who gave this response, 11 gave no other reason while 20 combined it with another reason. By way of comparison, Bottoms and McClean (1976: 112) report that 41 per cent of their interviewed defendants said they pleaded guilty because 'I was guilty' and 58 per cent said they pleaded guilty because of the police case against them.

Most of those who said 'I was guilty' were charged with offences which were apparently supported with substantial evidence that the accused believed he could not reasonably challenge. For example, an accused charged with impaired/over 80 mg pleaded guilty to impaired care and control, without legal representation. He stated, 'I had to plead guilty pretty well ... It was open and shut, I mean uh, you blow in the breathalyser, what can you do about that?' He said that he planned to plead guilty from the night of his arrest: 'What the hell ... what could I plead? Stupidity? Insanity?' This accused was among the many who saw the matter as foreclosed from the point of first contact with the police. They could not think of any reasonable alternative but to submit to police actions at the time of arrest. Similarly, they could not see any reasonable way to challenge the police action of charging once they reached the court stage. These accused immediately concluded that a conviction was in order, basing their conclusion on the realization that they did not have a choice in any case.

The second most frequently mentioned reason for pleading guilty was to get the court process over with as soon as possible in order to avoid the uncertainties and anxieties associated with delays. The 22 accused who gave this reason all offered it in conjunction with some other reason; in particular, along with a feeling of being guilty anyway (5), a belief that the matter was already foreclosed because of a written statement of confession (5), or the promise of leniency from the crown attorney (8).

Among those who said that they were guilty and wanted to get the matter over with quickly was an accused charged with possessing a small amount of marijuana. Without legal representation, he pleaded guilty on his first court appearance even though the crown attorney could not produce the drug analysis certificate: 'I wanted to get it over with, I didn't want to come to court in another three months, I knew it was hash ... The only thing I could see in pleading not guilty was just a lot of hassles, you know, go into court another day and get a lawyer and all that and there's just no point, I figured well I'll take what's coming to me.'

Eight accused said they decided to plead guilty to get the matter over with after an expedient and apparently lenient plea settlement worked out between their lawyer and the crown. For them, the choice was between a not guilty plea after remand for several months – with a significant chance of still being found guilty and possibly facing a harsher sentence than if a guilty plea had been entered – versus a guilty plea to get the matter over within the predictable scope of what the lawyer said about the agreement. Not surprisingly, these persons opted for expediency, especially since their lawyers formulated the settlement in comparatively attractive terms.

For example, an accused was charged with break, enter and theft and mischief, in connection with an incident he was allegedly involved in along with two accomplices. After three remands over two months, the accused said he was told by his lawyer that 'If I wanted to plead not guilty then okay, there still was a 50-50 chance on either side, but it would have been remanded again until after Christmas.' The accused believed the excessive delays were caused by the crown attorney, who required a police officer witness who had been unavailable because of an accident. He was offered a withdrawal of the mischief charge and a reduction of the break, enter and theft charge to attempt break and enter in exchange for a guilty plea. The accused accepted the offer even though he said he had been planning to plead not guilty up to that date. According to the accused's lawyer, his client would have been willing to plead guilty to the higher category (break, enter and theft) at this stage because he was so fed up with the dealings.

The pressures to get it over with were of course particularly marked in the case of those who were in custody awaiting trial. An accused in custody on charges of assault occasioning bodily harm, weapons dangerous, choking, and forcible seizure had 10 court appearances over 3 months. On his tenth appearance his lawyer arranged a plea settlement whereby the crown would withdraw the charges of weapons dangerous and forcible seizure in exchange for a guilty plea to two counts of assault occasioning bodily harm. The accused said his lawyer advised him to accept this arrangement. According to the accused, this 'advice' included telling the accused that if he pleaded guilty he could expect a sentence of 18 months in jail, and that if he did not go along with it he was facing another six months in custody awaiting trial plus the chance of being found guilty and receiving a more severe sentence. In interview, the lawyer described how he formulated the matter to the accused:

> I told him that 'You [are] looking at life ... Don't kid yourself, you're playing
> around with a penitentiary term' ... Enter a plea [and] there's a good chance
> you'll stay within a reformatory setting ... You understand that we could go to
> trial and you could get convicted of common assault. You're looking at about
> three or four months of doing dead time before your trial and you could still get
> up to a year, and you're gambling that [at a minimum] versus life. Do you really
> want to waive the trial?' he said, 'Yes.'

Not surprisingly, the accused did 'waive the trial' and entered guilty pleas on two counts of assault occasioning bodily harm (one of which was substituted for the 'choking' charge). He was sentenced to a total of 18 months' prison definite and 6 months' prison indefinite.

Fifteen accused mentioned as a reason for pleading guilty the fact that they had signed a written statement of confession to the police.[7] This reason was invariably combined with another reason – most often a desire to get it over with (five), a declaration of being guilty (three), or a plea agreement arranged between his lawyer and the crown (three).

Most of these accused equated their written statement of confession to the police with a guilty plea; that is, they felt they had 'pleaded guilty' to the police and that this foreclosed the matter of conviction because they were unable to contradict their statement to the police once they reached court. This was expressed in different ways in different circumstances, but the essential feeling of foreclosure was the same. For example, an accused stated '[Detective's first and last name] is the one I pleaded guilty to.' Another accused indicated at various points in the interview that his plea decision was foreclosed at the point of signing the confession statement:

> [Initially discussing why he did not call a third party]
> I signed a statement, a plea of guilty, so I figured there's no sense in getting a lawyer.
> [Discussing why he would not elect up and plead not guilty]
> I was guilty of it, you know. There's no sense in lying about it. I signed a statement and that. Probably if I did plead not guilty they would have been harder on me.
> [Discussing what he would do differently in retrospect]
> I'd get my lawyer before I'd do anything next time ... because I was talking to [my lawyer] and he says, 'You never plead guilty or anything. You're always innocent 'til proven guilty.' So, next time if anything comes in [I] don't sign nothing or anything 'til I talk to my lawyer ... If I had to do it all over again I wouldn't have been signing any statements or anything else, and I would plead not guilty.

Seven of the nine persons who gave as their first-mentioned reason for pleading guilty the fact that they had given the police a written statement of confession said that if they had it to do over again, they would plead not guilty by challenging the statement, or not give one in the first place. In light of this, it is important to enquire into why the 15 accused who said they pleaded guilty because of statements of confession to the police originally provided those statements. Four accused said they provided the statements as part of a 'leniency deal' with the police, 3 because they feared physical abuse at the hands of the police, and 2 because they feared further police investigations of their activities. These 9 accused can be viewed as having been pressured into their confessions and as having extended this into a guilty plea decision. Among the other 6 accused there were not similar signs of pressure:

3 said they gave written statements of confession because they were 'guilty,' and 3 said that other evidence was obviously against them and it was therefore expedient to provide a statement.

As indicated by the response of the accused cited above, the lawyer sometimes encouraged the view that statements of confession foreclosed the matter of conviction. In another case the accused, charged with one count of robbery, said he decided to plead guilty because his lawyer 'said I was already convicted on my statement.' In some cases this undoubtedly appeared as realistic advice, based on the prediction that the evidence was clearly in favour of the crown and that a guilty plea might be taken as a sign of co-operation that would pay off in a more lenient disposition than might otherwise be expected. However, as we discussed in chapters 2 and 3, in most cases the lawyer readily accepted the statement of confession as 'fact' with little or no effort at enquiring into how that fact was constructed. In some cases this undoubtedly led the lawyer to perpetuate the view that the statement had foreclosed the matter, when he might have used it as a basis for opening up quite different matters.

Several lawyers indicated in interview that they routinely accepted statements of confession as 'fact,' making guilty pleas inevitable, even though they were told of some irregularity by their client or otherwise believed there was some basis for suspicion about how the statements were produced. These lawyers displayed an unwillingness to upset their relationships with criminal control agents for the sake of defending persons whom they believed were guilty of something in any case. For example, a lawyer for two co-accused believed that the statements were improperly obtained and that one of his clients was not guilty to two of the charges he had given statements on. However, when he was asked at the conclusion of the case to comment on the police methods in obtaining the statements, the lawyer indicated that he made no effort to challenge them.

L: I don't know what the police did. Both accused said that they were beaten.
Q: Yes, you mentioned that at lunch.
L: Yes, that's all I know, if they were beaten that's obviously inappropriate.
Q: Did both of them give statements?
L: They both gave statements and they both said that's why they gave statements, because they were frightened.
Q: Do you believe it?
L: To some extent, yes.

Again, the feeling of this lawyer seemed to be that his clients should be convicted on something and that the important matter was to arrange what that something would be through plea transactions with the crown. It was of little use, and of possible harm, to challenge openly police procedures when everyone agreed that there should be a conviction on something.

In some cases the lawyers said that they did make enquiries into the production of the statements but satisfied themselves that everything was in order. In the case of co-accused who were both charged with and entered guilty pleas on one count of break, enter and theft, the nature of the enquiry and the basis for satisfaction were again indicative of the typical approach of lawyers. The lawyer for both co-accused said that he viewed the charges as legitimate because both of his clients had given the police written statements of confession on them. The lawyer initially described the police procedures as 'entirely proper and entirely in order,' although his later discussion of the statement-taking process revealed that they should only have been described as 'entirely *on* order': '[My clients] indicated to me that they felt obliged to make the statement. Uh, they indicated that they felt under some pressure to make the statement, but in going over it with them, I, we satisfied ourselves, all of us – that the statement was not coerced from them ... They did not feel that there were any threats of violence or anything like that against them. They just felt that if they wanted to get out of custody they had to make a statement.'[8]

It was not a practice of lawyers to challenge the admissibility of state-ments through *voir dire* hearings in court. Only one lawyer initiated this form of challenge, and his actions proved unsuccessful. Indeed, the only person to have his statement to the police ruled inadmissible in court was an accused who defended himself without legal representation. He argued that he had been threatened with other charges and continued detention until he con-fessed, and the judge accepted his argument as a ground for ruling that the statement was inadmissible. In comparison, a co-accused who alleged the same police practices in obtaining a statement from him did not challenge the statement because his lawyer advised against it. In interview, his lawyer stated that his client alleged improper police tactics in securing the confession, but the lawyer did not take these allegations seriously and made no effort to challenge the police either in or out of court: 'The information that I had received from [my client] and through one of the co-accused that I spoke with was that there were techniques that I might call "harrassing," "bullying," and yet I feel quite certain that no court would upset them. I think the technique that was used, was, "Look, we know you're guilty and you're not getting out of here until you sign the statement." There was also an allegation by one of the accused that they'd asked permission to call a lawyer first and that it was refused ... [My client] was concerned that there might be some abuse. But, it was his first contact with the police in this fashion and I would suspect that, you know, anybody in for the first time is going to feel intimidated.'

In sum, one accused felt intimidated and did something about it on his own: his statement was ruled inadmissible, and he was acquitted on one charge against him while the other charge was dismissed. His co-accused felt intimidated and consulted his lawyer: his lawyer passed off the complaints to inexperience in the ways of the system and had his client plead guilty to one charge (possession of stolen property under $200) as part of an agreement with the crown which involved the withdrawal of two other charges (possession under $200, theft under $200).

As we have previously argued, lawyers are unlikely to throw off balance a process which they help to engineer and from which they benefit. Lawyers routinely *accept* the 'facts' as they are constructed by the police, and consequently the 'truths' built upon these facts, even if they may not entirely *agree* with them. Lawyers inure themselves to the consistency of police accounts, because consistency means expediency; this is the case even if expediency might be at the expense of the accused. As ongoing members, lawyers do not wish to upset the ordering of justice; their primary commitment is to keep their client in order throughout the process in order to receive the 'going rate.'

Fifteen accused said that their lawyers' advice to them to plead guilty was at least part of their reason for pleading guilty. In two cases this was the only reason given. In the 13 cases where this was combined with other reasons, the most frequent additional reasons were 'I was guilty' (4), a plea arrangement for withdrawal of charges by the crown (3), getting the matter disposed of quickly (2), and the belief that a guilty plea would have a beneficial effect on sentence by not wasting the court's resources (2).

Only one accused said he pleaded guilty based on his lawyer's advice that nothing else could be done because of his statement of confession. This masks the complexity of the issues surrounding lawyers' advice and points to the advantage of having interviews with lawyers and tape-recorded data on plea transactions in addition to interviews with the accused. Research based solely on interviews with the accused may well underestimate the role of the lawyer in the guilty plea decision.

Twenty-two accused said that their decision to plead guilty was at least partly due to a plea agreement worked out with the crown. Nine spoke of charge withdrawal agreements, seven spoke of charge reduction agreements, one spoke of a charge withdrawal and reduction agreement, and five spoke of sentence recommendation agreements. These reasons for pleading guilty were invariably stated in combination with other reasons, in particular a desire to get the matter over with (eight), lawyer's advice (three), and the belief that a guilty plea would have a beneficial effect by not wasting the court's resources (three).

In comparison, Baldwin and McConville (1977: 28) report that in a sample of 121 accused persons who changed their plea to guilty at the last instance, 22 (18.2 per cent) said they did so because of an explicit 'plea bargain' entailing some form of sentence leniency. Empirical evidence suggests that judges do offer more lenient sentences in exchange for guilty pleas. Baldwin and McConville (1978) matched persons who had changed their pleas from guilty to not guilty late in the proceedings to persons who had pleaded guilty from the beginning and to those who had pleaded not guilty but were convicted, with respect to sex, age, offence, number of counts, record, and previous incarcerations. They found that 64.6 per cent of the late changes received custodial sentences compared with 50 per cent of those who planned guilty pleas from the beginning and 69.3 per cent of those convicted after pleading not guilty. Nardulli (1978) reports similar results in comparing guilty pleas to trials before a judge alone and trials before a jury, for the offences of murder, armed robbery, and trafficking in heroin. Custodial sentences were from two and one-half to four and one-half times greater after a conviction from a jury trial compared with a guilty plea. Sentences after a conviction in a bench trial were between the other two forms of hearing.

While 'lawyer's advice' was only infrequently mentioned along with a plea arrangement as a reason for pleading guilty, lawyers were instrumental in making the arrangements and then convincing the accused that the arrangements should be accepted. As documented in chapter 4, the typical practice was for lawyers to arrange a plea agreement for their clients and then to convince their clients that it was indeed a 'deal.' Since the accused was rarely in a position to judge the advantages or disadvantages of the arrangement, he typically went along with whatever his lawyer said was in order. As Baldwin and McConville (1977: especially 45ff) document, lawyers frequently formulate the matter in a way that effectively leaves the accused with no choice but to plead guilty. While the offer is one that could be refused, it is not likely to be refused because the accused acts solely on the basis of trusting his lawyer's judgments in out-of-court transactions with the crown.

In most cases it was routine for the lawyer to make the plea arrangement and then to get the accused's nodding agreement. Indeed, several lawyers took the view that once they were satisfied with the arrangement, they could order the accused to accept it. As we recorded in chapter 3, some lawyers said explicitly they would not allow their relationship with their clients to be otherwise. Other lawyers indicated their views in other ways. For example, an accused was charged with impaired/over 80 mg and break, enter and theft. The break, enter and theft arose when the accused allegedly broke into a garage compound to retrieve his motorcycle after it had been impounded by the police following the impaired/over 80 mg arrest. In talking with the police officer and crown attorney involved in the case, the lawyer made the plea arrangement and then confidently assured them that his client would go along with it. The lawyer simply proclaimed that he would order his client to agree and went on to concur with the detective's view that the accused was of a lower order:

L: What do you want, impaired or over 80?
CA: I'm easy.
L: How about over 80?

CA: I'll take the over 80.

L: Okay. What about the other charges, he's go ah –

Detective: How about just ah –

L: Mischief.

D: Yeah.

L: That's what he did, ah, broke a lock ...

D: It was his own bike.

L: Yeah, his own bike.

CA: So really a mischief.

D: Actually.

CA: You got him on a theft, charged him with a theft.

D: Yeah.

CA: We just got one where the fellow stole his own car.

D: Pardon?

CA: We just convicted a guy where he stole his own car.

D: Yeah. Like it's technically under s.4. Oh yeah, you've got the other file there.

CA: He's going to plead on the mischief, eh?

L: Yeah, he'll plead on that. As soon as he gets here and I tell him he's pleading to mischief.

D: It's just being dumb.

L: It's known as the unproclaimed stupid asses' section of the Criminal Code.

In interview, the lawyer described his client as 'passive' and agreeable to whatever the lawyer said was an offer. The lawyer also said that if he told his client to plead guilty to break, enter and theft, his client would have done so. Of course, given his exclusion from the plea transaction and his dependent position in relation to his lawyer, the accused could hardly be anything but passive and compliant. To reiterate, contrary to the view of the accused person as imperceptive, ignorant, frightened, and therefore passive (e.g. Dell, 1971), we see the accused's passivity as a reflection of his powerlessness within the ordering of justice.

Twelve accused who pleaded guilty gave as one reason for doing so the desire to create a favourable impression by not wasting the court's time in a trial. This reason was invariably combined with another reason, most frequently saying 'I was guilty' (three), as part of a plea arrangement with the crown (three), and on the advice of a lawyer (two). Most of these accused were aware of the legal fact that a guilty plea could bring sentence leniency because it shows a measure of contrition, a deference to the order of things. They learned of this through their lawyers. An example was provided by an accused who said his lawyer advised him to plead guilty because, 'He said that if I pleaded not guilty and they found me guilty, then I would have got more time for holding up the court, you know, remands and stuff like that.'[9]

Among the remaining reasons given for pleading guilty, five could be generally categorized as involving a belief that there was compelling evidence against the accused. Three persons said they wished to protect other persons who were culprits and therefore 'took the rap.'

Reasons for Pleading Not Guilty

Among the 20 persons who entered not guilty pleas, 15 said they did so because they were innocent. Among the other 5, 4 did not protest innocence but indicated that they had a plausible defence and/or were defending their legal right to a trial, while 1 provided no reason for pleading not guilty. In sum, most persons who pleaded not guilty said they did so because of a feeling of innocence rather than as a strategy to get off more lightly on something they admitted to doing. If they were seeking leniency, accused persons were more likely to plead guilty in the hope that they could parlay their co-operation into a lighter sentence.

Persons who said they pleaded not guilty because they felt they were innocent sometimes saw other benefits in going to trial. An accused charged with a fellow-worker for allegedly causing a disturbance at a strike picket line related that there were wider issues of labour unionism at stake and viewed his case as a union cause being fought by his union-hired lawyer. A first offender charged with mischief said that in spite of being innocent he did consider pleading guilty at one stage in order to get the matter over with; however, he continued with his decision to plead not guilty because he wanted to avoid having a criminal record.

Only one person took the view that he was out to manipulate the system and hired an expensive lawyer to 'get him off' completely on impaired/over 80 mg charges. The others who perceived that they might be factually guilty were committed to the idea that they still had to be proven guilty legally. For example, a person charged with driving while her licence was suspended, and then with failure to appear in court on this initial charge, took the attitude that she had 'nothing to lose' by pleading not guilty. She argued that there was a bureaucratic mix-up over non-payment of a fine which led to the licence suspension and that her failure to appear in court was an 'honest mistake' she had made in mixing up the court date.

Lawyers were not always successful at resisting wishes to plead not guilty, sometimes accepted these wishes, and occasionally encouraged them. However, only one accused said he explicitly overruled his lawyer's advice to plead guilty. He was charged with two counts of assault occasioning bodily harm and one count of weapons dangerous arising out of the same incident involving two victims. He believed that he was no more the 'offender' than the 'victims' and decided to plead not guilty because 'I guess I had to give them a fight ... Why not? Instead of just going up there and pleading guilty.'

The lawyer believed his client was factually guilty and said that he had a preconception of his client's guilt because of his reputation as a 'punk.' The lawyer felt his client was just 'playing games' by pleading not guilty: 'He has an almost oriental fatalism about the police and courts, you know. He got caught and he's going to screw the system around so long as he can and eventually, you know, take his lumps.' In most cases fatalism led the accused to give up at an early point; in this case, the accused was still fatalistic but decided to prolong the inevitable by forcing the game to the end.

The lawyer said he advised his client to accept a guilty plea arrangement. The lawyer predicted that the accused would have received 60 days via the guilty plea route, arguing 'There is a rule of thumb, I guess, that in cases which have an emotional overtone that you are much better off to plead guilty because of the sort of dull recitation of facts in a monotone by the crown attorney doesn't sound anywhere as near as severe as when the judge has an emotional interplay with the witness.' The lawyer said he told his client that a not guilty plea entailed the risk of antagonizing the judge and getting a heavier sentence, but the accused refused to accept the idea of a guilty plea arrangement with the crown. In the end, the accused was convicted on one count of assault occasioning bodily harm after the other two charges were dismissed, and he received a four-month reformatory term.

In another case the accused said he turned down a tentative plea agreement offer, but he had some backing from his lawyer rather than being faced with 'an offer you can't refuse.' He was charged along with a co-accused with possession of a weapon for the purpose of committing an indictable offence. Both accused adamantly maintained their innocence. The co-accused was in a particularly precarious position because he was a parolee who faced a three-year penitentiary term if his parole was revoked upon conviction for an indictable offence. At one point the crown attorney offered a plea settlement whereby the accused would plead guilty to the offence and the charge against the co-accused would be dismissed. The lawyer for the accused said he consulted with his client about his offer and they agreed to refuse it, and the lawyer said he countered with an offer that was not taken up. The counter offer was that 'they both could plead guilty to a summary conviction offence of being in possession of a weapon or something like that which would have avoided all these problems [parole revocation for the co-accused; excessive delay], but I kind of felt in the circumstances that they were kind of pushing a charge that there really wasn't a lot of substance to.' The accused said he would have no part of any 'deal' whether or not it might benefit the co-accused, and he had no difficulty in convincing his lawyer of this:

A: They had been talking to the crown, [the co-accused's] lawyer had been, because the fact was that [the co-accused] has just gotten off parole, forty months
parole, so if he got convicted he would have to do his forty months parole plus

whatever for this. So they wanted us to see if I could plead guilty and the crown said I would just get a fine – so [if] I pleaded guilty [co-accused] would be found not guilty. And I said, 'No because I won't change my story. Why should I? I'm telling the truth.' And at my preliminary hearing the judge took five minutes to decide if he should drop the charges on me or not, so I almost walked once, why should I decide to plead guilty now. And our lawyers, my lawyer told me, he says, 'Don't make a deal because you are going to beat it, there is no way they can convict you on what they have.'

Q: Both lawyers said this?

A: Yeah, so...the crown just wanted our conviction, some kind of conviction.

Q: Why did he want that?

A: Well that's his job, to get a conviction.

Q: At any point did any of you – your lawyers or you or [co-accused] at all consider the deal?

A: No, they just asked me to think about it. How good a friend I would be saving [co-accused's] neck, if we were found guilty; but my lawyer told me that, and I knew myself, as far as I was concerned that they just didn't have what they needed to convict us.

Both accused were acquitted.

In a few cases accused persons who seriously contemplated guilty pleas to get the matter over with were actively talked into not guilty pleas by their lawyers. For example, an accused charged with theft under $200 after a 'shoplifting' incident said he wanted to plead guilty so that he could relieve his anxiety about the case and not lose more time from work caused by additional court appearances. He said that he decided to plead not guilty after talking with a duty counsel:

> Like the two witnesses was there, you know. I said I had no chance to win the case. And he [duty counsel] said 'Try to plead not guilty' you know. So that is what I did, I pled not guilty because he told me. If it was my decison I would have pled guilty already, even the second time. Because when I got out through the door, you know I said, 'I am going to plead guilty.' And he stopped me again and he said, 'Why do you want to plead guilty?' So you know, well I said, 'They are going to fine me.' And he said to me, 'It's the judge's decision what he is going to do to you, fine you or not.' So I said, 'If they are going to fine me the same, I am going to plead guilty so to get it over with.'

This accused was found guilty and fined $75. In contrast, another accused charged with theft under $200 in similar circumstances pleaded not guilty on the advice of his legal aid lawyer and eventually had the charge dismissed after a trial.

Another accused who said he benefitted greatly from the advice of a duty counsel to plead not guilty was charged with common nuisance after an incident in which he and a co-accused had allegedly thrown beer bottles from a high-rise apartment balcony on to police cars. The accused, who went to court unrepresented, said he had direct discussions with the police and crown attorney about an out-of-court plea agreement:

A: [The crown attorney said] if I plead guilty, that [he'll] go for a mischief charge.

Q: If you plead guilty to common nuisance?

A: Yeah, he'll drop it down to mischief. And then he said, 'If you plead not guilty, [I'll] put it up to criminal negligence.' So I didn't know. I had to think about that for a while. If I would've pleaded guilty, I would have been [convicted] you know. If I pleaded not guilty – they never had no evidence on me at all for this. They were just going nuts.

Q: Yeah.

A: So, I was going to plead guilty, 'cause I didn't know –

Q: To common nuisance?

A: Right. I was going to plead guilty, and thinking maybe I can get off easier ... I thought if I had pleaded not guilty, I would have got [convicted], and you know, I would have got screwed or something.

Q: Yeah. So when did you decide you weren't going to plead guilty to common nuisance?

A: Well, I talked to the – what is he called?

Q: Duty counsel.

A: Duty counsel.

Q: So this is right after [the crown attorney] was trying to make this deal with you, you went in to talk to duty counsel? What did duty counsel say?

A: He goes, 'They're just trying to make deals with you. If you've never done it, go ahead with it [trial].' he says, 'They're scared.' I says, 'I know they're scared.' He says, 'Just go in there.' And I say, 'I want to get it over with right now. And I'm going to plead not guilty.' And so that's what I did.

The crown attorney substituted a mischief charge for the common nuisance charge and the case went to trial. The accused succeeded in having the charge dismissed.

These examples clearly point out that defence lawyers were not invariably oriented to the expediency of having accused persons plead guilty regardless of the crown's case. In a few instances it was the lawyer who forced the matter to trial as the most reasonable way of dealing with the case, even against the client's inclinations. Furthermore, as documented earlier, some lawyers involved in out-of-court plea negotiations with the crown *threatened* a trial as part of their strategy to have a plea settlement that was of possible advantage to their clients.

The Plea Decision in Retrospect

All the accused who entered not guilty pleas said that if they had to do it over again they would still plead not guilty. Even the seven accused who were convicted as originally charged after pleading not guilty said they would still plead not guilty if they were faced with the same decision again.

In contrast, 22 of 70 people who pleaded guilty said that if they had the decision to make again, they would enter not guilty pleas. Among this group, 11 pleaded guilty as originally charged, 9 pleaded guilty after the crown withdrew at least one charge, and 2 pleaded guilty after the crown reduced the charges. This indicates that dissatisfaction with the guilty plea decision was as prevalent among those who entered into a plea agreement with the crown as among those who did not.

In order to consider the reasons why these 22 accused would in retrospect change their plea to not guilty, it is instructive to examine the reasons they originally gave for pleading guilty. In Table 5.3 we cross-tabulate the first-mentioned reason for pleading guilty and whether or not in retrospect the accused would plead the same. This table includes the responses of 69 persons who originally pleaded guilty, excluding a person for whom there is no information.

The vast majority (20 of 33) of people who gave as a first-mentioned reason for pleading guilty the declaration 'I was guilty' would still plead the same if they had to do it over again. In contrast only 2 of 9 who said they pleaded guilty because of signing a statement of confession said they would still plead guilty. These persons had become educated during the course of their case to the fact that silence can be rewarding. They realized too late that it is extremely difficult to challenge a statement once given because it entails contradicting yourself and attacking the institutionalized credibility of the police. These accused came to appreciate that saying something to the police usually means there is little that can be said later; silence with the police at least keeps open the possibility of saying something in your defence at a later stage.

Among the six who gave as a first reason for pleading guilty the desire to get the matter over with, four said that in retrospect they would still have pleaded guilty. The two who would change their plea to not guilty were dissatisfied with the sentencing outcome and felt that they could secure a more lenient outcome via a not guilty plea. Both persons who gave as a first reason for pleading guilty a desire not to waste the court's time, in the hopes that it would yield leniency, said, in retrospect, that they would plead not guilty; again, the leniency they originally predicted was not perceived as forthcoming.

Among the 12 accused who gave as a first reason for pleading guilty a plea agreement worked out with the crown, 9 said that in retrospect they would still plead guilty. All 5 involved in agreements for charge withdrawal would still plead guilty, 3 of 5 involved in agreements for charge reduction would still plead guilty, and 1 of 2 involved in a promise of sentence recommendation would still plead guilty. In sum the majority of these accused were

TABLE 5.3

First-mentioned reason for pleading guilty and whether or not accused said in retrospect
he would plead the same

| First-mentioned reason for pleading guilty | Total | | Whether accused said in retrospect he would plead the same | | | |
| | | | Yes | | No | |
	N	%	N	%	N	%
I was guilty	23	33.3	20	42.6	3	13.6
Already signed police statement	9	13.1	2	4.3	7	31.5
Advised by lawyer	9	13.1	5	10.6	4	18.2
Get it over	6	8.7	4	8.5	2	9.1
Crown withdrew charge(s)	5	7.2	5	10.6	0	0.0
Crown reduced charge(s)	5	7.2	3	6.4	2	9.1
Crown recommended lenient sentence	2	2.9	1	2.1	1	4.7
Did not wish to waste court's time	2	2.9	0	0.0	2	9.1
Deal protecting accomplice	2	2.9	2	4.3	0	0.0
Defence strategy fell through	1	1.5	1	2.1	0	0.0
Other	5	7.2	4	8.5	1	4.7
Total	69	100.0	47	100.0	22	100.0

satisfied with their guilty plea arrangement with the crown attorney. However, it must be emphasized that this satisfaction was grounded in their
powerless position at a distance from the process by which the plea decision
was made for them by their lawyers. They were left to make their judgments
of satisfaction in their lawyer's terms, paying special attention to the sentencing outcome in comparison with what they were led to expect.

Among the 47 who said they would still plead guilty if they had it to do
over again, all but 7 gave the same reason as they originally gave for pleading
guilty. The 7 who gave different reasons all commented on the outcome
'working out well' from their perspective.

In conclusion we can say that in a minority of cases the accused's decision
to plead guilty was finally made *because of* an agreement made via the plea
discussion among the lawyer, the crown attorney, and the police. Other
studies have also shown that plea decisions by the accused are sometimes
arrived at out of apparent 'bargains' struck between lawyers and law
enforcers, although the extent of the practice varies enormously by jurisdiction. Regardless of the figures produced, reports on the quantity of plea
discussions leading to plea agreements (whether deemed bargains or not) are
lacking if they consider only samples of persons who plead guilty and ignore
the complex processes that have taken place up to the plea decision. For
example, if we consider our sample of 101 interviewed accused, we find that

20 per cent found it worthwhile to plead not guilty, mainly because they felt they were innocent but also in a few cases because they thought it was worth the effort to contest it or because it was not possible for their lawyers to reach a guilty plea agreement with the crown after an attempt to do so. Another 10 per cent had their charges withdrawn by the crown attorney prior to the point at which a plea decision had to be finalized. Among the 70 per cent who did enter guilty pleas, the clear majority (70 per cent) said they did so for reasons other than the nature of the agreement worked out with the crown. Paramount among these reasons was a realization of being guilty and/or a desire to get the matter over with as quickly as possible, two reasons which also undoubtedly framed the decisions of the other actors in the process. Many of these persons had extinguished their chances for future dealing when they signed a statement of confession to the police.

As we have demonstrated in our analysis of the process of plea discussion, most of the discussions involved routine administrative sorting out of evidence and relevant charges with little or no advantage accruing. The agreements involved mainly the altering of charges that were either questionable or insignificant in light of the main charges against the accused, and thus no 'big deal.' The agreements did allow the lawyers to *display* to clients that something was done and to sharpen their ability to predict the range of sentence. A substantial minority of accused said they were persuaded to plead guilty in light of these plea agreements, but nearly always in conjunction with other factors.

It is surprising that the accused do not mention more often the plea agreement arranged by their lawyers as a primary reason for pleading guilty. One explanation is that the ordering of justice vis-à-vis the accused is much more subtle than what other researchers have depicted. From the point of police contact the accused is managed in a way that makes him feel powerless, especially in the plea decision. Therefore, by the time his lawyer approaches him with a plea agreement it is not a 'deciding factor' in pleading guilty because he already been prepared for the realization that there is no choice. When he is thus prepared, even the hint of a concession in the plea agreement is likely to encourage him to think he has received a bargain. He has been made into a satisfied customer, not appreciating that in the process it is he who has been 'customized.'

6

Order in Court

Litigant, n. A person about to give up his skin for the hope of retaining his bones .
   Ambrose Bierce, *The Devil's Dictionary* (1881–1911)

There is something monstrous in commands couched in invented and unfamiliar language; an alien master is the worst of all. The language of the law must not be foreign to the ears of those who are to obey it.
   Speech by Learned Hand in Washington, DC (1929)

The order out of court – the bureaucratic pressures for expediency, the professional obligations which frame the process of plea transaction, and the formal rights and opportunities that the law gives to the crown and withholds from the accused (cf McBarnet, 1981) – prepares the accused to take up his dependent position in the courtroom. In the courtroom he experiences formality, rules of interaction, unavailability and inaccessiblity of information, and the various remedial routines used to produce order in court. In this chapter we describe and discuss the exclusion of the accused from active participation: his silence in court; his forced trust of the other actors, particularly his lawyer, to inform him, to make presentations on his behalf, and generally to act in his best interests; and his acceptance of and compliance with most of what is done to him. The court display is viewed as a dramatization of all the decisions, overt and covert, that preceded it, and as the ultimate demonstration of the role of the accused in the order of things.

The Court Setting

Agencies which handle large numbers of people daily usually display prominently a system of signs for the easy flow of traffic (Carlen, 1976, 1976a).

However, there were few such signs in the courthouses we observed. When he arrived at the courthouse the accused was confronted with a corridor with rows of doors on each side. Lists were posted outside with the name of the accused and the number of the section of the Criminal Code for the offences with which he was charged. He had to search each list for his name to ascertain in which courtroom he was to appear. As Friedland (1968) discusses, this has been the situation in courthouses across Canada.

In court, when the crown attorney or the judge suggested that the accused seek the help of a duty counsel or legal aid, he told the accused that the appropriate offices were either 'across the hall' or 'down the hall.' The only sign outside these rooms was 'Interviewing Room.' Nothing indicated that legal assistance could be obtained within. The court clerk would also often instruct the accused to report to 'the front counter' to sign recognizances, to sign probation orders, to surrender driver's licences, or to pay fines. At the beginning of the study, these instructions were meaningful because the 'front counter' was located near the entrance of the building. However, later it was moved to the end of the corridor at the back of the building. Nevertheless, the clerk still directed defendants to the 'front counter.' The accused could and did eventually find his way around, but in his already confused and anxious state, the lack of directions made him once again dependent on court regulars, such as the police, to get around.

Timing, like spacing, is another aspect of the court proceedings not in the defendant's control. Carlen (1976, 1976a; see also Foucault, 1977: 149ff) states, 'In the management of social occasions, time, like place, always belongs to somebody or some group.' In court the timing of the proceedings is controlled by the crown attorney and the police. The accused is told by the police to appear in court on a certain day at nine o'clock. He then waits for his name to be called so that he can set a date for trial or indicate that he will be pleading guilty. Since he does not know when his name will be called, he cannot leave the building. There is always an element of surprise because he does not know how the crown schedules the cases. If a trial date is set, he is instructed to return to court on that date at ten o'clock. When he returns he again waits for his turn. If he is pleading not guilty he is made to wait longer while those who are pleading guilty are dealt with first. As any court regular knows, one of the chief concerns of any accused is to get his case over with. Therefore, the hearing of the guilty pleas first can be seen as yet another incentive for the accused to plead guilty and as a sanction against pleading not guilty.[1] After he is sentenced, he once again must wait for the appropriate papers to be made out so that he can sign them. For the accused, it is a waiting game where the administrative priorities of the court and the crown's goal of conviction are primary.

The spatial display confronting the accused in the courtroom also indicates his dependent position.[2] As Carlen (1976a: 21) points out, the 'spacing and placing' of people in formal public settings not only affects their ability to hear and be heard but also emphasizes the realtive status of the participants.

It has been argued that the relative positioning of the various actors in court is necessary for maintaining the hearings as public (Atkinson and Drew, 1979). The spacing of the judge, the crown attorney, the defence counsel, and the accused allows for the easy identification by the public. Moreover, the formality of court is a necessary element for the appearance of orderliness, which in turn is a device for informing people of their place, and keeping them there, literally.

Lyman and Scott (1970: 167) point out that 'staged dramas require that the actor performs in the most dramatically advantageous position available to the character that he is portraying.' Robed in black, the judge sits behind a raised desk in front of an official crest and all eyes are on him. The crown attorney and defence counsel are seated behind tables equidistant from the judge. The accused is placed between the two, although closer to his counsel. In the courtrooms we observed the accused was not comforted by the shield of a table. The accused's position in the middle takes on meaning as the hearing proceeds. Rather than being an active adversary, he sits there mute while the crown attorney and his own lawyer talk around him and 'fight over the carcass' (Carlen, 1976a: 88), treating him like a dependent child who is to be seen but not heard.

The situation is dramatically altered when the accused is in custody. In such instances, he enters court through a separate side entrance preceded and followed by guards. He sits in the prisoners' box, sometimes behind glass, flanked by these guards. The positioning of the box is usually to one side of the courtroom and occasionally on the side opposite the defence counsel's table. Regardless of how it is positioned, the accused is not able as readily to communicate and to consult with his counsel. In these circumstances the accused must face the usual allegations made against him plus the additional implications that can be drawn from his status as 'prisoner.'

The judge is not only distanced from the accused by the elevation of his desk but also by the positioning of the court clerk between them. There is no direct contact with the judge since all evidence and reports are handed to him through the clerk. The authority and position of the judge is further emphasized by a number of other rituals. His entrances and exits through a private door are heralded by a clerk with the words 'All rise.' He is addressed with deference by the words 'Your Honour.' All testimony is directed to him and he alone can interrupt the otherwise strict code of questioning.

As an infrequent participant in the proceedings, the accused is sometimes confused about who the various agents in the courtroom are and about the nature of their roles. For example, even after four court dates and the dispositon of his case, an accused was confused about the role of the crown attorney:

A: No. The crown attorney always seemed like he was upstairs. Isn't that right?

Q: Upstairs?

A: Upstairs. No?

Q: What do you mean by upstairs?

A: Well, he, [lawyers] would always say that he would have to go upstairs and talk to the crown attorney about this or that and when he would come downstairs ...

Q: But in the courtroom, did you know which person was the crown attorney?

A: Well I would take a wild guess and say that the fellow that would talk to the judge. He had something to do with the court 'cause he was there every time I was there. So if, was he the crown attorney?[3]

His usual position as a 'one-shot' player means also that the accused is not well versed in the ceremonial rules of court. Occasionally in court when the accused's name was called, the court clerk had to direct the accused verbally to his position while all other participants knew their place. On occasion, the crown attorney, defence counsel, and the court clerk were observed to instruct the accused when to sit and when to stand. This could create embarrassment, as an accused related: 'There was a point there where they asked us, well [the crown] read off everything. Then he asked us to sit down, the crown attorney. And I was replying something back to the judge and I remained seated. And I didn't know that you had to stand up and bow or whatever before you talked to him.'

As a 'one-shot' player the accused also does not have the opportunity to develop membership within the crime control organization. His exclusion from the organization is apparent in a number of obvious ways.

All the actors except the accused dress for the formality of the occasion. The judge is robed, the defence counsel, crown attorney, and detective are well-suited and the police patrol officer is in uniform. The accused often cannot match these outward trappings because he cannot afford them. Moreover, if the accused is held in custody, he appears in the clothes he was wearing when arrested.

In addition there is an aura of respect and camaraderie among the official agents which does not extend to the accused. The judge is called 'Your Honour.' The justice of the peace is called 'Your Worship.' The crown and defence counsel call each other 'My learned friend.' The police are called by their rank. The accused has no formal title of address and is simply referred to as 'the accused,' or 'my client.'

The camaraderie of the crown and the defence lawyer was a source of some confusion and concern to the accused with respect to their roles: 'They seem to be more like friends than people who are working against each other, you know. Like when I was in court Thursday, the crown I had, kept calling [lawyer], "my friend over here," you know. When you're in court and you hear things like that it sounds like they're working together [rather] than against each other.'

As we learned in chapter 4, and as others have documented (e.g. Blumberg, 1967; Heumann, 1978; Utz, 1978; Macfarlane, 1982), the roles of the various agents in court appear to be based on a model of 'adversariness,' but backstage there are networks of co-operation among them. However, the accused only occasionally was aware of the linkages among the agents, indicating that appearances in court had their intended effect of reproducing the ideals of the process. Most accused did not believe that their lawyers were tied into the networks as were the police or the crown. On the whole, the image of the judge throughout remained relatively untarnished, largely because he was viewed as an unbiased umpire: 'He's the poor confused guy up there, that's up there. He's got to figure out, try and figure everything out, try and do the best for everybody.' Eighty-one accused felt that the judge before whom they appeared was neutral in their case, 12 felt that he was biased (11 felt the bias was against them), 5 could not make a judgment as to his impartiality, and there was no information available for 3 accused.

Even when the accused felt his sentence was too harsh, he justified the judge's actions in a number of different ways. For example, the judge was not always held personally responsible for the sentence he gave. As an accused stated, 'He did what he had to do, I suppose.' Alternatively, the judge, unlike the police or the crown attorney, was believed to be subject to temporary moods which affected his decisions: 'I think the judge woke up on the wrong side of the bed when he got me.' Or, he was believed to be influenced by the crown: 'I got no hard feelings against the judge ... because I think he was out to help me. Like, you know rehabilitate myself or whatever. And, uh, all's he was going on was, uh, what the crown attorney had dug up on my past, you know. He don't know any different. He was just going by what he was told. So, I, I wouldn't hold any feelings, uh, bad feelings against him.'

Moreover, according to the accused who was caught up in the idealization of justice, the judge was not influenced by extra-legal factors because he should not be. The judge and his role in the system were treated as a reified legal entity. When asked if being held in custody or not having a lawyer has any influence on the judge, an accused replied, 'I think he is very level-headed and nothing like this affects him.' Similarly, another accused blended the is and the ought in discussing whether personal factors in his background influenced the judge: 'Well, I think it should not affect, uh, you know. That's what I think. If it, this affects the judge, that's not justice.'

Casper (1978) reports similar findings. More than any other agent, the judge is distanced from the everyday 'grubbiness' of crime control and thereby has his legitimacy reproduced in the eyes of the accused.

The crown attorney was viewed by some as a pawn of the police and court. Some accused saw the crown attorney as the counsel for the police, and believed that the crown attorney is hired by the police.[4] Other accused viewed the crown attorney has having to cater to both the police and the judge: 'He's out of the scene. He doesn't know what's going on behind the scene. The police they are the ones that bring him the paper. The poor guy doesn't know what the heck is going on. He's like somebody between the judge and the police. And, oh, the police, they're going to give a punch in the head to him or the judge is going to give him a punch. So he's in between, the poor guy. And that's why I think he loses interest in everything. And he goes, "one, two, three, four, get going judge. Let me get out of here." '

Others talked of links between the judge and the crown, seeing them as courtroom regulars who routinely accepted each other's recommendations and otherwise worked hand in hand to dispense with the mundane daily workload.

Some accused attributed the essential power to the police. For example, in order to continue using an accused as an informer, a detective attempted to persuade the crown attorney to withdraw the charge against all three accused in the case. The crown attorney, who apparently was ignorant of the informant role of the accused, insisted upon prosecuting. The case was then remanded at the request of the accused. The accused-informant then contacted the detective, and on the day of the trial the crown withdrew the charges. In retrospect, the accused described the management of justice as follows: 'Okay, the magistrate sits ahead of the court. He is the one that's supposed to make the final decision. The crown attorney runs the magistrate, alright. He actually makes the magistrate's mind up with what he has to say. The police run the crown attorneys.'

In some instances the links between the court regulars were made explicit in court by the actions of judges who directed the prosecution and defence to meet together and come to some informal arrangement with respect to the charges. An example is provided in the case of three accused held in custody awaiting trial on a break and enter charge, plus an assortment of charges of theft, robbery, and unlawfully at large. On the third occasion in court, two accused had counsel and the third had just spoken to a lawyer in the courthouse cells with the intention of retaining him. The lawyer informed the court that he had not as yet been retained but that he would be in court the next two days in order to deal with it. The judge, addressing both the crown attorney and the three defence counsel said, 'You're all buddies now. We'll take an early lunch and you can discuss this matter over lunch in order to expedite this matter.' Over lunch a guilty plea agreement was arrived at, and after the recess the three accused entered guilty pleas in accordance with the agreement.

Except for the person with an informant status, the accused had no ties with the organization of criminal control. As Friedenberg (1975) describes it, they formed a 'conscript clientele,' the raw material that the network of crime control requires to perpetuate its existence. Set up to control criminal conduct, the agents of the system become dependent on it for their survival (cf Illich et al, 1977; Rothman, 1980; Chan and Ericson, 1981). The interdependence of and co-operation among the official agents is on the whole, however, not visible in court and as a result not obvious to the accused or the public.[5]

Understanding of Court Proceedings by the Accused

The accused's lack of resources and resourcefulness in court is also related to his poor grasp of specialist and 'recipe' knowledge. In the criminal law, nevertheless, there is a presumption of fitness and competence on the part of the accused to stand trial.

One of the few instances in which the accused's comprehension is questioned is if he is deemed unfit to stand trial and to conduct a defence because he is mentally ill, or if the balance of the mind is disturbed where the accused is a woman charged with an offence arising out of the death of her newly born child– Criminal Code sec 543(2) (a) and (b). The only other instance is where 'the failure to plead is due, not to wilfulness, but to a failure to understand or some other circumstances which make it unfair to call upon accused to plead or to stand trial' (Ryan, 1964: 907). The usual instances of this are when the accused is unfit due to insanity, or where the accused is deaf or dumb, or mentally so defective that he is unable to conduct his defence, or if he is a foreigner unable to speak or understand English. The last situation can be remedied by the use of an interpreter: 'In such cases accused is said to be mute, not of malice, but by visitation of God' (ibid).

It has been stated that in felony cases, and misdemeanour cases excluding exceptional circumstances, the accused should be present at his trial so that he may hear the evidence against him and answer it.[6] Again, the presumption is that an accused can comprehend the proceedings and is able to conduct a defence or instruct counsel to do so on his behalf. The problematic nature of this assumption is suggested in some empirical studies. Friedland (1975) found that the majority in a highly educated sample population (54 per cent were college students or graduates and the rest were high-school students or graduates) who were instructed on how to use legal statutes were not able to look up the law on their own successfully. Griffiths and Ayres (1967), in a sub-study of their New Haven research on the implementation of *Miranda*, report that among a sample of Yale University faculty members, graduate students, and professional school students who were arrested after a public demonstration 'few of the suspects knew of their rights in even the grossest outline.'

Seldom are attempts made to ascertain whether the accused understands. Given that the accused rarely speaks or is given the opportunity to speak, it is highly unlikely that a benevolent, well-meaning court would have any knowledge of the accused's comprehension. Rather than the court attempting to make the proceedings comprehensible, the onus is on the accused to inform the court that he does not understand. However, given the anxiety and stage fright that most accused suffer, this is unlikely. Carlen (1976: 109) documents that even when asked if they understand, accused are reluctant to say no because they feel powerless, they don't want to appear incompetent, and/or they are too nervous to say anything.

It might be assumed that it is the lawyer's role to ensure that the accused comprehends the court's discourse. On the contrary, the lawyer is usually left to 'do the understanding' for the accused and to order the accused in a way that does not encourage the accused even to seek understanding, let alone acquire it.

Among the 101 accused interviewed, 60 had previous experience with criminal court proceedings as accused and/or as witnesses, an additional 13 had watched one or more hearings in court (usually on the same day as their own hearings), and 25 had no experience with criminal courts.[7] Thirty-two accused said they did not fully comprehend their court hearings. Among this group, 15 said they did not understand the procedures and legal technicalities, 6 said they did not know who the court personnel were, 5 said they did not understand some of the language, 4 said they understood nothing, and 2 said they could not remember the hearing at all. Of these 32, 16 had been directly involved before the criminal proceedings and 5 had watched them previously.

While he is a perceptive person, the accused typically does not understand the court's formal rules, proceedings, and discourse. What he does understand is that the rules, proceedings, and discourse are further powerful vehicles to keep him powerless within the ordering of justice.

While 32 directly admitted ignorance concerning at least some aspect of the proceedings, many more accused claimed an understanding which was not reflected in parts of their interview. For example, one of the premises of the process is that the accused knows and understands the nature of the offences with which he is charged in order to prepare adequately a defence. Yet some complained about not knowing the full range of charges against them until they appeared in court.

Q: What did they charge you with?
A: They, I got a piece of paper which said, 'To a person who has not yet been charged.' And then it said, 'Theft under $200.' And that's well, when I was at the police station they said, 'Well, you're being charged with theft, theft under.' And he didn't say how many counts. He said, 'This is all, this is what we give

you.' And then he says, 'We'll sort it out later when it gets into court on how many charges' and things like that.

Q: So when was the first time you found out everything you were being charged with?

A: First time it went to court, I saw my name on the list, eight, ten times.

Q: But did you know what you were being charged with that time?

A: No, not exactly. I knew that it was theft but that was about all.

Others came into court knowing what they were charged with but then discovered that on the court docket outside the courtroom, their names appeared a number of times with only a three-digit number next to them. For persons not familiar with the Criminal Code, the section numbers of the alleged offences provided no information. An accused with five charges listed on the courtroom docket, but aware of only three of them, stated: 'No, there isn't another two. Like when I first got there I seen the five dots. So I went up to the front desk and I asked the lady if there's five little ticks below your name is that for all the charges and she goes, 'Yeah,' you know. I didn't have a clue what they were for, because there is no other two.'

The psychological effect of discovering that he is charged with more offences than he expects and not knowing what they might be, at a time when his anxiety is high, puts the accused at a disadvantage. Only those who were 'wise' in the ways of the system could anticipate that this was likely to occur. For example, an accused who was charged with one offence when he was released by the police and discovered three more on the court docket expressed no surprise:

Q: Now, when you came to court the first time to set a date and you saw three charges what did you think?

A: That they had drummed up a couple more charges. In case one wouldn't stick they've got something to fall back on, type of thing.

Q: Okay. Now how did you know that?

A: That's the way the police work.

In court the accused awaits the official arraignment of the case against him. Although this is not an everyday experience for him, it is a repetitive chore for the court clerk who reads off the charge in one long monotone with few distinctive breaks between words. Before he knows that the reading of the charge is over, the accused has been asked how he wishes to plead. An accused commented regarding his arraignment, 'The beginning was understandable. The, uh, middle sections were garbled and she was just rapping them off. She wasn't reading the end part of it and I didn't understand it.'

After the accused is arraigned on the charges, he is asked how he wishes to plead. This would, on the surface, seem to be straightforward. However, some accused were confused when it was all over as to how they pleaded. An accused charged with rape and possession of a restricted weapon pleaded not guilty to both. At separate trials he was acquitted on the rape charge and convicted on the weapons charge.

Q: Okay. Now, you pleaded not guilty?
A: To the gun (restricted weapon charge)? Yeah.
Q: Why?
A: I said I owned it. I don't think I pleaded not guilty.
Q: You pleaded guilty?
A: Of owning the gun–yes, I am pretty sure I did.

The confusion arose because, although the defence was not contesting the possession of the weapon, it was trying to establish that the accused was not aware that it was a restricted weapon and that it was not being used for a dangerous purpose. The accused alleged that he had purchased it as an antique and had it on display as an ornament in his home.

Another accused had been charged with both obstructing and assaulting a police officer:

Q: Was it the assault or the obstruct that she read?
A: The both.
Q: She read out both?
A: Yes–I think so.
Q: Did you plead guilty to both of them in court or just to the one?
A: Well, I, I think both. Both.
Q: Now, in fact, you were only convicted of 'obstruct police' and the crown withdrew the assault charge.
A: Is that what happened?!

Occasionally, efforts were made to make the proceedings fair to the accused. For example, the judge sometimes intervened on behalf of the accused in an attempt to balance the proceedings. However, the accused did not always understand the reasoning, and this sometimes led to increased confusion. For example, an accused was charged with shoplifting two items of men's clothing worth a total of $15. When he was brought back into the store and searched, no unpaid merchandise was found on him. The two store detectives claimed that he had concealed the items under his clothing and that when he was returned to the store in their custody, he discarded the items. In interview, the accused said that he felt he was innocent of the charge but pleaded guilty because he wanted to get the case over with to avoid taking any more time off work. He also felt that his case was hopeless because he had no witnesses to say that he did not pick up the merchandise. The judge, noting the hesitation in the accused's voice when he pleaded, halted the proceedings and suggested the accused speak to duty counsel. Duty counsel advised him that he should plead not guilty: 'He said, if you didn't stole those goods, you know, you shouldn't plead guilt. I told him, I said, "If I plead no guilty," I said, "I got no lawyer." I said, "Would you defend me today?" He said, "No, I can't do nothing for you today." '

The accused returned to court and pleaded not guilty, and duty counsel, who cannot represent an accused who is going to trial, coached him from the sidelines. The accused spoke English poorly and understood little of the proceedings: 'You just go inside the courtroom. They are talking. You don't know if they are talking good about you or they are talking bad, you know.' After being found guilty and fined $75, the accused related in interview: 'Well, I felt, which I told the lawyer, I told the judge which I had no chance. Like the two witnesses was there, you know. I said I had no chance to win the case. And he said, "Try to plead no guilty," you know. So that is what I did. I plead not guilty because he told me. If it was my decision I would have pled guilty already.'

The 'court' made all the legally correct moves but the accused did not understand them. However, justice was seen to be done.

The inability of the accused to comprehend the proceedings was in some cases partially attributable to the lawyer. An accused described the process by which he and his lawyer arrived at a plea. The accused, who had been charged with indecent assault (male), felt he was not guilty of the offence but possibly guilty of an attempted indecent assault. He said his lawyer concurred with this and stated that he would try and negotiate a withdrawal of the charge with the crown attorney. He reportedly advised the accused not to worry about his plea until he had a chance to discuss his case with the crown attorney. On his trial date, the lawyer arrived in court at 9:15 am and went immediately into the crown attorney's office. When he emerged from the office he informed the accused that the crown attorney had agreed to a suspended sentence in exchange for a guilty plea. Minutes later the case was called. The accused commented: 'One of the last things that I wanted to go to talk to him about was exactly, when he got in there, what am I supposed to do and so on and so forth. That was what I was hoping to be able to get a chance to talk to him about. What are we going to do on the date of the trial? But when we got there at a quarter after nine the first thing he said was you go have a seat. He was just on his way to talk to the crown attorney so that we really didn't get a chance to talk about it.'

As outlined in chapter 4, this sequence of events typifies a number of cases where plea transaction procedures were established in terms of the lawyer's practice and the crown attorney's day. The lawyer tells the accused not to worry about his plea until he gets a chance to talk to the crown attorney, but in the jurisdiction under study the case was not normally assigned to a crown attorney at the provincial court level until the day of the trial. As a result, most plea transactions were conducted in the hour before court commenced. The lawyer hurriedly told the accused the package he had arranged with the crown attorney, not the possibilities the crown attorney had either rejected or the ones that they had not discussed. At the 'eleventh hour' the accused had no time to question his counsel about these decisions and in the urgency of the moment typically agreed to the package.

Closely related to the knowledge of the accused of what charges he pleaded to is the knowledge of what charges were withdrawn by the crown attorney. In the interviewed sample, 51 accused were subject to the withdrawal of 1 or more charges. However, only 38 accused were aware that charges had been dropped and were accurate as to which ones. This poor understanding of the details of their case was in part due to the system of plea discussions transacted in the halls outside the court rooms (see chapter 4). The accused was usually told that if he pleaded to certain charges, the others would be withdrawn. However, given that he may not have had a full comprehension of the number of charges against him, it is not surprising then that he did not know what had been withdrawn:

Q: Why were these charges withdrawn? Do you have any idea?
A: No idea at all. He just went in there for about two minutes and he came out, and he says, 'Well, there's six of them.' He says, 'Well I tried for more, but the crown sort of said no.'

Another accused was completely confused as to which charges he pleaded guilty to and which ones had been withdrawn. He was one of the four co-accused who were each charged with ten counts of 'theft under,' one count of 'possession over,' and one count of mischief. Although not all four accused were involved in each of the incidents they were all charged with the theft of all of the items. On the trial date the accused, along with two co-accused, pleaded guilty to a package of five 'theft under' charges and one 'possession over' charge while five 'theft under' charges and the mischief charge for the others were withdrawn. In this accused's mind the six charges of which he was convicted merged into one:

Q: Were any charges dropped?
A: Yeah, most of them.
Q: What were you finally charged with?
A: Possession over.
Q: And that's it, none of the others?
A: The others were dropped– I think [there] were five counts.
Q: The only charge that you were convicted on was the possession over?
A: Yeah.

Apart from the problem of making decisions based on misinformation, in this case the accused now was left with an inaccurate perception of the extent of his criminal record.

Another decision the accused may face at an early stage of the proceedings is his election choice: trial by provincial court judge, trial by county court judge, or trial by a county court judge and jury. Of the 36 accused who had to make an election choice, 30 said they understood the election when it was put to them. However, even though they may have understood the wording of the election as read out by the court clerk, they did not necessarily grasp the procedural advantages of one alternative versus another (see chapter 3).

Silence of the Accused in Court

One of the most obvious manifestations of the powerlessness of the accused is his silence. Although most accused plead guilty and there is no adjudication of the facts, there are two points during the hearing where it is deemed appropriate for the accused to address the court. The first opportunity arises when the crown attorney finishes submitting his evidence and the judge turns to the accused or his counsel and asks, 'Are the facts substantially correct?' The second opportunity, in cases involving indictable offences, arises immediately prior to sentencing when the accused has the right to address the court personally (Criminal Code sec 595). At both of these junctures the accused is most often silent.

The apparent passivity and non-involvement of the accused have been well documented. Bottoms and McClean (1976) report that only one-third of their interviewees 'struggled' in the sense that Packer (1968: 149) put forward, while one-third of them were categorized as 'passive respondents.' Baldwin and McConville (1977: 83) point out that 'Paradoxically one of the most immediately striking findings to emerge from our interviews with defendants, all of whom were legally represented, was their profound sense of non-involvement in, if not complete alienation from the legal process in which they had been concerned.'

As emphasized previously, the passivity of the accused reflects a realistic assessment of his powerlessness. The structure of the system inhibits and dissuades active participation by its 'clients' (cf Christie, 1977). The court is experienced as a fearful place that is deferred to rather than *used* by the accused. The accused lucidly summarized the feeling:

> Well, it's not–a place you go very often ... It's a very forbidding place, you know. The judge sits way up there and everything is all–you're kind of a low man on the board ...
>
> I know there were people at the back there but I didn't know– it was all I could do to – thank goodness they had a chair for me to sit down ...
>
> Well, all I heard was you are charged with and then my mind sort of went blank. And she asked how I plead and I couldn't even answer. I had to look to [lawyer] there.

Some accused were intimidated to the point of remaining silent even though they could not comprehend the proceedings. The third accused was afraid to interrupt the court to ask his lawyer for an explanation in case it might negatively affect the outcome: 'If I had delayed matters – that – it might have put the judge in a worse mood, perhaps, that, he may not have been so lenient.'

Some felt that once the decision to plead guilty was made, there was nothing they could do to alter their fate. This led them to opt out mentally early on in the proceedings:

Q: Was what the Crown said basically correct about your charge?
A: No, I just plead guilty and never listened to him.
Q: OK. Now. after he talked, he asked you if what he said was basically correct and you answered 'yes.'
A: Don't make any difference, I guess.
Q: Why doesn't it make a difference?
A: Big spiel to tell you the truth – I don't know – once I go – I plead guilty – I figure I'm pleading guilty so well, I'll just let it go.
Q: You don't think it's important to listen?
A: No, I never pay attention.
Q: But, I mean, it could have a great affect on your life, doesn't that matter?
A: Still doesn't shorten my sentence, does it?
    ...
Q: Weren't you concerned?
A: It was just like a formality, like you know. You go through it before you get your time and that's it.

The focus of the accused on sentence outcome was common (see chapter 5; see also Newman, 1956; Casper, 1972). Thus, an accused related that his only thoughts in court were, 'When is it going to be over with? Can't the guy just stop flapping his gums and give me my sentence, you know.' The accused only regains focus when he hears the very plain words about how he is being disposed of:

Q: Did you understand the things that everybody was saying? Your lawyer, the crown attorney, the court clerk?
A: Ah, not really. Because he's – he used ten dollar words, sort of thing.
Q: Who didn't you understand?
A: Well the only person I did understand was the judge.
Q: Would you have felt better if you did understand them?
A: Well, I couldn't really say because I – I'm not really listening to what they're saying. I just want to – I'm just waiting for what the judge is going to say.
Q: OK. Why don't you listen to what they say?
A: Well, because, uh, I'm more worried about what I'm going to get than what they're saying.

The accused's withdrawal and passivity reflect the anxiety, despair, and alienation that arise from the strangeness of the proceedings.[8] The court discourse is not his discourse, but its powerful effect in making him dependent is clearly understood. It is the power of this alien discourse, not any general problem with being articulate, that keeps the accused silent in court.

Those who do address the court under oath feel constrained by it. The legal rhetoric not only minimizes the accused's understanding of the proceedings but also restricts him from giving accounts in words that are meaningful to him. His definitions of reality are therefore not given expression and are typically replaced by the system's definitions. Of course, this situation is not peculiar to the court structure, although it is accentuated there. Mueller (1970), in analysing the repressive communication imposed in total institutions, describes how 'the individual's interpretation of reality is temporarily suspended since it is not judged as corresponding to what is defined as reality by the institution' (p 105). Similarly, legal discourse is repressive in that it contains concepts that are not included in the everyday language of the accused. Deprived of his usual mode of discourse, the ability of the accused to define the situation in his own terms is weakened, as is his ability to question the legitimacy of the law.

Carlen (1974) argues that the formal language of the law creates the boundaries of formal symbolic control in court. For instance, a restricted linguistic code is created by the written and codified rules of procedure. However, for the most part judges and lawyers use an elaborated code. The accused tries to use an elaborated code only when challenging official definitions. On the rare occasions when such a challenge is forthcoming, the restricted linguistic code is enforced by the judge to put the accused in his place (ibid: 104).

The regular courtroom participants, who are well versed in the legal rhetoric used to orchestrate the rules, have a monopoly on use of them. The accused seldom acquires this knowledge in time. His inability to participate reaffirms his dependent status. As a result, his definitions and interpretations are given less acknowledgment.

Carlen (1974, 1976) suggests ways in which social control is achieved in the context of magistrates' court in London. 'Remedial routines' are mobilized when the substantive dimensions of legal absolutism, which portray legal processes as 'homogeneous, unproblematic, external, inevitable, essential, and eternal,' are about to be revealed by the accused as 'pluralistic, problematic, intentional, contingent, phenomenal, and temporary.' Judges and lawyers can invoke a variety of rules to account for the application of legal rules, but the accused cannot. Hence his challenges to either the ritual, the administration, or the legitimacy of the law can be portrayed as either 'out of place, out of time, out of mind or out of order.' As Roland Barthes (cited in Carlen, 1976: 112) stated in 1972: 'To rob a man of his language in the very name of language: this is the first step in all legal murders.'

The process of denying the accused in his own language and therefore his own account and interpretation of reality and substituting the formal restricted code of the courts and the official definitions of reality is similar to the process of 'nihilation' described by Berger and Luckmann (1966: 132ff). They outline two ways in which nihilation denies the reality of phenomena or interpretations that do not fit into the universe in question: all definitions of reality existing outside the universe 1) are given an inferior status and 2) are ultimately redefined into concepts derived from the universe in question, thereby rendering them meaningless.

The universe and definitions of the accused are denigrated and redefined in a number of different ways. To begin with, the style of discourse in court is not bilateral. In addressing or questioning the accused, the judge may use terms that, if used by other members of society, might be considered slanderous. In addressing the judge, the accused must show respect and deference. It is true that the accused's 'adversary,' the crown attorney, must also display the appropriate amount of homage to the judge but it is important to keep in mind that the crown attorney's behaviour and reputation are not in question.

In her trial on the charge of failure to appear in court on the date specified, the accounts of an accused were not accepted. The accused, who was not represented by counsel, admitted to the facts of not appearing on the specified date, but not to the intent. She explained to the court that she had heard the judge say the thirteenth of the month rather than the third. Since it was her first court appearance ever, she thought the court would send written confirmation of the date. On the sixth of the month when she still had not received confirmation, she called the court and discovered that her appearance date had already passed. She immediately turned herself in to the court. Although the accused described her actions as due to an honest mistake, the crown and judge redefined it as forgetfulness and negligence.

Crown: [citing case] An honest mistake is acceptable but Judge ——— has said that
negligence wasn't. Because of the importance of the obligation to attend court,
she has an obligation to remember the date. Her submissions are not a defence
to the charge but a mitigation towards sentencing.

Judge: The courts draw the distinction between an honest mistake and negligence.
Forgetfulness leads to negligence. Forgetfulness destroys the courts because it
leads to delays. The accused could purposefully forget dates. [Judge goes over
evidence.] There is no obligation on the court to inform you of the date. Being
your first time you should have been more careful. That you forgot is negligence. I make a finding of guilt.

The judge then asked if the accused wished to say anything toward sentencing. The accused asked the judge if he thought that it would be beneficial to issue a notice to the accused, to which he replied 'no.' She then explained that months can go by between court dates, to which he replied, 'I'm not going to argue with you.'

In interview, the accused said that she did not think she was being argumentative. She reported that in discussion with the investigating officer after her trial, he had told her that he didn't find her to be argumentative although he indicated that 'I was being forward, that I should have backed off a bit. And maybe it would have come out better.'

Another method for redefining the situation is in the control of information in the form of questioning used in courtroom examination and cross-examination. Atkinson and Drew (1979) describe the form of conversation used in court where the turn-taking sequence and the type of discourse are predetermined by the rules of evidence and are therefore not locally managed. One of the noticeable features of courtroom talk is the occurrence of questions which set up a preference for an answer expressing agreement at the next turn and therefore, the second-position turns are shorter in length than those in the first position. Because discourse is patterned into a sequence of pairs of questions and answers, silence on the part of the accused to an accusation can be construed negatively. Also, given that a denial is anticipated, the accusation can be constructed so that a flat denial can be seen as unsuccessful. Atkinson and Drew further point out that lawyers are instructed in ways to design questions so as to restrict answers and thereby control the production of information. As a result lawyers are better skilled at phrasing their challenges into questions than accused people are in phrasing their rebuttals in answers.

A number of accused commented on the constraints imposed by the form of courtroom questioning. When an accused was asked whether he felt he had enough opportunity on the stand to explain himself, he replied, 'On the stand I don't think anybody does because you've just got your yes or no questions and the lawyers can rearrange what you say to what they want you to say.' Another accused commented that while he felt constrained by the 'yes/no' answers, he also felt that no answer at all could be detrimental: 'There are some questions that you had to answer, you know. Like, you couldn't sit there and say nothing. Like you had to say "yes" and some questions you had to say "no" ... He was almost putting the words in your mouth for you, you know. Like you got to say them.'

Evidence in court must appear to be precise. The police and other 'expert' witnesses are well versed and rehearsed on how to give evidence in ways that seem objective, factual, and consistent. In bail hearings, the crown attorney asks the police officer to 'outline the facts.' The police invariably reply, 'The facts of the case, sir, are ...' When pleading guilty the accused is asked, after the crown reads in his evidence, if 'the facts' are substantially correct. The police are allowed also, in giving evidence, to refer to their notes made at the time of the arrest. Regardless of the problems of how these notes were constructed in the first place, by the time the court hearing comes up, they are accepted as fact. Similarly, other experts (e.g. psychiatrists, social workers, and probation officers) tend to give their evidence in the context of official reports which creates an objectification of their evidence. The accused, however, is not allowed any of these props and instead gives descriptions in everyday language which end up sounding like a story.

An accused who pleaded not guilty to obstructing a police officer, compared the police testimony to that of one of his own witnesses: 'See his was the same thing as the other officer, right. Like, you know. They knew what they were talking about. I guess they talked before they went to court, you know. And they made sure that what they were going to say was the same, eh ... Everything [my witness] said was correct, but it's the way he said it, eh ... he wasn't too sure.'

Occasionally, the accused finds that his everyday style of conversation is turned to his disadvantage. An accused who took the stand described his impression of the crown attorney's cross-examination of him: 'Mainly they get up there and they say you don't really know what happened. You don't know if you was round about ten feet away from him or if you was a hundred feet away from him. Do you really know. And he tries to make you look stupid. And then he'll say, you know, like if you was driving down the street and you hit a kid. He'll say didn't you know that the kid was in front of you. No. You mean you really didn't know that the kid was in front of you. And he's over-exaggerating. He try and make you really feel like a dummy. You just can't get up there and say, you know, like "F off" and go fly a kite and this. And you can't talk back.'

Another accused commented on how the style of questioning in court left little room for him to present a favourable image of himself. 'It's just the way that he [judge] asked me questions, I didn't talk to him for any length of time ... All he did was ask me direct question and I could either say "yes" or "no" to them. There was nothing I could have said then to impress him.'

As Atkinson and Drew (1979: 8) point out, the form of discourse used in court can be regarded 'as the product of continuing and determined efforts to find principled solutions to identifiable practical problems posed by ordinary discourse.' However, the practical effect is to exclude, to control, and to redefine the accused and his universe; as a result, taking the stand is not an attractive choice for most.

In the sample of 101 interviewed accused persons, only 23 took the stand or addressed the court personally. Of these 23, 9 said they spoke at their hearing to give their version of the offence with which they were charged. For example, an accused who was charged with 'assault causing bodily harm with the intent to wound' pleaded not guilty to the wounding but guilty to the lesser included offence of 'assault causing bodily harm.' After both the crown attorney and the defence lawyer made their submissions with respect to sentencing, the judge began to speak to sentencing. The accused interrupted the judge saying that there were a few things he wished to explain and spoke for over half an hour. In interview the accused explained why he spoke out: 'I just felt things were getting a little out of hand. I had to get some, some understanding here somewhere ... I, I just felt there was more had to be said myself. When, when the crown attorney was up there, he was saying that ah, this man wasn't, obviously wasn't a match for [victim]. And uh, they didn't say nothing about the two people attacking me or anything, and the way he escorted me out the hotel or nothing ... they were just putting everything on me. Just I think, just to make a conviction really, I don't know. Just 'cause I had a knife. I really felt there was more to be said I know. It's, I don't know, it's kind of like an open and shut case, maybe. I knew that myself that they always look at you as if being, uh, being the worst. Worse than what it is, maybe. And what your job is to try and prove, prove it's not.'

This accused believed his lawyer wasn't in a position to say what he wanted said, 'Because ah, nobody really knows but me.' For this accused, the whole proceeding took on a different light in retrospect because of his opportunity to address the court. At a number of points throughout the interview, he complained about the bias and unfairness of the evidence presented against him but when he was asked later how he felt during his trial and sentencing day, he replied:

A: I felt, uh, I felt pretty good ... Because, well, I've been wanting for so long now to wait for that trial to come and say my word in it. And then after I've said it, he just nonchalantly, come out and said, 'six months' and I just felt good.

Q: Why did you feel good?

A: Maybe because, uh, I felt that I got across to him that I really wasn't going to hurt anybody.

Even when the accused pleaded guilty and was not contesting the crown evidence, and even when represented by counsel, the small input he may have had by addressing the court was important to him. An accused who did not speak up in court expressed his regret in retrospect:

Q: Would you have ever liked to have talked to the judge directly yourself?

A: At one point, yes.

Q: What point was that?

A: Just before he gave my sentence.

Q: And why would you have wanted to talk to him then? What would you have said?

A: Just let him know how I felt personally, myself – about the whole situation.

Q: Now, why do you think it would have been important for you to tell him, rather than your lawyer?

A: No, I don't think it would have been important. I would just have liked to have said something, you know. If I were to have spoken up like that, you know, I would have said it. But, ah, you know, I just didn't say anything. I let my lawyer handle it.

Of the 23 people who addressed the court, 8 said they did so on their lawyer's instructions. In some of these cases the lawyer told the accused to take the stand to explain his side of the incident. In other cases it was because the lawyer saw some strategic value in putting his client on the stand; for example, a lawyer said he had his client take the stand because 'she was the kind of witness that would appeal to Judge —— .' Other who took the stand on their lawyer's advice thought they had no choice in the matter: 'When he [the lawyer] asked me to take the stand I figured I had to go up there and tell what I did.'

The remaining 78 accused did not address the court in any way. All charges against 11 persons were withdrawn and as a result taking a stand in court was not an issue for them. Among the remaining 67 accused, the reasons given for not addressing the court included: it was of no obvious benefit (23), no one asked him to (14), it might negatively influence the outcome (8), the lawyer thought it might damage the case (6), the lawyer said it was not necessary (5), the accused was too nervous (4), and two idiosyncratic reasons.[9]

One of the major tasks of the defence lawyer is the orderly presentation of his client in court. Often his job is made easier if the accused is silent. As explained by the lawyer for 1 of the 11 accused who said they did not speak in court because of their lawyer's advice on the matter: 'I deliberately didn't [have the accused take the stand]. If you want me to elaborate on that – my feeling is that if your client doesn't testify and is not in the position of being disbelieved, you can always still fall back on the proposition that he was entitled to test the crown's case. When you put him in the witness box, as you know there is a classical problem of whether or not to put him in the witness box, having elected to do that, you in a way go along, across a line. Or put it in another way, you go down a corridor and there is doors closing behind you as you do the trial. Putting him in the witness box closes a lot of doors behind you and you can't get out.'

Accused frequently believed it was of no benefit to speak out in court because of their position at the bottom end of the hierarchy of credibility. In particular, many accused talked about the 'believability' of the police compared with whatever accounts they could offer. An accused stated, 'It was one hundred per cent against me. No, you just cannot testify against a police officer. They are the law. There's no two ways about it.'[10]

The judge is often caught in a dilemma of delicate balance. He has to give the impression that he is impartially weighing the veracity of two competing versions, that of the police and that of the accused, and at the same time is fully aware of the repercussions and implications of not believing the police evidence. This is sometimes reflected in his summations before sentencing. For example, before passing sentence on an accused who was charged with obstructing two police officers, pleaded not guilty, and was convicted, the judge stated,

J: There is no evidence that [the accused] struck the police officer and the officer was very dramatic when giving his evidence. How many children do you have?

Husband of A: One four-year old.

J: Do you work?

A: Yes [she says what her work is and for how long she has been doing it].

J: I am impressed that you didn't lie. A hundred and fifty dollars fine or thirty
       days. You can have thirty days to pay.

In this short exchange, the judge re-establishes the hierarchy of credibility
in two ways. Firstly, the police do not lie. The worst that they can be accused of
is giving evidence 'dramatically.' This euphemism is the closest he can come in
saying that he doesn't completely believe the police evidence. In so doing, he
does not undercut the authority of the police which is crucial to the system of
crime control, but rather reproduces the power of the police. This is especially
important when order maintenance charges such as 'obstruct police' are
involved. Juxtaposed to this comment, the judge implies that the testimony of
an accused person is normally unreliable by saying that he was impressed that
this particular person did not lie. The ramifications for the concept of the
presumption of innocence are obvious.

The husband of this accused was charged in the same incident with
assaulting a police officer. He pleaded not guilty and was found guilty.
According to the accused, he had been beaten by the police and had attended a
hospital for his injuries. When he tried to get copies of the hospital records they
were missing. A few days after the incident, the accused said that one of the
officers involved had threatened him if he, the accused, pressed charges against
him. The accused explained that he did not refer to this at trial because, in the
judge's eyes, it would be unbelievable.

Q: But what about all those other things? I mean why didn't you just bring them
      out in court? It would probably – would have gone in your favour.

A: It might have went in my favour. Like as the judge said – like there was no
      fantastic story and in my mind if I had to tell them exactly what happened, they
      think it would be a fantastic story.

The complaints of the accused against the police fail not only because he
has low credibility, or because he is challenging the very legitimacy of the
system, or because he is inept in the rules of the courtroom, but also because, as
Emerson (1969) puts it, denunciation has traditionally been thought of as a
dirty business. People should not tell tales or make derogatory statements
about other people, unless it is their business to do so and they have a structure
of legitimacy within which they can carry out their work.[11] The accused belongs
to no such official organization. Therefore, his challenges to the police version
are likely to be seen as self-aggrandizing slurs and once again the accused
remains silent.

Traditionally, the right to 'allocutus' allows the accused to talk to the judge
and inform him of any mitigating circumstances relevant to sentencing
(Criminal Code see 595). However, the section also states that an omission on

the part of the trial judge to comply with the section does not affect the validity of the proceedings. In reality, a conviction was generally registered and the accused was for the most part sentenced without saying a word. Moreover, no one had asked him if he wished to address the court.[12]

While 11 accused did not take the stand on their lawywer's advice, others said they did not because they received no advice. Fourteen said they wanted to say something in court and were waiting for their moment, but no one indicated the appropriate moment. An accused said he was waiting for the judge 'to say, uh, "You got anything to say," and he never come out with it.' Another accused said he expected his lawyer to instruct him when to speak, but the only instructions were of a different order:

Q: Did you take the stand at all?

A: No.

Q: Why not?

A: I don't know. I was never called up there.

Q: Did you and your lawyer ever discuss whether or not you should take the stand?

A: No, all he said when we walked in, he said 'All you're going to have to say is "guilty" six times and leave the rest to me.'

When the accused wanted to say something in court, their requests were sometimes cut short. For example, an accused who pleaded guilty to a charge of impaired care and control proceeded without the assistance of a lawyer although he had consulted with a duty counsel before his case was called. During his hearing the duty counsel came up to the accused and asked if he wanted him to speak on his behalf. The accused agreed. The duty counsel proceeded to make submissions on the defendant's behalf, informing the judge that the accused was unemployed but made furniture in his basement.

J: Fourteen days. You've been down this road before.

L: Can he serve it on weekends?

J: There is no point since he is unemployed.

     [Accused tries to say something and is being silenced by the duty counsel]

A: Your Honour, may I serve on weekends? The only way I can make money–

J: You're unemployed.

A: I make furniture in my basement.

J: All right.

A: I was impaired ...

     [Accused tries to give an explanation but is interrupted by the judge]

J: You pleaded guilty.

The accused in an interview explained: 'Well the judge told him, he says, "No, we'll get him in there for two weeks. Then he can get it over with 'cause he's unemployed!" And then, so well that's when I spoke up. And he, the legal that runs, the duty counsel, he says, "Shhh – shhh, he says, that's the minimum sentence." He says, "Shhh, quiet." '

Owing to the number of cases that a duty counsel must deal with, it is not surprising that he does not have a complete understanding of his client's circumstances. The problem arises when the lawyer forgets his limitations and like all the other official actors in court deals with the accused like a child, best seen but not heard. In the second part of the exchange, the accused tried to explain to the judge that although he was impaired, he had not been driving. He had parked in a shopping plaza parking lot to sleep off the effects of alcohol. The duty counsel, before court, had advised the accused to explain this to the judge and that as a result the judge might be lenient with him. The accused never at any point in the interview denied his guilt to the charge but said that he merely wanted to explain that he had at least done the right thing and not driven. However, any statement that seemingly contradicts a guilty plea is aborted in court; cf *R.* v *Sumarah et al* (1970) 5CCC 317 (NS Co Ct). The suppression of ambiguity is yet another way in which the accused is prevented from explaining his position, and the court definition prevails. As Carlen (1976: 115) observes, everyday life is full of ambiguities but in court ambiguities are not only not tolerated but also must be eradicated. Matters that have as many shades as a chameleon in a box of crayons are made into black and white. The accused is not even allowed to suggest that there is a residue of grey.

In another instance, an accused who was charged with impaired driving was unrepresented and pleaded guilty. After a conviction was registered and the crown attorney had indicated that the accused had no record, the accused attempted to explain to the court that because the breathalyser test was not given until two hours after he was arrested he might not have been drunk at the time that the police had stopped him. The judge asked the accused if he was disputing his guilt. The crown attorney informed the judge that the breathalyser was taken approximately one hour after the accused was arrested. The judge then passed sentence. In interview, the accused explained that he didn't feel he had enough opportunity to explain himself: 'If I had pled not guilty I would have had more chance to say everything I wanted to say ... Well isn't that what the judge told me? He said, I can, when I told him about the time element, he said if I wanted to put the case for trial it's okay with him.'

Guilty with an explanation is not a legal concept. Some accused recognized this and pleaded not guilty in order to be heard. As one accused expressed it, 'We expected really to be found guilty but we wanted to get our side out.'

Other accused who wanted to speak out in court silenced themselves for fear of being out of order. They felt that their counsel had not represented them well or had misrepresented them, and that because of their counsel's presence, the judge was less likely to listen to them. In sum, they believed that when their lawyer spoke it could be mitigating, but when they themselves spoke it would only be aggravating. However, when they attempted to have their lawyer voice their concerns on their behalf they were frequently told to be quiet. Not knowing when to speak or how to speak, they felt the risk of being in contempt of court:

A: I wish he [lawyer] had of talked to him because, uh, he had all his facts mixed up on the whole case. He had me working for this guy we robbed and that's why I got the sentence I did because it was breach of trust ... And I couldn't get up there and say nothing.
Q: Why not?
A: There was no mike.
Q: What do you mean?
A: I–I tried once to say it. Like– OK, once before, I was in court and I tried to view my opinion and I just about got charged with contempt. And there's no way I can stand there and say 'Hey Judge listen. It's like this.' Uh– I was in enough trouble as it was. I didn't want to get charged with contempt.

The role of the lawyer as the 'mouthpiece' of the accused was often reinforced by the court's rules of interaction. Many times the following scenario was observed: the judge would ask defence counsel for some pertinent piece of information about the accused, defence counsel would turn to the accused repeating the question, and then turn back to the judge informing him of the accused's answer. As documented in chapter 3, lawyers also perpetuated their role as the voice of the accused by persuading their client that it was in their best interest if they remained quiet and let them do the talking. Our finding that the accused also began to think this way is hardly surprising.

A few accused who did not take the stand, and some who did, also saw speaking in court as detrimental. Rather than being merely a passive omission, not taking the stand was sometimes used as a strategy. Many were afraid to speak in court on the chance that they would say something that would harm their case. For example, an accused said that he would have liked to have explained the incident to the judge but felt that it was safer not to: 'I believe, under the emotional pressure that I was at the time– I could easily have said something that, you know, wasn't warranted.'

An accused who understood the procedural rules realized that he could not be compelled to be a witness and used this to his advantage. He and his co-accused had been charged with the possession of weapons for the purpose of committing a robbery (Criminal Code sec 83). They both pleaded not guilty and elected a trial by county court judge alone. After the crown attorney presented his evidence, counsel for the accused called no witnesses and presented no evidence. The accused explained why: 'Well, we didn't have to. We could have just pled no evidence and have it judged on what evidence they had, which was lousy. And as far as the judge knew we were, he kept referring to us as "boys." He knew [co-accused] was on parole but not exactly for what. He didn't know if I had any previous record. And if we got up on the stand, the crown would have made us look as stupid as [the police officers] looked. And it would have either, we could get up there and explain our story and make it better for us or make it look worse.'

Here, the accused was well aware of the crown attorney's skill at turning the accused's evidence to his disadvantage and the possibility of destroying the judge's image of them as 'boys' by having their criminal records divulged. He understood that not taking the stand was a gamble, but in this case his strategy was arguably the correct one as both accused were acquitted of the charges.

Other accused believed that having a voice might damage their case by aggravating the judge or other court agents. An accused who appeared without a lawyer wanted to question the crown witnesses and to present a counter argument to the crown evidence, but he said very little: 'In the court I could have asked a million questions that was going through my mind. Like, you know, I could have argued with the officers, the crown attorney. I could have objected to a lot of things he said. But I can't. I'm just up to defend myself, like, which a laywer–now perhaps he could. But, like, I couldn't take the chance of getting, you know, the crown mad or the judge mad. You know, that ended off there.' The structure of the court system is such that it made some accused feel that they had no right to their rights.

Others felt that maintaining their silence would be less damaging than risking explanations in court phrased in words other than legal rhetoric. Indeed, as documented in chapter 3, accused people believed that one advantage in hiring a lawyer is his ability to express himself in 'legalese': 'Well, your chances are a little better with a lawyer you know, because you can't express yourself like the lawyer can ... If you don't know how to talk for yourself, right, then you are going to end up in trouble because you – you are spitting up words that don't mean anything, you know.'

Moreover, in taking the stand, the accused must first solemnize the occasion with an oath promising that he will be truthful. Similar oaths are not required of those who question him. Moreover, the 'conversation' between the accused on the stand and those who question him is circumscribed by rules of evidence of which the accused is largely ignorant.

Most accused who did not take the stand said they did not do so because they believed it would be of little consequence to the outcome. This was particularly so for those who realized that a finding of guilt was inevitable. Thus, an accused stated that he did not take the stand because 'Well, I pleaded guilty in the first place, that's the end of the case. If you're guilty, you're guilty.' Similarly, another accused argued, 'If they've got you they've got you no matter what you say or talk. It won't do much good for you.'

Sentencing: The Trial of Moral Character

After the conviction is registered, the crown counsel and defence counsel prepare to make their sentencing submissions. These submissions are 'contests over moral character' (Emerson, 1969) aimed at influencing the final disposition of the case. Each side attempts to present the accused as a one-dimensional entity, submitting pieces of information selected for their consistency with the particular character portrayal they wish to put forth. The product is a reified version of the human being before them (cf Scott and Lyman, 1970: 108).

Defence counsel spoke often to the interviewer of the selective reconstructions of their clients' background and the deviant act in question. Thus, a lawyer said he saw himself as a 'mechanic with a set of facts ... a salesman. I'm selling a product that has defects to someone and I'm trying to emphasize the good parts.'

The lawyer generally adds or deletes information according to whether it might be beneficial to the characterization of the accused. A lawyer said he presented a lot of character evidence to the judge in order to avoid having a pre-sentence report ordered, a report which would have been unfavourable and 'would have gummed up the works.' Another lawyer said he did not submit an unfavourable psychiatric report because it recommended treatment in an institutional setting.

In forcing the accused into a caricature of himself, the lawyer is aware of the distancing effect it might have on the judge. He therefore also uses various strategies to present the accused as an individual to whom the judge can relate. Thus, a lawyer said he had his client's parents stand up in court 'so that he's just not a body, the judge actually might be able to identify better if the parents stand up.' Another lawyer pointed out to the judge that the wife of the accused was present. He did not call her as a witness because he felt that she would not have been 'impressive,' but at least the judge could visualize the accused as an individual in a family situation.

Lawyers also consciously tailored their submissions to the particular judge. This practice can begin early in the process when the lawyer tries to manoeuvre the case to avoid appearing before a particular judge. In the jurisdiction under study, the practice was to inform the lawyer of the identity of the presiding judge only on the morning of each day. A few lawyers talked about requesting a remand or considering electing a higher court to avoid appearing before a particular judge. More often, lawyers talked about keeping the presiding judge in mind when preparing their submissions. Thus, a lawyer stated, 'I directed submissions in such a manner that I knew they'd be receptive to Judge —— ... [It was tailored] to my knowledge of Judge —— .'

Carlen (1976) documents various factors in probation reports that are affected by knowledge about the magistrate: the length of the report, the language used, the manner of referring to the client, the types of argument used, and whether or not a firm recommendation was made. She also argues that tailoring submissions is done not only to benefit the client but also to maintain the lawyer's credibility with that judge. In this vein, a lawyer for an accused in our study felt he could not represent his client again when he was charged with theft of an auto shortly after he had been sentenced on the original charges: 'I didn't take him this time because I felt that I'd shot my bolt with respect to representations on his behalf ... and I just, my reputation, I just wanted the judge to know that when I say something it's because I've hopefully saved him a lot of time by trying to put myself in a position where I can project to him my assessment. And if he can't rely on my assessment then he can't rely on me. And I lose my effectiveness and that was one of the main reasons even though it's going to be in a different jurisdiction.'

The lawyer's credibility is one of his marketable assets. A lawyer said he instructed his client on dress and other aspects of behaviour in court as much for his own reputation as for the accused's benefit; these blend together, as the lawyer's reputation can enhance the prospects for the accused. Another lawyer asserted what he believed to be the ideal, stating that he does not need to call character witnesses in the cases he defends because in court 'they accept my word.'

It is difficult for the accused to establsh respectability credits for much the same reason as it is difficult for him to project credibility given his ascribed status at the bottom end of the 'order of things.' The courtroom interplay is what Scott and Lyman (1970) call a 'defensive face game' where the accused whose character has been discredited attempts to protect valued aspects of his identity. There are not many avenues open to him in doing this. Giving first-hand evidence is one way that the accused can inform the court about himself, but as we saw earlier, this was not a route frequently pursued. As one lawyer said of his client, 'I'm evaluating him as a witness and discovered that I thought he would make a rotten witness but he could likely call enough character evidence to make up for his personal weakness.'

The alternatives were to have the lawyer make the 'respectability presentations' on the accused's behalf, the submissions being more believable because they came from someone other than the accused and someone who was a respectable member of the community; or to call in character witnesses to testify to the good character of the accused. These two modes are usually given added credence because they may seem less self-serving than the submissions of the accused.

Occasionally, the lawyer believes he himself may be seen as biased and therefore calls character witnesses as an alternative. Thus, a lawyer called the father of the accused, the detective who investigated the case, and two probation officers who had dealt with the accused before, to give evidence at sentencing. He gave the following explanation for this course of action: 'I can stand up there and I can make submissions until I'm blue in the face about how nice this girl is, about how she's reformed, etc., etc. But they're self-serving evidence. What I mean is, it's in effect the accused standing up and telling the judge what a nice girl she is, which is not great. It's not independent.

It's not objective evidence. So what I have to get is somebody that's aloof and independent of the situation to give an analysis of what's going on. In this case, I had the ideal witness; that is the opposition, the detective.'

In various cases, relatives and other respectable associates were brought in to give evidence on the defendant's basic good nature, to convince the court that the accused was basically a law-abiding citizen, a good community member temporarily gone astray, or to point out to the judge that there were people out in the community who cared and who were willing to supply a stable environment. For example, a lawyer called to the stand the father-in-law of one accused to inform the court that the accused had married his daughter and had obtained employment. Another lawyer excluded the boy-friend of the accused because 'He wasn't a very good witness. His work record was poor. His appearance was very scruffy looking and his method of communication was leaving a lot to be desired. And I think if the judge knew that she was associating with this person, he would have had some doubts about her future.' Sensitive to the problem of submissions appearing self-serving, a lawyer had the local justice of the peace speak on behalf of the accused and had obtained several letters of reference. All the letters were favourable except on one point. The lawyer commented, 'It's always nice to have something not favourable. It adds to the credibility of anything.'

This is yet another instance where the accused is not an adversary. The crown attorney does not face a problem of credibility with respect to his evidence since most of his witnesses are agents who are higher in the hierarchy of credibility and have special licence to discredit.

Since the accused rarely speaks in court, the moral judgment being passed on him is based not only on the evidence the lawyer presents but also on his demeanour. Demeanour is 'that element of the individual's ceremonial behaviour typically conveyed through deportment, dress and bearing, which serves to express to those in his immediate presence that he is a person of certain desirable or undesirable qualities' (Goffman, 1956: 489). From the way an accused handles himself in court, the other agents and, in particular, the judge make interpretations about his behaviour from which moral attributes are derived. As Jerome Frank (1949), quoting Wigmore, says, 'The witness' demeanour is always ... in evidence.'

The demeanour of the accused informs the court about his attitude towards the moral-legal order. Any disrespect shown through either his dress or behaviour which may question the legitimacy of the hearing or the moral order on which it is based affects the court's response to his case. An accused said he felt that his behaviour in court was important because 'If you have complete resentment for the proceedings going on then you're getting the judge uptight, you're getting the crown attorney uptight, you're getting everybody uptight in court.' A deferential attitude is critical. Any defiance of or autonomy from the hearings asserted by the accused by staring at the judge, not using deferential forms of address, laughing, or grinning is a threat that must be punished. An accused related his lawyer's instructions concerning how to behave in court: 'He told me to, when I was sitting up there to just hang my head, you know, and not look around or look back or anything like that.'

Although deference must be shown to the judge by the accused, it is not reciprocated by the judge. The judge is allowed to cast aspersions against the character of the accused, but if the accused forgets his place he is quickly reprimanded for being out of order. An illustration is provided in the case of an accused who appeared in court for the third time to set a date for his trial and still had not retained a lawyer. The accused informed the court that he had been advised to wait a week for legal aid and then to choose a lawyer. The justice of the peace enquired from the accused about his activities during the 52 days since the time of the offence:

A: I've been looking for work. I'm on unemployment insurance and I have to keep looking for work and keep a list.

JP: You mean you haven't been able to find work or a lawyer in 52 days! I'd advise you to get out of bed in the morning and start looking. Get a little bit of independence, a few shekels in your pocket. You've got all your faculties. It shouldn't take you this long to find work.

A: Well, it has. I'm not here to be insulted and listen to this sarcasm. I'm not going to stand here and be insulted – with all due respect.

JP: Yes, 'with all due respect.' You've heard that from defence counsel here and it's with the greatest respect we'll put it over to set a date.

The accused, having transgressed the boundary that delineates his position as a 'dummy player,' was put in his place by the justice of the peace. At a later date, the defence counsel who was eventually hired by the accused indicated to the crown attorney that he would guide his client back into place: 'Give me a little time to work on him. He's just a little different. Apparently last time he was here he just went nuts, yelling at the judge.'

Even though the accused may not comprehend the proceedings, the ceremonial rules of deference and demeanour demand that he at least feign full attention to the proceedings. While attending to the hearings the accused believes that he must also display an attitude of concern: 'I went in there with a long face, a solemn look ... and if there were any spots of humour that came up in the trial, not to take it too seriously. Like, ah, if someone made a, a statement that was humourous, well, then I wouldn't just burst over laughing. It would, uh, I don't know, just wouldn't look good in a court of law, that's all. Maybe snicker or grin or something like that and show that I, at least, had a sense of humour.'

The solemnity of the proceedings must not be broken by the accused. One lawyer explained to the interviewer that he had to reprimand his client twice for laughing in court. The accused must not reduce the impact of the display by questioning its legitimacy through any disrespectful behaviour. An accused commented that he was the only person heavily constrained by these rules of demeanour. He said his lawyer had instructed him to 'look humble,' and added that judges 'like people to be humble just to go along with what they say, not, you know, like lawyers can be snotty but people, defendants can't.' This can be construed as yet another reason for retaining a lawyer: the lawyer is allowed more leniency in discourse and demeanour than is his client.

Both lawyers and accused persons felt that moral judgements concerning character were also made on the basis of dress. As a result, lawyers instructed their clients to wear a suit and tie, to get a hair cut, and dress up, to change a Rastafarian hairstyle to look more 'everydayish,' etc. The accused was also aware that sometimes his manner of dress was the only avenue of influence open to him, underscoring the interpretation that the whole process is concerned with the manipulation of appearances: 'After the first appearance in court, my lawyer came in. He says, "All right, at least you have one thing going for you." I said, "What's that?" "You come in a suit." '

Dress to some accused signified signs of respectability, remorse, and rehabilitation. An accused who was instructed by his lawyer to wear a suit said, 'Probably it looks better on you. The judge figures, "Well, he must be trying to straighten his act or something, you know." ' Another accused, who was held in custody for a bail hearing, had his mother bring some good clothes to the jail for him to wear in court: 'It's just if the judge is sitting there and he looks at a guy with jeans on, looking really grubby and everything, I think he'd feel that he belongs in jail more than the guy that's dressed nicely, nice cut hair, you know.'

Occasionally, the reverse strategy was used, as some accused purposefully dressed down hoping to avoid a heavy fine. One accused, by dressing down, understood the utilitarian bias inherent in the courts. Crime is never condoned, especially if it is not motivated by dire need: 'Really doesn't matter if you dress really fancy, well. The judge he takes that, like, this guy must have lots of money. "Why is he out robbing places?" you know. That's how they [lawyers] made us throw on some old clothes and it looks like you don't have enough money and it looks better on you.'

Perhaps the most crucial attitude the accused must show in court is remorse. The courtroom ceremony is structured to cast the accused into the status of wrongdoer. The accused is pressured by the fear of heavier sanctions to conduct himself in a contrite, repentant manner. By so doing he acknowledges his own guilt. Verbal expressions of his contrition are not enough. He must show total commitment to the role of wrongdoer by conveying a deferential and remorseful attitude by his demeanour. As a result, he is pressured into becoming personally involved in his own discrediting (Emerson, 1969). Goffman (1971: 100) argues that those who have transgressed a rule must do some remedial work to show that their offence is not uniquely expressive of them and that they have a proper relation to the sanctioning system. Carlen (1976: 101) comments that the accused is made 'to engage in a paradoxical process of mitigation (of his own offence) and vindication (of the law).'

Each act of contrition reproduces the legitimacy of the law and its moral basis by indicating that the accused is willing to rehabilitate himself and become once again a person who is in order. Thus, an accused pleaded guilty to dangerous driving after two counts of failure to remain at the scene of an accident were withdrawn. By not only condemning himself, but also imposing punishment on himself, the accused seemed to be viewed more favourably by the judge:

Defence counsel: The accused agrees with a penalty. He is 28 years old, married, and lives in — . He has been in Canada for five years. He is employed as a machinist for the past year. This whole incident has cost him money and he has lost his own car, the equivalent of losing $1,000. He hasn't driven since the accident and he doesn't want to drive for years. The accused was also held in custody for two days. My client is asking for a substantial fine and a licence suspension ... In all other aspects he is a good citizen. His wife does not speak English. He is asking for a fine and to keep him off the road.

Judge: Counsel has said what the courts feel and I note his self-prohibition on driving.

By his self-imposed punishment the accused gave license to the courts for the action they took against him.

The representation of the accused to the court must also include the element of rehabilitation. An accused explained that the only reason he felt that he was released at his bail hearing was because he indicated a willingness to reform:

And then he [duty counsel] told me, like, he says, you know, I'll, this was while I was down in the cells, he says, 'I'll give you time to think about it,' you know. 'If you figure you've got a drinking problem, when you come up to the court and I ask you, "Would you consider joining AA?" you either give me a yes or a no.' So when I went up to court, they had asked me a few questions. Was I employed? or, where was I living?, things like this, and then he asked me if I would consider joining Alcoholics Anonymous. And I said yes, and then the JP read off what he was doing, what my bail was. He says 'I'm letting you out on the conditions that you do join AA 'cause I figure you need help.' And I think that's the only way I got my bail ... I don't like that at all because I was more or less talked, not talked into it, but, you know, if I didn't say that, I wouldn't be granted bail. So therefore if I wanted to get out, I would have to say it, right. So I really didn't like that, but if that's what they want to hear, that's what I was going to tell them.

Aside from what the accused can do for himself through his acts of contrition, his counsel can make submissions to counteract the assault on his client's character made by the prosecution. Both the crown attorney and defence counsel employ similar techniques, focusing on the same critical areas. The crown attorney attempts to establish that deviance is a salient characteristic of the accused, that his deviant act is consistent with his biography and a prelude of worse things to come. The defence counsel, to counteract these submissions, tries to show that the act in question is an isolated spontaneous event in his client's life, or due to a particular set of circumstances, and that the actor's essential self is divorced from the act. The lawyer stresses the youth of his client, or his lack of a criminal history, or that he has been involved with a bad substratum of society, or that there are some mitigating circumstances that contributed to the deviant act (e.g. alcohol or drugs), or that the client is compelled by circumstances (e.g. stealing in order to pay the rent or buy some goods). He tries to establish that the accused is a member of the community with roots. He does this by informing the court that the accused has a job and a home. He further attempts to establish that the accused is on a path of rehabilitation. This is indicated by the remorse the accused shows for his past act through his demeanour in court, by pleading guilty to his charges, by co-operating with the police, and by making restitution. The lawyer then tries to show that his client has not contravened the law since the offence in question and has plans for the future. Moreover, the experience of the accused with the system in connection with this offence is presented as being punishment enough and as a deterrent for the future. All the above submissions indicate the degree of commitment to a 'normal' utilitarian code of behaviour, with a respect for the formal rules and the agents that enforce them. If the lawyer can display the proper *signs* that order has been reproduced, the most lenient sentence possible can be expected. The following account by a lawyer includes the appropriate elements for display:

> Number one, she's a young girl, number two, she's been away from the house. She's got no parental guidance and she herself is a new mother. She's caught in the situation where she's thrown into the harsh world without proper guidance. Without economic means and she finds herself in dire economic straits. I think that was the submission that I made, and rather than take the appropriate route, she fell into the trap of doing a break and enter to pay her rent because of the unexpected departure of her roommate and that was basically what I played upon. And then, in addition to that, there had been a full year, perhaps fourteen or fifteen months that had gone by since this incident. And she had conducted herself well by all reports and she seemed to be in fact getting much better because she's going to —— , etc. Those were two things. The third thing which played heavily, more heavily than I thought it would in my favour was the fact

that she turned herself in and she helped the police recover all of these goods. You know, the judge kept referring to Detective —— 's evidence. Plus the other mitigating factor was that we had a plan for her in the future. There was people that were concerned about her and, perhaps could guide her in the future whereas she had no guidance in the past, you know. Those things.

The role of the accused in all of this is silently to appear to be in accordance with the manipulation of appearances about him. In doing so, he collaborates with the agents of the court in separating his self from the objectified being upon whom the sentence is about to fall. Moreover, he enables the agents to separate their selves from what they are doing. Having shown the correct relationship to the order of things, the accused is deemed ready to take his punishment.

Perception of Outcomes by the Accused

Despite their concern about the sentence, some accused were confused as to what took place at their sentencing hearing, including the actual sentence they had received. For example, an accused pleaded guilty to two charges of over 80 mg and one charge of failing to appear in court. The judge registered a conviction on each of the three charges and suspended the accused's licence for a year; however, he remanded sentencing on those charges for five months. Meanwhile the accused was to use this time to get employment, attend Alcoholics Anonymous, see a doctor, and 'stay out of trouble.' The judge warned the accused that if he failed to meet these conditions he would sentence him to six months in jail when he returned for his sentencing. The accused's lack of understanding as to what took place is revealed in the interview.

Q: What did he suggest you do till April?

A: Well, stay away from the alcohol and maybe attend a few AA meetings and stuff. And when I come back in April I have to have a letter, reference saying that I haven't been drinking or have someone there with me from AA or something.

Q: OK and if you have done all that he's asked you to do in April, what will he do?

A: He'll drop the other charges.

Q: The other charges? What other charges?

A: The other impaired driving. He only charged me with one, right? Charged me with one and I still have the other.

Q: Charged or convicted?

A: Well he convicted me with one, I guess. Because he suspended my licence for a year. But he said if I, you know, stay out of trouble and don't drink and every-thing, when I come back he'll drop the other charge.

Q: And if you don't what will happen?

A: He'll charge me with it. I'd probably lose it [the licence] for another year.

Q: The other 'impaired'?

A: Yeah. And the 'fail to appear.'

When the accused returned for his sentencing he was given a suspended sentence plus two years' probation on each charge to run concurrently. As revealed by the above excerpt the accused did not fully appreciate that having pleaded guilty to all three charges, a conviction was then registered against him on each.

In another case the accused was charged with two counts of theft under $200 after allegedly shoplifting some items from a department store. Represented by duty counsel, she pleaded guilty to one count on her first court appearance. The judge then remanded sentencing in order to obtain a psychiatric report. When she returned to court for sentencing with a privately retained lawyer, no report was submitted. Instead her lawyer told the judge that the psychiatrist had informed him that the accused had no problem that would excuse her behaviour. The judge subsequently sentenced her to four days' imprisonment. In interview the accused demonstrated considerable confusion with respect to the sentencing proceedings:

Q: Why didn't you have a report. Why didn't he [the psychiatrist] give you a report to give to the judge?

A: He don't give it?

Q: No. Your sister asked for a report and you don't know whether he [the psychiatrist] gave one?

A: No.

Q: Well it wasn't in the court that day.

A: No?

Q: No, there was no report.

A: Who said?

Q: ... the judge asked for a report and there was no report.

A: No?

Q: No.

At the end of the interview the accused asked the interviewer whether she thought the judge would now make her pay a fine. The accused did not realize that on release from the reformatory the next day it would all be over.

The fact that little effort is made to enquire into the accused's state of understanding makes the presumption that the accused understands the proceedings a hard one to dispel. His lack of knowledge and comprehension contributes to his exclusion from a process that is ostensibly centred around him.

The vast majority of the accused felt that they had been dealt with fairly by the courts when the question was put to them generally. Seventy-one had felt that they were dealt with fairly and a further 16 felt that they had been dealt with fairly on the whole with one reservation. Only 11 said that they were not dealt with fairly. (There was no information for 3 accused.) As illustrated previously, the accused did perceive an imbalance in the system in terms of their ability to participate and to affect the outcome. Nevertheless, there was a general acceptance of the 'system.'

One accused who had an accepting view in retrospect had been charged along with a co-accused with possession of an offensive weapon for the purpose of committing an indictable offence. They were held for a bail hearing and were denied bail. A month and a half later they were released from custody after a bail review. Their case came before a county court judge 15 months after they were charged with the offence. They pleaded not guilty and after the crown's case was heard and having called no evidence themselves, they were acquitted. In answer to the question, 'Do you think your case was dealt with fairly?,' he replied: 'I guess so, yeah. We didn't have a proper bail hearing to begin with. It should have been over with in our preliminary hearing. And, uh, if we were going to make any kind of deal at all, we would have done it then, not a year late. So it took too long to get it over with, with those kind of bail restrictions– like reporting.'

Although there is discontent with the parts of the system, the whole remains relativey unscathed. The 'majesty, justice and mercy' (Hay, 1975) of the law are maintained through 1) the ceremonial ritual in court; 2) charge withdrawals, charge reductions, and the occasional finding of not guilty; 3) leading the accused to believe that he will receive a harsh sentence by reference to the Criminal Code maximums, or by simply making up a figure, thereby making him feel grateful when he receives the going rate.

The majority (75 per cent) of the accused were pleased with the sentence they received. Much of the relief was a result of a general expectation of receiving a worse outcome. For example, 14 accused were expecting a jail term of over a year on the offence most salient to them whereas only 6 were given incarceration of over a year on those offences.

The lawyer was a key contributor to a client's anxieties. For example, an accused said he was satisfied with his sentence because he was told by his lawyer that he could receive up to five years. He was sentenced to 21 days to be served intermittently plus a $75 fine.

A similar process is at work in relation to judges. Emerson (1969: 180) describes how judges stage court so that their sentencing decision appears to 'save' the accused, and Carlen (1976) asserts that the judge not only must make the appropriate legal judgment but it must also be seen as such. In one case a mother and her three daughters each pleaded guilty to two counts of theft over $200 and one count of possession of stolen property over $200. The judge put all four into custody for two hours before sentencing. When they were brought back before the court, he said, 'I'm going to put the matter over, one of the ladies' husband doesn't know. I'm considering a jail term and they need time to put their affairs in order ... Before imposing a sentence on her and the others, arrange your affairs so that you can be away from home for a period of time and I will allow your lawyer to change my mind on the date of sentencing.'

On the day of sentencing, the judge fined the three daughters and sentenced the mother to seven days in jail. The lawyer for the four women felt that his submissions had little effect because the judge had made up his mind after the facts had been read in. In addition, he stated that the two hours in custody was to give his clients a taste of jail and the remanding of sentencing was to scare them.

Aside from the formal sanctions handed out in court the accused is also subjected to hidden penalties. Feeley (1979) discusses the costs of time and money to the accused associated with taking time off work to appear in court, hiring a lawyer, pre-trial detention, and attending various rehabilitation programs in hopes of ameliorating the sentence or having the charges withdrawn. As Feeley documents in the context of a Connecticut lower court, the cost in time and money for each of these factors far outweighs the cost in time and money for pleading guilty immediately without a lawyer. In addition, for some accused the court process was sufficiently anxiety-provoking to be punishment enough. For others, the police processing, the fingerprinting, the taking of official photographs were sufficiently stigmatizing to be punitive. For those charged with shoplifting, there was often the added penalty of being banned from the premises where the offence had taken place. Others lost their jobs because of the criminal charges. Still others felt that they had to take unattractive employment that they otherwise would have not in order to present themselves as employed in the sentence submissions. Moreover, all accused were sensitive to the ramifications of having their entanglements with 'the law' permeate their personal lives.

The hidden penalties also afflicted those who were found not guilty. An accused found not guilty waited 15 months for the disposition and during this period was held in custody for several weeks and then released on restrictive bail conditions:

A: I was wondering if, ah, you knew of any way I could get any kind of compensation towards all this, all the reporting I did, the gas, time. I couldn't get a job on afternoon shifts. I had a car, a different car than I have now. I got in a car accident one night on my way to reporting. If I didn't have to report I would never have been there, in that situation.

Q: I don't know. Have you talked to [lawyer] about it at all?

A: Ah– not really, no. My attitude towards it actually was that it's like you can't fight City Hall or whatever, you know. Like because they are bigger than you are. Or they would just say to you, the court would turn around and say be glad that you, that you beat the charge and are lucky with that, 'get lost don't ask for anything else.'

Q: What do you feel about that?

A: Well I feel I was not guilty, I pleaded not guilty all the way. I was not falsely arrested because they, ah ..., in their minds they had certain– it was there and they couldn't just let that go kind of. But overall should have had, should have got bail to begin with, shouldn't have spent two months in jail and being scared of elevators and stuff like that. Then I was looking for jobs afterwards, I couldn't accept shift work. I would have to explain that to unemployment, whoever, why. And anybody you explain stuff like that to, they figure you are guilty until you are proven innocent. And ah, I had a lot of weekends I couldn't go anywhere to visit relatives or something because I couldn't leave until after I reported on Saturday and they couldn't understand why it was three times a week, and why it was taking so long. And it was 88 miles per week, that's a lot of gas over a year and three months or whatever and that came out of my pocket. And now they finally said you are not guilty, fine, you know, forget about whatever it cost you all that time ... I think if I was over there and got stopped or ended up getting charged with something or other again with the [police], I think I would even have twice as hard a time with them, because the way this one went.'

When the accused loses by being found guilty or pleading guilty, he is expected to repay the state for his wrongdoing. When the state loses by the accused being acquitted or charges being withdrawn, the state is not expected to compensate the accused for its questionable or wrong accusations.

The ordering the accused experiences from the point of contact with the police onward is reproduced in the public forum of the court. The physical setting of the court, the rules of procedure, the discourse, the implicit and explicit instructions of officials, and the manipulation of appearances for sentencing all distance the accused from the proceedings and ensure his place as an object to be put in order. It is a testimony to the skill of the court actors, and the structure within which they work, that they reproduce an aura of legitimacy that is usually accepted by the accused.

The 'majesty, justice, and mercy' of the criminal process *work* in reproducing the individual accused's deference to authority. The criminal process thereby also *uses* accused persons in the aggregate to help define the relationship between the individual and the state, to reproduce a social order well beyond the doors of a local court and its ordering of justice.

7

The Reordering of Justice

Laws are like spider's webs which, if anything small falls into them they ensnare it, but large things break through and escape.

Solon (7th–6th century BC), quoted in Diogenes Laertus, *Lives and Opinions of Eminent Philosophers* (3rd century AD)

The reasonable man adapts himself to the world: the unreasonable persists in trying to adapt the world to himself. Therefore, all progress depends on the unreasonable man.

George Bernard Shaw, 'Maxims for Revolutionists,' in *Man and Superman: A Comedy and a Philosophy* (1903)

Summary

Accused people in the criminal process are dependent upon the actions of others in taking actions and producing outcomes. They are treated as objects with their wishes often being read as symptoms of their suspect character. They lack organized means of altering their dependent position, in the face of an organization of criminal control that is very large and powerful in its own right and backed up by all the power of the state with its legislative apparatus.

As the agents of the state work on the accused's case, they redefine it and transform it in terms of the criminal law and also use the criminal law to regulate the process of resolution. In doing this, criminal control agents have power *over* the definition of reality, as well as *through* the definition of reality they decide upon. They take over the accused's trouble or conflict and make it state property (Christie, 1977; Ericson, 1981), leaving the accused to await an outcome via a process that to him is complex, difficult to comprehend, and mystical and which makes him powerless.

To be sure, the accused is asked to participate in this process at several points along the way. Of greatest apparent importance are the many decisions he is asked to make, e.g. to give a police statement, to obtain legal counsel, to elect a court for the hearing, to plead, and to appeal the outcome. However, as we have documented, and as others have observed, 'What appears externally as a "decision" to be "made", may not appear in such a way to the defendant' (Bottoms and McClean, 1976: 8–9). Matters are foreclosed first by the police, and then by the lawyer, often to the point where only one course of action seems reasonable. With one course of action there is no choice, and therefore no decision. In a system and a society which profess to make the individual decision a central element of existence, the reality for the accused is that he rarely has a decision (choice) to take, and when he does, it cannot be viewed as an 'original' decision because it reflects submission to pressure from others and to structural arrangements.

The accused is also asked to participate by being physically present at *some* of the locations at which his case is decided. The accused must appear in court at some scheduled hearings, or be represented by an agent in the case of summary conviction offences; if he chooses not to appear, he is subject to an additional criminal charge for not appearing and increases his chances of being held in custody awaiting his next appearance date. At court hearings, the accused typically stands by while a remand is arranged by his lawyer, or stands up to enter guilty pleas, or stands by while his moral character is first dissected and then pieced together again to show the judge that he is still a whole person (although slightly fractured), who justifiably deserves less than what the Criminal Code maximum sentence threatens him with. In requiring the presence of the accused, the court acquires his 'consent' to what is being done to him (cf Shapiro, 1975).

The fragmentation of the criminal process helps to maintain its ideology. The accused does not appear in the crown attorney's office, judge's chambers, or other sanctified locations where transactions are carried out among his lawyer and criminal control agents. He is not to observe the loose organization of personal relationships and situational constraints by which the property that was once his conflict is carved up and capitalized on by these others. He is to see only the majesty of the courtroom, where formal legal rationality is displayed for all to observe even if all do not understand it. Of course, for the vast majority of accused the picture in court is a 'short' rather than a full-length feature because they plead guilty without a trial. Moreover, if they are too persistent and demand a double feature the accused are excluded from any participation: appeals heard at the supreme court, the most majestic of them all, allow the accused to be a spectator but not a participant. At the lowest level of deciding cases (out-of-court case transactions), and at the highest (appeals before the supreme court), the accused is absolutely silenced.

In the context of structured dependency, we find the accused forced into a passive, indeed submissive state. At each stage of the process the accused not only fails to take what externally appear as his formal decisions, but he also does not take advantage of his formal rights because the costs of doing so are structured so that they usually exceed the benefits (Feeley, 1979). The accused typically complies with police searches whether or not they have the authority of a warrant, usually does not remain silent in the face of police questioning, infrequently seeks or obtains access to a third party while in police custody, often does not obtain a lawyer, rarely demands a trial, often does not speak out in court when he has the urge to do so, and very rarely entertains an appeal of the outcome, let alone actually seeks one. Instead of expending the effort to do these things, the accused distances himself from the process and concentrates upon the outcomes. He becomes a pragmatist, focusing upon a few immediate personal costs involved in the matter rather than taking issue with his rights, or the agents' wrongs. In doing so, he acts much like the pragmatic police officer or other criminal control agent who operates in ways which have the least potential for causing strain (cf Chambliss and Seidman, 1971).

As Balbus (1973: especially 258-9) has shown, accused plead guilty and receive the short-term gain of a relatively light disposition instead of taking the risk of furthering their long-term interests through an adversarial struggle (see also Galanter, 1974). For the accused charged with shoplifting, or possession of narcotics, or assault, or a few break and enters, the cost of challenging the process – even if there appear to be options available – far exceeds the cost of 'giving in' and taking whatever tariff prevails among the agents of the court.

As Feeley (1979) cogently argues, for the vast majority of accused in the lower courts 'the process is the punishment.' The easiest way to avoid the full impact of possible punishment is to avoid as much of the process as possible. One obvious way of doing this is to confess to the police, confirm this through a guilty plea at an early stage in court, and accept the tariff of the court. While he is ignorant of much that goes on in the criminal process, the accused is smart when it comes to a cost benefit analysis. Why hire a lawyer when his fee will only add substantially to the 'fine' one will receive anyway? Why hire a lawyer who, because of his own scheduling, might remand the case when one wants to get it over with? Why hire a lawyer when he might trade off one's case for concessions on another client's case? What will be the penalty for refusing to confess to the police: more investigation? investigation of one's friends? embarrassment to one's family? If the case is repeatedly remanded, what are the costs: in psychic and anxiety terms? the economic costs of losing time at work? the personal costs of 'dead time' in custody? the economic costs of losing interest on bail money? As Feeley (1979: 277) concludes, 'Ironically, the cost of *invoking* one's rights is frequently greater than the loss of the rights themselves, which is why so many defendants accept a guilty plea without a battle. This situation is true for defendants who are or consider themselves innocent as well as for those who readily acknowledge their guilt ... When the costs of invoking the safe-guards of the process are likely to be greater than the eventual criminal sentence, there is little incentive to engage fully in the process in an effort to vindicate oneself or minimize the sanction.'

We find that on the whole the accused expresses satisfaction with the process, and especially with the sentencing outcome and with the judge who pronounces it. His satisfaction results from the impact of his appearance in court: regardless of what took place up to that point, the order and aura of the court serves its mystical function and makes the accused a true believer. Moreover, the accused is lead to believe that matters could have been made far worse, and his disposition is assessed in this context. Refusing to co-operate with the police can lead them to lay more charges of a 'contempt' variety (e.g. obstruct police, causing a disturbance) or a 'kicker' variety (extra charges arising out of the same incident), or to retaliate in other ways (e.g. prolonged custody, opposing bail). Going to trial can cost more in time and lawyer's fees and can lead to more severe penalties if found guilty. Speaking out in court can make matters worse in the judge's opinions for sentencing, or even lead to charges of contempt of court or perjury. The accused is bright enough to know when he is stonewalled. Conservative like most of the rest of us, his motto is better safe than sorry. The 'majesty, justice, and mercy' of the law work their wonders on him, and ultimately through him.

The Nature of Reform

In the previous chapters we have documented the structural sources of the dependency of the accused. Similar to other people who are outsiders to the system of criminal control, the accused is left judging the system in terms of the rhetoric rather than the law itself and its pragmatic implementation. As McBarnet (1981: chapter 8) argues, a legal system based upon case law is able to bridge the gap between the ideological rhetoric and the application of the law to specific cases by allowing for uncertainty and providing for discretion in a particular case in a manner that still allows the more general abstract principles of the rule of law to remain intact. Thus, the law is viewed as a legitimate vehicle across the political spectrum, embraced by 'lawandorder' advocates on the right, civil libertarians, and the reformist left. Public knowledge and public debate go on in terms of the rhetoric, and the reality of the law in the books and the law in action remains largely untouched.

Ultimately, the rhetoric of reform itself is an integral part of the criminal process, and contributes to the dependency of the accused. This is the case because 'reform chatter' and 'policy talk' are carried on in terms of the 'majesty, justice, and mercy' of the law rather than in terms of what the law actually does as an instrument of social control to keep the 'lower orders' in their place.

A typical reformist response in light of the analysis we have undertaken in this book would be to propose changes which might make it appear that the system is more adversarial in nature and more just. How could we move the accused away from being dependent toward being independent? This might be done by changing some of the rules of the game, making them more visible and rigid and therefore more predictable for the defence. It might be done also by using alternatives to the criminal process in handling the troubles of the accused, including various official 'diversion' schemes and the alternative of doing nothing. In what follows we examine typical reforms of the adversarial and due process type and the decriminalization and diversion type in order to show that they hold no promise for altering the fundamental nature of the dependent position of the accused.

Law is governmental social control, discretion is power, and rights are limits on the discretion to use law. In the past two decades, particularly in the United States, there has been a resurgence of a great liberal lineage that emphasizes the rights of citizens in their encounters with the state. In part, this is a reaction to, or perhaps even a backlash against, the 'progressive' movement of behaviourists and administrators who advocated and achieved maximum discretion for authorities with little concern for procedural due process (Rothman, 1980).

Obviously, libertarian values underlie this rights movement. The apparent desire is to minimize arbitrary action by state agents and resolve conflicts within a framework of rules which ensure predictability of action on both sides. Ideally the system is concerned more with freedom than with winning, although this is admittedly difficult to accomplish in a society that is achievement-oriented with attendant fantasies about upward mobility.

In this quest for asserting and preserving the rights of citizens, the sphere of crime control stands at the forefront of the debate. This is perhaps explained by the dramatic aspects of crime control, which make it the primary arena in which the public assess the role of the state as a moral agent. Thus, there is much talk, at least in middle-class libertarian circles, about the need to control the powers of the police, prison administrators, parole boards, and the like. The prison is a particularly interesting context in which to explore many of the same issues discussed in this book. While reform rhetoric concerning the needs and rights of inmates is part of the very program of the prison (Foucault, 1977), there is a massive apparatus of secrecy ensuring that the prison is insulated from public (and legal) scrutiny and that inmates do not know the rules or how to obtain what they are entitled to (cf Cohen and Taylor, 1978; Feltman, 1981).

Those who advocate greater rights for the accused person in the criminal process employ an adversarial model of that process which includes a system of rules to ensure that each side in the conflict has roughly equal opportunities for a fair hearing. A major obstacle to this, as documented in our own research and in other research (e.g. Heumann, 1978; Feeley, 1979; Ericson, 1981, 1982), is that legal rules are not the only rules which frame the processing of criminal cases. Rules of the organizations that comprise the criminal process, and the relationships they sustain, create a set of 'recipes' for action which fundamentally affect the production of case outcomes. The accused, excluded organizationally, does not have access to this 'recipe' knowledge and at best (or worst) must rely upon his lawyer's 'recipe' knowledge and ability to use it. Thus, for the accused all the knowledge in the world about the formal rules will not allow him to engage in rational calculation and predictable action in relation to the rules of the particular criminal control organization be comes caught up in. Unless accused persons can be convinced of the value of reading academic treatises on organizational theory and the processing of criminal cases, it is difficult to see that this situation will change.

One change proposed by rights' advocates, and implemented in several American state jurisdictions, is a movement in the direction of fixed penalties. Given the orientation of the accused to outcomes and his lack of real participation in the process by which outcomes are arrived at, this appears a viable reform. It can apprently reduce arbitrariness in sentencing and make it appear as if one can really make a punishment fit the crime according to standards approaching just proportion. The fixed-penalty system is a direct reaction against progressives or correctionalists who champion the indeterminate sentence.

Early correctionalists saw a fixed-penalty system 'as completely discredited and as incapable of a part in any reasoned system of social organization, as is the practice of astrology or ... witchcraft ... The time will come when the moral mutilations of fixed terms of imprisonment will seem as barbarous and antiquated as the ear lopping, nose-slitting and hand amputations of a century ago' (Lewis, 1900, cited by Rothman, 1980: 59–60). The time has now come, or come back, when it is regarded as enlightened to advocate a fixed-penalty system (e.g. Morris, 1974; von Hirsh, 1976; American Friends Service Committee, 1971). In keeping with the model of the penitentiary (Foucault, 1977: 232), a fixed-penalty system is ideal 'in a society in which liberty is a good that belongs to all in the same way and to which each individual is attached.' It is equitable, allows for proportion, and provides a model for other forms of social organization: 'It reproduces, with a little more emphasis, all the mechanisms that are to be found in the social body' (ibid).

A fixed-penalty system is supposed to make the punishment more specific to the offence and less specific to the offender, on the assumption that using the characteristics of the offence is somehow less arbitrarily conceived and implemented than using the characteristics of offenders to make judgments. However, in spite of appearances to the contrary, it does not fundamentally alter the discretionary power of officials. For example, under California's Uniform Sentencing Act, which is a movement in the direction of fixed penalties, specific criteria are still invoked to increase or mitigate a penalty. Moreover, discretion is likely to be transferred to the prosecutor from the sentencing authority (Alschuler, 1978), giving double entendre to the word 'fixed' penalty (see also Greenberg and Humphries, 1980). Under this type of system, the accused is still likely to see the process as mysterious and punitive.

If we choose to use our imagination a little more than we are usually called upon to do, we can suggest the limits to an equitable adversarial system of justice. Under an equitable system, there would be equal resources allocated to the defense and to those bringing the allegation, instead of the present situation where the police receive 66 per cent of criminal control spending, correctional agencies 21 per cent, and legal aid a paltry 1.6 per cent (figures from the Solicitor General of Canada, 1979). We would have mobile defence counsel who, like the present mobile police, would be equipped with a sophisticated communications system so that they could be on the scene of a conflict within minutes, ready to defend the citizen who is the subject of allegations of wrongdoing. Just as the mobile police officer has access to the computerized CPIC (Canadian Police Information Centre) system for data on suspects, defence counsel would be equipped with a CDICK (Citizen Defence Information Concerning Kops) system, which would detail the police officer's career record, including such things as previous allegations of brutality against him, and whether he is in an 'observation' or 'suspicious' category. The citizen subjected to allegations would say nothing to the police. He would either be summonsed and released or immediately taken to another official for determination of release. All cases would go to trial. Persons found not guilty would be compensated by a Criminal Control Injuries Compensation Board.

Absurd, you might say. It is absurd because we have too little practice in the exercise of our imaginations. It is absurd because in light of our research findings it would be fallacious to expect that this system would make things fundamentally different for the accused. The defence bar would ascend to greater heights of professional power, taking control of cases as their property from the very beginning. Patterns in organizational co-operation and co-optation among the control agencies would continue, as would the accused's dependency. Trials would necessarily become even more ritualistic than they are now, and court appearances would have the same impact as they have presently (see chapter 6). Finally, and most fundamentally, it is absurd because the idea of the criminal process as an adversarial system based on due process is a myth.

The ideal of an adversarial system is that the accused is innocent until proven guilty, with the onus on the state to prove guilt according to fair (due process) procedures embodied in the principle of legality. While this creates the potential for combat as a case proceeds, there is nothing in legal theory or implicit in the rules of criminal procedure that would suggest that even the ideal function of the criminal process is full-blown adversarial conflict in every case (Feeley, 1979: 268). Indeed, *some* articulated ideals of due process and the rule of law do not have an identifiable empirical basis (Black, 1972: 1090). They are ideal standards set up, or made up, by researchers and legal commentators who attempt to use them to asses some particular aspect of some particular system of criminal control, and who thereby contribute to the rhetoric of that system.

With the vast majority of cases being disposed of by guilty pleas after out-of-court plea transactions, the general belief is that adversariness is on the decline and that we are moving closer in practice to the inquisitorial system of certain continental European countries (e.g. Heydebrand, 1977). These arguments ignore historical data showing that guilty plea decisions have been the norm since the formalization of criminal control at the beginning of the nineteenth century (see Friedmann, 1978; Heumann, 1978; Feeley, 1979). They also ignore the fact that until the relatively recent introduction of legal aid plans accused who were indigent pleaded guilty without the availability of a lawyer to suggest whether a challenge was possible, or worthwhile. In some cases the arguments offer no more than the tautology that good procedure protects the accused (and symbolically the rest of us) against the oppressiveness of bad procedure.

The criminal process is designed so that it does not give the accused more rights than would upset the operation of criminal control in the interests of the state. Nimmer's (1978) model of the 'hierarchy of importance' within the criminal process suggests reform proposals are most likely to be made, and are most likely to be successful when implemented, if they reflect the criteria of 'maximum general importance' which clearly serve the interests of administrators and agents and not the accused. The system, including the process of reform, will keep the accused relatively powerless, ensuring his dependency within the pre-trial process as well as during the time he serves his sentence to requalify as an (often still-dependent) citizen. The idea that legal provisions of due process will separate law from order and act as a bulwark against an oppressive order is a gloss; these provisions are integral to 'lawandorder.' 'Due process is *for* crime control' (McBarnet, 1976, 1979; see also Carlen, 1976: especially 42; Ericson, 1981: chapter 6). The legal system, not the rhetoric, *is* the law and operating procedures and the way the system operates forclose what formally might appear as choice until there is no choice for the accused. Placing the onus of proof on the crown does not mean much since the crown establishes the framework for the case to begin with in a way that makes it predictable that the accused will be unable to raise a reasonable doubt. The procedural law itself directs agents of law enforcement to treat differently various types of offences and offenders. As McBarnet (1979: 39) states, 'Legality requires equality; the law discriminates against the homeless and jobless. Legality requires that officials be governed by law; the law is based on post hoc decisions. Legality requires each case be judged on its own facts; the law makes previous convictions grounds for defining behaviour as an offence. Legality requires incriminating evidence as the basis for arrest and search; the law allows arrest and search in order to establish it. Legality embodies individual civil rights against public or state interests; the law makes state and the public interest a justification for ignoring civil rights ... Deviation from legality is institutionalized in the law itself.' Apparently the law can be developed to protect the citizen from everyone but the state.

The legal rules of due process are also enabling for crime control because of the nature and the use of rules within organizational contexts. It is a common feature of bureaucratic organizations that rules intended to influence the actions of agents are routinely absorbed by the agents to conform with their existing practices. Efforts to place legal limits on the discretion of school principals to suspend pupils are absorbed and the level of suspensions rises (Gaylin et al, 1978: 136ff); efforts to give legal rights to inmates in disciplinary hearings are accommodated within the existing manipulative practices of prison guards (Harvard Center for Criminal Justice, 1972); efforts to develop rules relating to the right of the accused to silence while in police custody are absorbed and made useful to the police (for reviews, see Greenawalt, 1974; Zander, 1978); efforts to review and control police search practices have no effect but to legitimate what the police wish to do (Ericson, 1981, 1982); procedures to allow judicial review of decisions by prosecutors to withdraw (*nolle*) charges result in invariable 'rubber-stamp' approval (Feeley, 1979: 129); efforts to increase penalties for those having firearms while engaging in major crimes result in these penalties being absorbed into the existing tariff for the accused's package of offences (Heumann and Loftin, 1979); efforts to have judges curtail their use of prison sentences by giving suspended sentences result in more persons being sent to prison because judges decide to use suspended sentences as an alternative among non-institutional dispositions (Thomas, 1974: 145); and so on. Procedural rules are for the *use* of law enforcement agents in their efforts at criminal control. All procedural rules must be understood in the organizational context of their use. Doing so allows us to appreciate how rules of procedure are designed and/or implemented on behalf of the forces of 'lawandorder,' and how the accused will inevitably experience the process as punishment.

As stated earlier, in a large number of the relatively petty cases that are dealt with at the lower court level, it is not worthwhile for the accused to invoke his rights even where they appear to exist. In these cases the greater availability of apparent rights is practically meaningless because they can mean greater costs to the accused than simply accepting a conviction and sentence: 'The pat solution to the problems of adjudication – to expand "due process" in the adversary system – might produce negligible results or even be counterproductive. Expanding due process might give the illusion of improvement even if there were none, and also contribute to a set of standards and controls so remote from the existing system that they would be inapplicable and meaningless in all but occasional cases' (Feeley, 1979: 277).

Introducing one or two 'rights,' like all liberal tinkering reforms, serves not as change but as an excuse for not changing. It is the same as altering the payout sequence on a slot machine. Players might believe that their chances for success have improved, but most still find that their luck eventually runs out. Of course this is what one would expect in a system where the house alters things only in a way that predictably ensures that the house always comes out ahead (cf Nimmer, 1978). Furthermore, a flood of rights will result in excessive legalism. Excessive legalism might lead people to mistake due process for substantive relief from tyranny. It will also fill the pockets of lawyers, while still leaving most accused– especially poor ones who cannot afford much legalism– with a feeling of emptiness (Friedenberg, 1980a: 7).

In addition to those who argue that we need a system of rights for accused, there are those who advocate that our primary concern must be the person's needs. The basis of their opposition to a primary emphasis on rights is articulated well by Rothman (1978: 94; also Rothman, 1980). A focus on rights can give legitimacy to neglect. It can also lead to greater professionalization and attendant control of the process by lawyers, a matter which must be examined in the context of contributions of other occupational groups. Furthermore, the greater the degree of adversarial conflict generated in the process, the greater the likelihood that the accused as the least powerful by definition will lose. 'How absurd to push for confrontation when all the advantages are on the other side' (Rothman, 1978: 94). Finally, courts do not have a consistent history of advancing the position of underdogs; other forums might serve their needs in a better way, if that is what one is interested in doing.

Realizing that even with a rigid code of formal procedures, legal officials are still able to be flexible (arbitrary) in their practices, and that such codes frequently legitimate selective practices, some argue that we should seek alternatives to the formal process. Conflicts should be taken out of the hands of self-interested professionals operating according to the inertia of bureaucratic organizations and put back in the hands of the accused and victims whose troubles are at stake (Christie, 1977). This can be done by complete 'decriminalization,' removing the behaviour in question from the substantive criminal law and dealing with it otherwise; or, in a compromise to those who continue to delude themselves into believing that a problem can be solved most adequately if it is subject to criminal law, by 'diversion' schemes which keep the criminal process as a back-up mechanism to other methods of resolving disputes.

In recent times decriminalization and diversion have been rationalized and justified by ideas from the labelling perspective (Schur, 1971, 1973; Ericson, 1975a, 1977), although the same ideas accompanied by similar policy recommendations have been with us for a very long time (Scull, 1977; Rothman, 1980). The basic argument is that we can at least do good by doing less harm than we have been doing with existing programs. In the last century the penitentiary was heralded as a giant step forward in the historical evolution from barbarism to civilization, in contrast to the neglect, torture, and executions that preceded it (Foucault, 1977; Ignatieff, 1978; Rothman, 1980). Today prison is the symbol of all that is wrong with the system, and we are urged to take another giant step forward by using it economically, saving our money and our souls through 'community' alternatives (Chan and Ericson, 1981). Beyond this, the argument goes, the criminal process itself may be bad, or at least inappropriate, as a means of dealing with citizens' troubles or troublesome citizens. We should save some types from the punishment of the process itself.

Within the present order of things it is difficult to conceive of complete decriminalization as a viable option. It would in theory yield a state of anarchy and in fact could not occur because we are interdependent, not independent. We are interdependent through bureaucratic forms of organization with a highly specialized division of labour which makes us dependent and not symbiotic. Anarchy exists at the extremes of independence or symbiosis, and we exist somewhere toward the middle (Black, 1976).

Even decriminalization of specific offences is difficult for people to conceive of because the criminal law bestows upon a behaviour a lasting sense of wrongdoing. The criminal law also helps people to think that the problem has been solved, or at least is being contained with the most potent mechanism available to the state. When there is talk about removing a particular offence from the criminal law, it is often an offence that is of a minor nature in the eyes of many citizens (e.g. possession of cannabis), or an offence that is already decriminalized *de facto* through non-enforcement (Feeley, 1979: 294). Decriminalization of offences that are rarely enforced will do little to alter the daily menu of the courts.

Furthermore, decriminalization often implies some other form of law (governmental social control), which is likely to perpetuate rather than alleviate the process. For example, since the report of the LeDain Commission (1973) on the non-medical use of drugs, there have been recurrent proposals to control possession of cannabis via the Food and Drug Act rather than the Narcotics Control Act, along with a possible lessening of the penalties. However, this is unlikely to change matters substantially because the penalties have already been routinized on a minor tariff scale (Erickson, 1980), and changing the act under which control is legitimated is unlikely to affect the organizational emphasis the police give to control (Ericson, 1982: chapter 6). Moreover, even if possession of cannabis were made as 'legal' as possession of alcoholic beverages, control under a cannabis control and licensing act would still bring under-age persons, bootleggers, and persons consuming in restricted places, etc, within the ambit of the police and courts in ways similar to the current operation of the Ontario Liquor Licence Act and Liquor Control Act (ibid). Indeed, as we shall emphasize shortly, easing the legal basis for control can have the effect of increasing the number subject to control.

The same view can be taken of efforts to keep offences as criminal matters, but to expedite their disposition through summary mechanisms. For example, Feeley (1979) and Solomon (1980) advocate the use of penal orders similar to those now employed in West German jurisdictions. The accused receives a summons with a specified penalty established by a prosecutor and possibly ratified by a judge, and can choose either to pay the penalty without going to court, or appear in court for a trial with a promise that the penalty upon conviction will not be any higher than the one on the original summons. Feeley (1979: 295–7) argues in favour of the system on the grounds that it would reduce the stigma for the accused, although at an earlier point he contends that most accused are lower-status people who do not experience stigma in the manner that middle-class academics think they do (ibid: 201–2). Feeley seems also to overlook his own data, which suggest that the accused in the Connecticut lower courts he studied receive summary justice anyway (*no* trials in 1,640 cases). Granted, in the system Feeley examined the accused are expected to appear in court and they could avoid this 'punishment' if they simply had to mail in a summons. However, a substantial minority (one-third) who did not appear in court were never convicted for not appearing if they were brought before the court again. Feeley also fails to discuss the potential for the increase and dispersal of control that may come from easing the enforcement task even more.

In Canada most recommendations and experiments have been of the 'diversion' variety. In the early 1970s diversion was the pet word and pat answer of the Law Reform Commission of Canada (1974, 1975) in its work on criminal law reform. Dozens of projects have been developed within the umbrella of this concept (for a list and summary see Solicitor General of Canada, 1979a). In particular cases, the court process is to be used only as a back-up mechanism to a diversion program set up by a staff who receive cases directly from the police. Part of the rhetoric of the programs is that 'the community' has resources and capabilities to deal with the culprit in more economical, effective, and humane ways than do the organizations that comprise the criminal process. In spite of a major sociological critique of the 'community' concept–showing how fallacious it is to expect a return to the days when human interdependence was close and approached symbiosis––those who promote diversion state a faith in the community as healer. Moreover, within the community certain institutions are promoted as being at the core of the effort, especially the nuclear family. The family is put up as *the* halfway house between the individual and society, part of the 'carceral continuum' (Donzelot, 1979). It is the family, and its integrating role in the community, that will 'make corrections work' (Waller, 1979).

We do not have the space to engage in a full-scale critique of diversion programs. The project of mounting a critique was already underway in the United States (e.g. Greenberg, 1975; Scull, 1977; Feeley and Sarat, 1980) even while diversion was being touted as *the* reform for Canada, and the critique has since been picked up in Canada (Ericson, 1977) and Britain (Cohen, 1979).

Advocates of diversion, in keeping with all reformers, have a bias in assuming that whatever exists is a 'bad thing.' For certain types of cases and culprits, the criminal process is a 'bad thing.' The view this encourages is that criminal control officials involved in these cases are automatons with no power: when their actions are always wrong, we must doubt the existence of choice and hence the existence of power. Of course, even without formal diversion programs criminal control agents *do* divert cases themselves and make choices, moral and otherwise, in doing so. There is much work to be done on the criteria of decision-making by criminal control agents before we consider whether they should be required to turn over their decision-making to other agents whose operations will be even more mysterious. Advocates of diversion wish to substitute informal procedure for the formalities of criminal procedure, but in most cases the criminal process, up to court appearances, operates with a degree of informality, and sometimes casualness. Diversion programs may formalize what is now relatively informal, starting at the point of the diversion hearing itself: 'Neighbourhood justice centers and community courts are currently gaining great favor ... They try to substitute informality, understanding, and the perspective of local community opinion for the formal, rigid procedures of the courts. But their proponents fail to realize that lower courts do *not* operate according to rigid formalities; they operate with flexibility and concern for substantive justice. Thus these new centers may end up doing in a time consuming and cumbersome manner what the lower courts do more quickly and more effectively' (Feeley, 1979: 293–4).

Another fundamental critique is that diversion programs may not only lead to more cumbersome procedure, but may also increase the number of persons subject to control and even the intensity of control. As stated previously, advocates of diversion are biased in claiming that the criminal process is in some cases a bad thing. However, critics of diversion are also biased in implying that more control by diversion project staff is necessarily a bad thing. Advocates of diversion agree at least that state agents other than the traditional agents of the criminal process should be in control; critics disagree with this, but they rarely go on to suggest alternatives and they thus lend support to those who advocate models of due process and legality *within* the criminal process. It may be that critics do not come up with alternatives to the traditional agents because they know that diversion usually gives more control to the traditional agents as well as adding new agents (Feeley and Sarat, 1980).

There is now a wealth of evidence that diversion programs can expand the numbers under control and intensify the nature of control. When one member of a family is arrested and diverted into a program, other members of the family can be compelled to participate and be subject to further penalty if they do not conform (Blomberg, 1977; Donzelot, 1979: especially 215). Diversion has come to mean 'referral to' instead of 'diversion from,' with the ironic effect of increasing costs, caseloads, and the eventual involvement of the criminal control prosecution system against defaulters (Klein, 1976; see also Bohnstedt, 1978; Feeley, 1979: especially 233–4). This much could have been gleaned from the historical record, saving a lot of bother for both practitioners and for the researchers trying to convince them (see especially Foucault, 1977; Donzelot, 1979; Rothman, 1980).

One type of system of control explains another. Conditions created in one system routinely generate clients for another system (cf Friedenberg, 1975; Black, 1976). Control systems are interdependent, and from the viewpoint of their general mandate to order and improve the population and to put people into working order it does not matter much how they get their cases as long as they have an ample supply to work on. Despite the rhetoric, the first item on all of their agendas is regulation, not relief, and this means that they will devise, implement, and perpetuate policies of convenience over matters of conscience (Rothman, 1980). Ultimately diversion programs along with other reforms are more about wider social processes, including the occupational interests of various control agents and their efforts to control each other, than about the people they bring within their ambit. *The* question concerns control of the process, not what the process is supposed to do. Who are we to trust with the reproduction of order? social workers? police officers? psychiatrists? lawyers? teachers? judges? parents? probation officers? any of the above? all of the above? none of the above?

Prospects for Change

> We have hanged thieves, chopped off their right hands, used branding, stocks, pillory, transportation, penal servitude, imprisonment, whipping, fines, proba-
> tion, and discharge, absolute or conditional. And that is not a complete list.
> Thieving continues.
> R. Jackson, *Enforcing the Law* (1967): 213

It is a curious thing that no matter what reform measures are talked about or implemented, the phenomenon of crime and an apparatus of control are perpetuated. This leads one to suspect that reform talk and policies are about something other than eradication. It also leads one to suspect that beyond the rhetoric there may not be much difference between due process-adversarial models and correctionalist models. They are both for crime control. All agents of the law (governmental social control) are in the same business of classifying, containing, and resocializing selected members of the social body who exhibit dangerous energies. The particular governmental agency and type of sanctions to be used for specific tasks in this project are a matter for dispute among professional and occupational groups. The relative role and influence of these groups do change with reform efforts, while the types of persons subject to control and their position of dependency remain relatively static.

The system of criminal control is able to use the rhetoric of reform to insulate itself from substantive change in relation to those it processes. A range of theories, justifications, or excuses can be called upon by agents of the system to account for what they do with the case or issue at hand. Regardless of the organizational interests in dealing with a case in a particular way, the method can be justified in terms acceptable to the organization, and in terms of a range of socially acceptable theories about crime and its control. The public can be made content with a display that something is being done, but rarely want to know what is being done. They are left to conclude that there must be 'criminals,' since so many of them are being dealt with by the courts every day.

The need for a display of doing something leaves the way open for perpetual chatter about reform, and for reform rhetoric to become an integral part of the process of criminal control. One of the functions of all control agencies is to engage in reform rhetoric that mystifies and misleads. They 'mislead by their very existence. Indeed, it is their social *function* to mislead, just as a neurotic ritual serves to spare an individual unbearable insights even as it reveals what is going on to an observer with a less vested interest in misunderstanding it' (Friedenberg, 1975: 92).

The rhetoric of reform takes into account three elements: costs (in terms of resources economically derived), the effectiveness of various alternatives, and the humaneness of various alternatives. The ideal combination of these elements represents the holy trinity of reform. These elements have framed the discourse of reform for more than a century (Foucault, 1977; Scull, 1977; Ignatieff, 1978; Rothman, 1980), although in recent years the arguments have been bolstered by a burgeoning cadre of criminologists who, often under the guise of liberation for the dependant, provide the agencies with further rationalizations.

As Rothman (1980) argues, reform is no more than the favourite program of a particular interest group at a particular historical juncture. The rhetoric of a reform proposal– that it is less expensive, works better, and is less offensive to the moral sensibilities of the time– serves to allay the conscience of control agents and any members of the public who may also be interested, while perpetuating practices that are convenient for agents in their administration of the system. Moreover, once they are implemented under the protective veil of the rhetoric, the programs continue even in face of massive evidence of their failure. Regardless of how many probationers recidivate, probation is still useful as a lever for the prosecution in plea transactions, and as an additional power in the hands of judges. Regardless of how many parolees recidivate, or how much parole mechanisms increase the length of sentence, or how oppressive parole is for the parolee in terms of uncertainty, parole remains useful as a disciplinary control device to prison administrators and as a regulator of numbers in prison. Regardless of how token an educational program in prison might be, it is useful as a device to take care of the excess labour pool who cannot be put to work elsewhere in the institution. And so on. Things seen as major issues and as exciting reforms by government policy advisers and some academics are translated into mechanisms of convenience by control agents and relegated to their pragmatically appropriate place within the agents' scheme of things.

The translation process by which reforms become used as matters of administrative convenience is eased because policy-makers and drafters of legislation collaborate in mystifying what the reform is really intended to do. This is particularly evident if one examines the many misnomers which permeate and support the system. A few examples illustrate the point. We have a Bail Reform Act which, at least according to some media accounts and police protests, gives the accused greater rights for release from police custody. In fact the act directs the police to discriminate in terms of specific criteria of offenders (e.g. criminal record, place of residence) and to seek custody on grounds of *potential* danger. The proper name (and one used in other jurisdictions) is 'The Preventive Detention Act.' We have a Protection of Privacy Act which makes provisions for the police to *invade* the privacy of citizens via wiretapping. We have an 'insanity defence,' but the word 'defence' is misused because the accused in practice gives up any defence by pleading insanity and thereby puts himself at the mercy of a prolonged period in custody at the lieutenant-governor's pleasure. We talk about plea 'bargaining,' although usually what this refers to is discussions among lawyers and control agents which may or may not broach the topic of plea, or result in an agreement, and which is often not seen by the defence as a 'bargain' (see chapters 4 and 5). We talk about guarantees of rights for the accused within an adversarial system, but the accused is frequently 'punished' if he exercises his rights' options (Feeley, 1979), or the rights are removed entirely (McBarnet, 1981: 38), and even if he does go to the trouble and is eventually found not guilty he receives no compensation for the trouble he has been put to by the state. We talk about 'treatment' for the 'criminal' ailments of the accused, but upon closer scrutiny treatment turns out to be punishment without sensitivity to justice or proportion. We call the accused a defendant when his position in the criminal process is as a dependant.

Protected in so many ways by the rhetoric, agents of criminal control can come to see justice in terms of justifications. They can take an action which is organizationally appropriate with the assurance that there is some theorizing, some rule, some rhetoric, to justify it. Beyond this, the agents have at their disposal the common organizational rhetoric of 'resource problems' which can be used to explain away their divergence from what others might expect of them (cf Drucker, 1973). In the face of massive expansion of police (Chan and Ericson, 1981; Solicitor General of Canada, 1979), and evidence that increases in police expenditure and size are translated into increases in the rate of indictable convictions (cf McDonald, 1976: 194), the police call for more resources to reduce the rate of crime (e.g. Toronto *Sun*, 25 June 1980, quoting the head of the Ontario Association of Chiefs of Police). In spite of evidence that apparent increased caseload pressures on courts do not explain high rates of guilty pleas and the process of plea transaction itself (Heumann, 1978; Feeley, 1979), caseload pressure is referred to as a reason for giving less attention to cases than some might desire, or deserve (e.g. Toronto *Globe and Mail*, 11 April 1977: 5; Toronto *Globe and Mail*, 1 September 1978: 92).

While they are quite willing to treat accused persons *as if* they have free will and therefore as responsible for their actions, agents sometimes slip into a very deterministic view of their own actions. In blaming workload, inadequate funding, and lack of staff, agents have a very elastic justification to cover any apparent deficiencies. It allows them simultaneously to displace responsibility and achieve more resources, as if what they are doing now is satisfactory except for the 'fact' that more of the same is needed to reach perfection. Confident that the public views them as being successful at doing whatever it is they have always been doing, they can also ask, 'If we don't do it, who will?' However, in a period of many professional agencies in competition for slices of the control business, it is better not to ask this question too loudly or too often in case some other agency comes up with an alternative that appears more economical, effective, and humane.

The proliferation of occupational groups with an interest in the business of crime control means that there is considerable competition and conflict concerning control of the process itself. Psychiatrists, social workers, and other 'specialists of the invisible' (Donzelot, 1979) have entered the business and compete for the resources of law enforcement and the 'concessions' trade associated with it. 'Criminologists' also participate in this enterprise. A recent development is the formation of 'The Canadian Association of Professional Criminologists.' This association publishes a magazine called *Panopticon*, the first issue of which contained a special tribute to Jeremy Bentham as a pioneer in criminology. In titling the magazine and giving testimony to Bentham, the association is either oblivious to the message of Foucault (1977), or is being admirably forthright and honest about the purpose of the enterprise.

No matter what else might be involved, all reform alternatives include an added role for some group of professionals. This is *the* axiom of reform. To repeat a point made earlier, change comes in the form of which professional group is doing the controlling, not in the position of those subject to control.

In industrialized societies professionalization has become *the* mode of buying into the control business. Even those bodies which have traditionally had control of the process, especially the police, have had to adopt the trappings of professionalism in order to sustain their control. Professionals take an increasingly active role not only in providing an expert service, but also in defining the needs of those being serviced (for recent data concerning the medical profession, see Naylor, 1981). This comes about through subtle selling techniques over a period of time, so that the 'client' as consumer changes preferences and replaces one form of dependency with another, e.g. nineteenth-century women allied with medical doctors, improving their power position in the family while becoming dependent on the medical profession (Lasch, 1980). It can also come about through more coercive practices. As Friedenberg (1975) observes, many agents of the law have to 'catch' their clients before they can administer 'help' to them. Regardless of the technique and how it is legitimated, professional involvement by definition means that the client's control of the matter is given up. The client gives up his usage rights in the hope of obtaining benefit rights (Coleman, 1973). In the sphere of crime control, the agents take over citizen conflicts and make them their organizational property, working to define the conflict out of the matter according to their own professional interests.

While ideology can be read into any professional policies and practices, professional groups are not *directly* in the business of ideological work. Their primary interests are pragmatic: displaying competence and thereby securing resources that serve their own interest. In this sense they are as parasitical as the persons they work on. They both depend upon the generosity of the welfare state to dole out money from the services' side of the gross national product. While selling themselves as 'client savers,' they are also saving themselves. In consequence, professionals sell themselves in terms of their ability to manage particular troubles and crisis, not in terms of ideology. It matters little if crime is explained by political oppression or by the absence of firm political control (a slackening of 'lawandorder'). Professionals will be there to do their duty, easily accommodating to shifts in political and journalistic fashion (cf Lasch, 1980).

With the burgeoning of professional bureaucracies involved in the criminal control business, a picture emerges of organizations that are 'loosely coupled' (on this concept, see March and Olsen, 1976; Meyer and Rowan, 1977). The shifting patterns of relationships and influence among the organizations make it difficult to specify the connection among intentions, actions, and outcomes. This creates problems for evaluating their contributions, for judging which group has the most substantial influence in particular areas and how this is accomplished. The control bureaucracies thereby seem to have a collective degree of autonomy from outside influence and are left to compete among themselves using various strategies and tactics of interorganizational and intraorganizational control. This is a model of conflict, albeit petty conflict among self-interested professionals.

This model is useful for viewing the day-to-day transactions of criminal control agents (Manning, 1980), for aggregating data on the products of their labours (Hagan et al, 1979; Hagan and Albonetti, 1980), and for understanding historically how control bureaucracies reproduce their institutional hegemony (Rothman, 1980). However, it seems evident that their transactions, petty conflicts, and shifts in power do not take place in a pluralistic vacuum, however much analysts who believe in pluralism wish they did. It is arguable that a wider structure and attendant social processes frame the limits of their conflict (cf Scull, 1981) and ensure that they are all, after all, involved in the same project. The conflict is over the means of reproduction, not over what is being reproduced.

The core values of the structure include pluralism and individualism. These values have increasingly permeated the organizations of criminal control, and indeed all forms of state control, preserving a sense of individuality and personal initiative while legitimating professional intervention and supervision. Criminal problems are viewed as individual problems, requiring individually tailored measures to correct them. The whole business of selecting the cloth with the proper label, cutting it up, and then sewing it back together to suit the offender's apparent new image is called 'corrections.' What is required from the very beginning of this task, and as it continues and is repeated when the old suit wears thin, is maximal discretion for all the specialized suit-makers. 'Discretion is indispensable to any legal system in which individualization plays a significant part' (Thomas, 1974: 139; see also Davis, 1969). A central element of reform policies in this century has been and continues to be discretion for the professional or occupational group vying to implement it: 'All Progressive programmes assumed one outstanding feature: *they required discretionary responses to each case*' (Rothman, 1980: 6, emphasis in original). Equipped with discretion backed up by the value of individualization, control agents can hardly go wrong. Differential selection of citizens according to citizen characteristics and other individual circumstances of the case is not regarded as 'extra-legal' at all and certainly does not constitute discrimination. Control agents are both legally and organizationally directed to act in this way, and they simply follow suit.

The translation of individualization into the discretion of control agents is most obvious, and has been most discussed, in the areas where the correctionalist-progressive model has appeared to be the most triumphant, e.g. dealing with the mentally ill, the juvenile justice system, and family crisis intervention. However, it has increasingly permeated the practices of agents processing accused persons through the adult criminal courts. The agents of the courts establish and use their own tariff to reach an outcome that both satisfies their sense of justice and is justifiable organizationally. After chatting and obtaining agreement *among one another*, they are free to pick and choose because the system enables them to do so through a wide range of officially accepted justifications to legitimate what they want.

Feeley (1979: especially 284–6) argues that the lower criminal courts for adults operate in a manner 'strongly related to the practices and theory of juvenile courts.' In spite of all the formality in court, most convictions are sealed and sentences are made predictable during informal encounters out of court. The practice of plea transactions out of court is entirely in keeping with the emphasis on individualization that has permeated the entire criminal control system. It is legitimate for the defence lawyer, police, and crown attorney to discuss what the accused deserves (or needs) in terms of who he is, has been, or may become. The pre-trial process ensures that the accused's confession to the police, and confirmation of this confession in pleading guilty, are seen not as a violation of a right against self-incrimination and a right to a trial, but as the first necessary step toward 'rehabilitation,' and is rewarded as such.

Some might feel reassured that conflicts among professional groups in the control business at least lead them to do some policing of each other. In addition civil servants, academics, and journalists occasionally venture far enough into the operation of the criminal process to raise some important questions about what is and is not going on. Increased research attention to 'plea bargaining' and related aspects of the pre-trial process is in keeping with research attention to institutional and community-based corrections. Perhaps the proper corrections are not taking place, or are taking place improperly. Perhaps individualization has resulted in too much power in the hands of one group from whom we want to take it away and give to someone else. Note however that the vigilance over professional activity does not go farther than suspecting everything in practice, while justifying everything in theory. The critique does not go any farther because of a pragmatic interest in not biting the hand that feeds.

While the criminal control occupations have enhanced their power through the societal value placed on individualism and all it entails, their work is of course directed at producing anything but unique individuals. They are in the business of inducing and producing conformity. They are out to make everyone like the 'middle Canadian' in theory and like the 'working Canadian' in practice. Above all, the job is to classify, contain, and resocialize errant members so that they are put into working order, literally. The correctionalist approach and the due process-adversarial approach are simply different models for achieving the same result. There is no imperative to use the criminal law in much of this activity. Diversion to agents of other law (governmental social control) might do just as well, or even better administratively speaking because criminal law does tend to be bothersome with all of its form. Choosing one model or the other, or some combination, makes some difference in terms of which professional groups will do the job, but not in the coercive effect of the means they employ, not in the ends they pursue, and not in the dependent position of those they work on.

In other words any reordering of justice has been and continues to be a matter of tinkering with the machinery of the loosely coupled organizations that constitute the apparatus of control, not a matter of altering the wider social order of things. As Foucault (1977, 1979) and Donzelot (1979) argue, the criminal control system ('the judicial') serves as the model for all government control systems standing at preceding points in the 'carceral continuum.' Educationalists, social workers, psychiatrists, health care specialists, and others involved in the modern apparatus of resocialization employ models based upon the judicial, and use the criminal control alternative as a threat or as a back-up sanction if their own efforts are unproductive. Everyone is in the business of policing, defined in terms of its original meaning as all methods for improving the human stock of the nation in order to strengthen the state. In this task, agents of criminal control are guarantors and executors of the entire apparatus on behalf of other agents.

This system is designed to do everything but eliminate the person. Since there is no intention of eliminating the person, there is no prospect for eliminating his behaviour, including that which may be labelled criminal. Sanctions – the hard core of social inequality (Dahrendorf, 1961) – are employed to label, distribute, and use the person in a more general economy of power (cf Chan and Ericson, 1981). The person is made useful both as a cog and as a product of the system, labouring for the system and producing signs of its features (Foucault, 1977). This was embodied in the vision of the reformers who established the penitentiary (Ignatieff, 1978), carried on in reformed institutions such as the prison described by Teddy Roosevelt as 'a manufactory of citizens' (Rothman, 1980: 266), and adopted as the model for all governmental efforts at containment and improvement of the population (Foucault, 1977, 1979; Donzelot, 1979).

The dependent person learns to labour for capital, which includes establishing his own self-sufficiency. He is taught to fish in a stocked pond rather than be provided with fish, in the hope that the compulsion to do so will eventually come internally. When the fisherman falls asleep out of the boredom of it all, or seeks escape to serve other personal needs, or uses forbidden lures, or casts too big a net, the criminal sanction end of the carceral continuum is threatened or used to add just a measure of external compulsion to what he is supposed to be doing for his own 'needs.' If the person eventually starves in spite of all the state's efforts, he is deemed to have eliminated himself. The refusal of the system to accept that it is responsible for eliminating someone is one reason why it continually appears constipated.

During the processing of his case, the accused is reminded about just how dependent he is. In receiving his sentence he is coercively taught, and used to teach others, the economy of a power relation. If he does not internalize the lesson he can expect to be repeatedly brought into the remedial cycle for further doses of aversion therapy.

Chatter about whether this therapy works, or is costly, or is humane misses a fundamental point. The system is not motivated by profit, but by the economy of a power relation (Foucault, 1977). 'The enterprise justifies itself:

there is hardly any point in asking about "success"–this is not the object of the exercise' (Cohen, 1979a: 358). In terms of the dependent position of the accused at the bottom end of the criminal control system–which simply mirrors his position in society's scheme of things–there is no contradiction between efforts at surveillance/custody and efforts at rehabilitation, and no contradiction between rigid rule/due process/adversarial and progres- sive/correctionalist efforts. All of these are used singly or in combination in the everyday justification of practices, allowing agents of control to make what they can out of the accused and his case. As discussed earlier, even the California system of 'uniform sentencing,' a relatively 'fixed' system of formal rules governing the process, still allows for specific criteria of the offender to be used in aggravation or mitigation. It simply shifts the locus of power among agents, as do all reform efforts. In *any* system the accused is ordered to do what others say is best for him and is used to reproduce the order of things.

Of course one should not expect otherwise. To call for a reordering of justice from the viewpoint of the accused would be to deny the very raison d'être of the system and the society it represents. Who would support giving more to accused persons when we do not give more to other dependants who have managed to stay respectable? Certainly not other dependants and those close to being in their state. Ever since the inventions of Bentham, persons respectable but dependent or nearly so have been led to believe that the only thing worse than dependency is death. These are the people whose idea of an escape from the dull routines of life is to go for one week to a holiday camp where the penalty of time, place, and activity is reproduced in exacting detail. These are the people who believe that a protest against government consists of debate over the raising, or lowering, of the age of eligibility for legal consump- tion of alcoholic beverages. These are the people who fail to appreciate that retributively condemning the offender does not constitute compassion for the victim. People who slave to keep just out of the reach of dependency (cf Gaylin et al, 1978, especially the discussion by Marcus on Dickens's novel *Our Mutual Friend*), and who condemn those who appear to have given up the struggle, however temporarily, are one of the most important constituents of state power. As Friedenberg (1975: 129) comments:

> Such social mechanisms as these insure that as one descends the socioeconomic
> scale the prevalence of people who are obliged to justify their own alienation by
> equating obedience and conformity with maturity and what they call a sense of
> responsibility will increase. So will their vehemence in denouncing as violence
> resistance to the State and responsiveness to one's own conscience, and
> denouncing as intolerably libertine spontaneity in life-style. This relationship
> holds true all the way to the bottom of the socioeconomic scale. At the bottom
> are convicted and imprisoned felons who, of all people, have experience of the

State's incomparable capacity for cruelty and violence and the strongest possible reasons to reject its value judgements about themselves, but nevertheless have long been notoriously patriotic, hostile to political prisoners and, especially, to sex offenders, and tightly conventional in their attitudes toward the society that is, as they well know, destroying them.

Beyond the way in which they are used *for* state power (cf Wolin, 1980), these people are kept effectively powerless within the political process. Similar to their consumer perspective with regard to material goods, they adopt a consumer perspective to the various agencies of the welfare state. Whatever their ailments– physical, emotional, criminal, mental–they are dependent upon the service professionals, whose job is to see through them, prior to seeing them through. This consumer perspective on government and its services further removes the citizenry from participation in government (Lasch, 1980), contributing to the docility that is so valued in a system professing first and foremost peace, order, and good government.

Directions for Further Enquiry

There is growing recognition that the process by which persons are made dependent in the criminal control system is interconnected with the process by which persons are made dependent in the mental health control system, the welfare control system, and the other areas of governmental social control. These control systems collectively constitute a major force of interdependency, and source of dependency, in our society.

Some observers conceive of this control apparatus in monolithic terms. This conception has historical routes in the visions of reformers during the industrial revolution. They saw the machine-like qualities of the factory as an ideal form for the penitentiary, which in turn was useful as a model for other forms of governmental social control (see generally Ignatieff, 1978). As Marcus (1978: 52) relates regarding the visions of Bentham: '[He] saw that his all-purpose building, the Panopticon, originally planned as a penitentiary, could do good service as a workhouse [by which the convict and the pauper became interchangeable]. Bentham was against abolition, but he was for radical institutional reform, systematical and on a national scale. He proposed an analytical division of the whole country; as an ideal, five hundred great workhouses would be built, each 10 2/3 miles apart, so that no man would be more than half a day's march from one. Economy of scale would thus make for great savings. As for questions of settlement, he proposed that all infants be branded, painlessly and indelibly, with name, place, and date of birth; hence identification for settlement and a score of other useful purposes would be easily ensured.'

Foucault (1977) uses an analogy with the control system set up to contain the plague to emphasize his view that we have been placed increasingly under a monolithic 'social quarantine.' He emphasizes also how the penitentiary has become *the* model for governmental social control, creating a 'carceral city' (see also Donzelot, 1979; Cohen, 1979a). Governmental social control has become an integrated, routinized part of everyday existence, woven like invisible thread into the social fabric. Substantial numbers of people make their living as 'tailors' in this business, including doctors, policemen, social workers, parents, researchers, private security agents, teachers, and, yes, university personnel (e.g. Ku and Blew, 1977).

As emphasized in the last section, the quest is for an inoffensive, docile, and useful social body produced through the ceaseless refinement of techniques for standardization and predictability. That liberty may be compromised or lost in this project is a matter of concern for a token few of the technicians, but this concern is a little too removed from the pragmatic thinking of most to retard the ceaseless thrust toward making every body the same.

The research arm of the apparatus typically adopts similar attitudes, apparently in the interests of science but obviously in the interests of control. For example, wishing to obtain a good assessment of whether alcoholics were responsive to 'treatment,' researchers in one project had subjects subject themselves to random breathalyser checks in their homes (Hunt and Azrin, 1973; for a general appreciation of this research mentality, see British Journal of Criminology, 1979; Ross and Gendreau, 1980). Research and commentary by a few concerned citizens occasionally address the effects of all this on the people concerned. The dehumanizing effects on the accused and other recipients of coercive governmental social control are becoming well documented. The dehumanizing effects on the agents, whose mundane task it is to process fellow humans according to alienating bureaucratic criteria and form, is less well documented and needs to be appreciated more.

In terms of analytical focus and topics of concern, the way forward for research has become obvious. Analytically we must continue attempts to bridge the gap between what takes place in the daily transactions within the control apparatus and the structures which frame the limits of those transactions. This can be accomplished by a thorough analysis of the legal and other rules which are part of the reality of control and how these are translated into the actions of control agents. It can also be accomplished by examining, as we have done, the actors' viewpoints and structural considerations as they are used to constitute action. Doing so allows one to appreciate how apparently tenuous and transitory transactions are the building blocks for the structures that come to appear as 'givens,' 'the system,' 'the natural order of things,' and which in turn bear upon the transactions (cf Gerson, 1976; Strauss, 1978; Foucault, 1980). The study of the everyday transactions which make up the control network obviously entails emphasis upon observational methods and organizational analysis. The study of the structures reproduced from these transactions requires an analysis of the 'macro' level of organizations and the 'macro' level of the relationships among the organizations that constitute an institution and the relationships among institutions. This requires comparative analysis of contemporary structures, as well as social historical analysis.

The topics for study must go beyond the narrow appreciation that can be gleaned from studying one type of control agency in one place at one time. An understanding and appreciation of any particular control system can come best from comparing it with other types of control systems at other times in other places. As Cohen (1979a: 340) argues, studies of single control agencies 'are often curiously fragmented, abstracted from the density of urban life in which social control is embedded. It is not so much that these agencies often have no history: they also have little sense of place. They need locating in physical space of the city, but more important in the overall social space: the master patterns of social control, the network of other institutions such as school and family, and broader trends in welfare and social services, bureaucracies and professions.'

Systems of criminal law, mental health, and welfare control can be studied as they intersect with non-governmental forms of social control. In this connection, some of the insights of Black (1976) may be helpful. Black offers the proposition that 'law varies inversely with other social control,' and provides a schema of four styles of social control (penal, compensatory, therapeutic, and conciliatory) in terms of five key elements (the standard, the problem, initiation of case, identity of deviant, solution) (ibid: 5). This model appears useful in developing a comparative map of agency control styles. In terms of historical research, one could trace shifts in the styles for controlling different types of troubles, and also look for the ascendancy of a particular style at a particular time and for convergence among the styles. For example, there appears to be overlap among the penal, compensatory, therapeutic, and conciliatory styles in today's criminal control system.

The possibilities for research are many and have only begun to be articulated and explored (e.g. Black, 1976; Foucault, 1977; Scull, 1977, 1979; Gaylin et al, 1978; Donzelot, 1979; Rothman, 1980). As criminologists, we have much to learn from the comparative study of control systems. A few examples suggest the range of enquiry possible. Many times more people are subject to non-criminal incarceration under the state's powers of benevolent treatment than are subject to criminal incarceration (Kittrie, 1971: 6–7). A mixture of criminal and civil procedures penalize the (usually lower-status) person who cheats the Unemployment Insurance Commission much more than the (usually higher-status) person who cheats the Department of National Revenue (Hasson, 1980). The Canadian government comes close to violating its own criminal law on property by using civil process to argue against Inuit land claims 'on the grounds that the Inuit had no conception of property rights and private property and therefore have no basis for a claim that can be pressed in Canadian courts' (Friedenberg, 1980a: 158). The same progressive-correctionalist movement that altered procedures for criminal control also influenced the control of juveniles and the mentally ill (Rothman, 1980) and additionally was a basis for the women's movement as it sought reform in the control of the family and contributed to the role of the family in state control efforts (Degler, 1979; Donzelot; 1979; Lasch, 1980). These are only a few of the mechanisms and processes that are open for exploration in the comparative study of social control.

This is an emergent field for enquiry that can take us well beyond the modest contribution of our study, and similar studies. We, along with others, have at least begun the process of making visible the ordering of relations producing dependency in one sphere of life. Moreover, in this chapter we have indicated that new sensibilities about social control, which lead to new reform rhetoric and eventual tinkering with the practices, typically hide the old. Mental hospitals and prisons serve as functional equivalents to the poor laws. Diversion programs divert only in the sense of drawing attention away from the coercion they entail or they simply signal neglect. A call for the return to adversarial rights for the accused misses the point that they never had many, if any, in practice, and that in practice the rights of the accused are primarily a means of professional privilege. Moreover, new sensibilities tend to hide the reality that no matter what the rhetoric and the practices it justifies, the accused and his similarly situated fellow citizens will continue to be kept in place as dependants. This will be so whether they are subject to the ordering of justice or to any of the other mechanisms geared to the social ordering of the population.

Notes

CHAPTER ONE: The Ordering of Justice

1 The research design is outlined in the final section of this chapter.
2 Further details of this case based upon police observation data are presented in Ericson (1981). As described in Ericson (1981: chapter 3), the researcher observing the detectives who were assigned this case noted that the detectives undertook 23 hours of continuous investigation of the suspect after he was turned over to them by the arresting uniformed officer. In this period the accused was interrogated by the detectives for one-half hour, then for a further 40 minutes after he confessed to the initial attempt rape offence. He was then interrogated by a detective sergeant, and the two detectives alternating, for one and one-half hours. The accused was then placed in a holding cell for four hours, after which there was a further six hours of interrogation involving different combinations of a detective sergeant, the detectives assigned the case, and a policewoman. Following this, there was a one-hour gap before a different detective sergeant took up the interrogation. All of these interrogations after the initial confession were directed at confessions to the outstanding indecent assault (female) occurrences, but the accused did not confess to these and was not charged in relation to them.
3 The lawyer's opinion is supported by some research evidence. Rosenhan (1973) demonstrates that a psychiatric patient's diagnosis is fundamentally shaped by the environment and contexts in which diagnosticians observe him. Babigan et al (1965) report that in-patient settings dispose clinicians toward a diagnosis of psychosis. For a general review of literature on the reliability and validity of forensic psychiatric work, see Ennis and Litwack (1974).
4 Compare the rules of penitentiaries in the mid-1800s under the Auburn system: 'Convicts are to yield perfect obedience and submission to their keepers. They are to labor diligently and preserve unbroken silence. They must not exchange a word with one another under any pretense whatever, nor communicate with one another, nor with anyone else, by writing. They must not exchange looks, wink, laugh, nod or gesticulate to each other, nor shall they make use of any signs, except such as necessary to explain their wants to the warders. They must approach their keepers in the most respectful manner, and be brief in their communications. They are not to speak to, or address, their keepers on any subject but such as related to their work, duty, or wants [Punishment for infractions of these and many other rules included solitary confinement and public whippings.]' (Inspectors of the Provincial Penitentiary, *Rules and Regulations respecting Discipline and Policy* Statute 4

Wm ɪᴠ ch 37, quoted in Beattie [1977]). For accounts and analyses of contemporary systems of prison rules, see Zellick (1980), Feltman (1981).

5 The term 'versions of the truth' indicates that the ascription of truth value is relative. It does not necessarily entail lying. What stands for truth for a particular actor is a result of his interpretations and accounts of events. Although there may be consensus among some actors as to the validity of a particular version, other versions must be treated as valid since they are products of different interpretive schemas. The version of truth which becomes dominant is especially dependent on the relative power possessed by the particular actor or organization that produces it.

6 Perhaps the earliest efforts in Canada to consider the offender's perspective were those associated with commissions of inquiry into prison conditions. However, the offender's views were not taken seriously by some officials. For example, in their response to prisoners' accounts of prison life contained in the report of the *Royal Commission to Investigate the State and Management of the Kingston Penitentiary* (1913), the inspectors of penitentiaries stated: 'In the absence of reliable evidence, the scum of Canadian criminality and even insane convicts were called, their sworn "evidence" recorded and published in the local press as facts. The publication of these scurrilous, false and filthy statements was continued for days and weeks under the caption of "Startling Revelations", "Disgusting Disclosures", "Hell in a Hollow", and other hysterical headlines, with the obvious intention of discrediting the institution and injuring the "reputation of officials" ' (Canada *Report of the Inspectors of Penitentiaries for the Fiscal Year Ended March 31, 1914*, Sessional Paper No. 34, Ottawa: King's Printer, 1915; cited by Whittingham [1981: 163]).

7 A detailed description of the research design for the detective study is contained in Ericson (1981), and for the patrol study in Ericson (1982).

8 The 'appreciative focus' is associated with sociological ethnography, especially in the Chicago and California traditions of symbolic interactionism. General references to this orientation include Blumer (1969: especially chapter 1); Matza (1969); Rock (1979). Many of the methodological points made by Glaser and Strauss (1967) are also relevant.

We distinguish our work from that of Bottoms and McClean (1976), who claim to be taking an appreciative stance but end up treating many issues, rules, rhetoric, and so on as unproblematic. This takes them away from appreciating the accused's perspective and position as dependant rather than defendant (see the critique of Bottoms and McClean in McBarnet [1977]).

9 Indeed, in addressing the question of the validity of the accused's version, Klein (1976: 143) points out: 'Offenders have no more of a vested interest in making the system of negotiated justice look bad than do those who are expected, if not required, to espouse the official morality have in making the system look good. With the above in mind, we shall tentatively accept the proposition that the offender's perception of the system is no more inaccurate that the perceptions of others who operate within the system.'

10 The inferior status of the accused is often mirrored in the writings of criminologists. For example, Grosman (1969: 407) states: 'The two individuals who remain with a case from beginning to end are the detective in charge of investigation and the defence counsel.' This statement, while being incorrect (the lawyer is rarely present at the beginning at the police station and the detective is usually not present at the end of the sentencing of the accused), reflects by omission the accused's position in the world of crime control and social science.

11 The other books pertain to the work of patrol police (Ericson, 1982), detectives (Ericson, 1981), lawyers (Macfarlane, 1982), and crown attorneys (Wilkins, 1982).

12 As Fromm (1965: 125) observes, 'We forget that, although freedom of speech constitutes an important victory in the battle against *old* restraints, modern man is in a position where much of what "he" thinks and says are the things that everybody else thinks and says; that

he has not acquired the ability to think originally – that is, for himself – which alone gives meaning to his claim that nobody can interfere with the expression of his thoughts.'

CHAPTER TWO: Police Orders

1 Criminal Code sec 29 requires a police officer to tell a suspect when he is under arrest and to state the reasons for arrest. However, an arrest is still held to occur even if no verbal statement is given and even when a person is not physically taken hold of by a police officer, if the party generally submits to the power of the police officer. For a legal analysis see Freedman and Stenning (1977); for an empirical analysis see Ericson (1981, 1982).
2 Cf *R*. v *DeClercq* (1966) 2 CCC 190.
3 The Canadian Bill of Rights (1960 sec 2) provides that 'No law of Canada shall be construed or applied so as to ... deprive a person who has been arrested or detained ... of the right to retain and instruct counsel without delay.' It is noteworthy that the Bill of Rights has no overriding legal authority and has never been used to override a criminal statute.
4 For a recent discussion of the issues regarding third-party access in Britain, see McBarnet (1981: 61 – 7). Wald et al (1967: 1557) found that suspects were rarely denied a third-party call, while Baldwin and McConville (1977: 68) state that the police denied six out of every seven requests made by their respondents. In our police observational studies (Ericson, 1981: chapter 6; Ericson, 1982: chapter 6), we found that most suspects did not make third-party requests, and that when they made requests they were frequently refused. In the uniformed patrol study, the fieldworkers recorded only 14 of 170 suspects 'further processed' who were observed asking the police for access to a third party. Among these, 7 asked to consult a lawyer: 2 were granted permission immediately, 1 after a delay, and 4 were refused. A further 7 suspects asked to contact persons other than lawyers: 5 of these requests were granted without delay, 1 was granted after delay, and 1 was refused. In the detective study, the fieldworkers recorded that 19 of 96 suspects were known to have asked for access to a third party. Of these, 6 asked to consult a lawyer: 3 of these requests were granted immediately, 2 at a later point, and 1 was refused. A further 13 asked to call persons other than lawyers: 8 had their requests granted without delay, 4 after some delay, and 1 was refused.
5 See McBarnet (1981: 57 – 8), who describes the case of an accused convicted under the 1968 Theft Act (England), which requires the accused found in possession of stolen goods to explain himself if he is not to be assumed guilty. In this case the prosecution's evidence was that he showed a 'couldn't care less' attitude, refused to produce a driving log-book or answer police questions, and asked to see a solicitor.
6 Medalie et al (1968) report that a project in Washington, DC, where lawyers were available to assist suspects in the police station at all hours was not successful. Suspects felt that access to a lawyer did not apply in their case or that the lawyers had associations with the police. Moreover, the police often delayed in calling the lawyer or in allowing him to see the suspect until it was too late.
7 See the description at p 63. Further details of the accused's decision to plead guilty, and his lawyer's involvement in this decision, are reported in chapter 4.

CHAPTER THREE: Lawyers' Orders

1 This quotation is taken from a personal communication sent to the authors by Michael McConville in response to an earlier draft of this book. It is cited with permission.
2 Newman (1956), Zander (1969), and Dell (1971) state that although the majority of accused plead guilty, unrepresented accused are more likely to forego their rights to trial.

However, as other researchers (Blumberg, 1967; Baldwin and McConville, 1977; McCabe and Purves, 1972; Bottoms and McClean, 1976) have illustrated, the presence of counsel does not ensure that the accused makes use of his legal rights. Some accused in these studies gave lawyer's advice as reason for their decision to plead guilty.

3 There is missing information for one accused whose charges were withdrawn in court. Neither the accused nor his lawyer was present at this court appearance. It was not possible to contact the accused for the second interview and we were therefore unable to ascertain if he had contacted a lawyer.

4 This was one of only three cases in our sample which included a judge in out-of-court transactions regarding plea and sentence. Two of these cases involved the lawyer under discussion, both at the provincial court level.

5 Rather than making the proceedings comprehensible and therefore accessible to the accused, an institution of professional or expert guides to the legal maze has been established. As the legal profession expands annually (Burnett, 1977: 70) a simplification of legal proceedings may be seen to be counterproductive. It is usually the legal profession which institutes legal changes – e.g. the eighth annual report, 1978 – 79, of the Law Reform Commission of Canada states that the chairman, vice chairman, and the remaining three commissioners of the commission were all members of the legal profession; in addition, three-quarters of their panel of consultants and research personnel were members of the legal profession or legally trained. Such reforms would be tantamount to cutting their legal throats. As an example, legal practitioners opposed the codification rather than the substance of the rules of evidence proposed by the Law Reform Commission of Canada in 1975. Brooks (1978: 315 – 16) argues that the opposition may be based on the position that codification would make the rules more accessible to people outside of the legal profession: 'To suggest that the Code would simplify the law of evidence to the point where lawyers would be unnecessary is, of course, pure hyperbole. However, there is little doubt that the Code does set forth a law of evidence which is more accessible and understandable than the present law. Further, it is clear that lawyers have a vested interest in maintaining the complexity of the law. In modern jargon, the complexity and consequent mystification of law results in its privitization, to the undeniable benefit of the profession. For this reason, it is unlikely that the impetus for simplification will come from lawyers, and it is realistic to predict that common law lawyers will remain hostile to all forms of codification.'

6 Two accused – one who ultimately obtained a private lawyer and one who ultimately went unrepresented – stated that they had engaged duty counsel for particular court hearings, but the duty counsel failed to show up for the hearings.

7 This was the only accused known to have initiated action against his lawyer at the completion of his case. One other accused took the action of firing his lawyer in mid-stream, and hiring a new one. He was angry with his lawyer's handling of the case, especially because he wanted his lawyer to 'judge-shop' to avoid a particular judge, but his lawyer was apparently unable to carry out his wishes. He fired his lawyer after pleading guilty to two charges in exchange for withdrawal of others and hired a new lawyer for sentencing purposes. He said he further retaliated by refusing to pay the remaining instalment of $450 on the $700 bill he owed to the first lawyer.

8 In producing outcomes the lawyer is, of course, not freed from other sources of influence and constraints. He is bound into limits imposed by the agents of criminal control and the organizations they represent; the lawyer must work within their orders both in and out of court. (See our previous discussion at pp 77–8 and chapters 4 and 6).

9 The accused's decision about plea is influenced by his lawyer and therefore could appropriately be discussed in this chapter. However, as we saw in chapter 2, the police frame the limits to the plea decision. In addition, the plea decision is transacted among the lawyer, the crown attorney, the police, and occasionally the judge in the out-of-court discussions

that take place in the absence of the accused. The accused's decision concerning the plea is influenced by all that precedes it and by what can be predicted to follow from it. Therefore, we consider the accused's plea decision in the context of the plea transaction process as outlined in chapters 4 and 5.

10 Bottoms and McClean (1976: 78, 84) report that 95 per cent of their interviewed defendants who had an election choice chose a summary trial, and that 27 per cent of this group did not know prior to entering court that they had a choice.

11 One of the 20 accused who discussed an appeal with his lawyer was unrepresented at his original court hearings.

CHAPTER FOUR: Order out of Court I: The Process of Plea Transaction

1 'The guilty plea process, much more than the trial, encapsulates the steps immediately preceding and following conviction. Both the charging decision and sentencing merge into the conviction decision, particularly in the negotiated plea, so that concerns at this stage are not uniquely those of adjudication, of final guilt or innocence, but are intertwined with the prosecutor's discretion and the sentencing discretion of the trial judge' (Newman, 1966: 232).

2 Cf Note (1973).

3 The legitimation of plea bargaining in the United States has culminated in legal procedures set down in Rule 11 of the Federal Rules of Criminal Procedure. An outline of this is provided in Note (1976). Reviews of the legal position in the United States are provided by Heumann (1978) and Utz (1978). The existence of plea bargaining in the earlier part of this century, and its functions for the agents of criminal control, are documented by Rothman (1980: especially 98 – 109) and Friedmann (1978).

4 Lord Parker, CJ: '[Defence] counsel must be completely free to do what is his duty, namely, to give the accused the best advice he can, and if need be the advice in strong terms. This will often include the advice that a plea of guilty, showing an element of remorse, is a mitigating factor which may well enable the court to give a lesser sentence than would otherwise be the case.' An earlier decision legitimating the fact that a guilty plea can mitigate sentence is *R*. v *DeHaan* (1967) 3 ALL ER 618. Other cases have legitimated the use of different tools to expedite guilty pleas. For example, regarding election, in *R*. v *Coe* (1969) 1 ALL ER 65, Lord Parker, CJ, stated 'No doubt it is convenient in the interests of expedition, and possibly in order to obtain a guilty plea, for the prosecution to invite the justices to deal with indictable offences summarily.' In Scotland, the law is explicit in stating that a guilty plea justifies a more lenient sentence (see McBarnet, 1981).

5 E.g. *Attorney-General of Canada* v *Roy* (1972) 18 CRNS 89 (Quebec QB); *Perkins and Pigeau* v *The Queen* (1976) 35 CRNS 222 (Quebec CA); *Regina* v *Wood* (1976) 26 CCC (2d) 100 (Alberta SC). There have also been decisions which affect plea discussions and agreements because they control multiple (overlapping) charging practices. See for example, *Kienapple* v *The Queen* (1974) 15 CCC (2d) 524; *R*. v *McKay* (1978) 39 CCC (2d) 101.

6 *R*. v *Houchen* (1976) 31 CCC (2d) 274.

7 Detailed attention to the role of the police in producing court outcomes through their charging practices is provided in Ericson (1981, 1982). See also Klein (1976); Feeley and Lazerson (1980).

8 For example, Reiss (1974a: 67) argues that it is difficult to assess possible benefits to the accused resulting from plea transactions 'partly because cases disposed of by both means [guilty plea or trial] are not strictly comparable but also for other reasons. In trial by jury, some defendants are found "not guilty" and, therefore, escape altogether the stigma and sanctions incurred by a plea of guilty. There is evidence, moreover, that the finding of "not guilty" would be substantially greater for cases where pleas of guilty are

entered. Often the evidence is weaker in these cases or there are violations of the defendant's rights that would lead to a finding of not guilty or a dismissal of the charges. These very weaknesses in the substance and procedure of the prosecutor's case are a major incentive to accept a plea of guilty to dispose of the case. Finally, were all cases to go to trial, there is no evidence that the penalties imposed would be as high on the average as they now are for those that go to trial. What is clear is that a plea of guilty is a cost to a minority of defendants who would otherwise be found not guilty; for others there remains a question of whether they gain at all by plea bargaining.' Especially in minor cases in lower courts, there can be considerable costs in invoking rights and going to trial. 'The process is the punishment,' and the easiest way to minimize it is to plead guilty and accept the tariff (Feeley, 1979).

9 However, see Utz (1978) who builds this possibility into her model by conceiving of out-of-court 'trials' as adversarial in a manner similar to what in court trials are supposed to be.

10 The other case is the one described in chapter 1.

11 The intensity of police involvement in 'making a deal' has previously been documented by Klein (1974: 219), who states: 'The police were involved in 79% of the 202 cases of bargaining described by our [penitentiary inmate] informants. In fact, they were the *only* officials directly involved in conducting the negotiation with the offender in 52% of the cases.' Klein's figure is much higher than ours because he also includes 'deals' between police officers and suspects made prior to charges being laid and prior to the entry of a lawyer into the case. However, it confirms the basic fact that the police are active in the negotiated outcome of the case from the point of contacting the accused through to court disposition.

12 For example, a crown attorney prosecuting another case, after accepting a plea settlement between detective and lawyer that involved charge reductions from robbery to theft, stated, 'If what they're saying sounds outlandish, I won't go along with it. I take time to look over and recess it, and take some time on it. But other than that, that's all I can do, I'm really low man on the totem pole and I have basically nothing to exercise my discretion on, even if I get a chance to look at the files, law school just doesn't prepare you for that sort of stuff.'

13 All narcotics charges are prosecuted federally.

14 For dangerous use of a weapon the election option rests with the crown attorney, whereas for possession of a dangerous weapon the defence has the election option.

15 According to statistics produced by the Solicitor General of Canada (1979), pertaining to expenditures on criminal control in Canada for the 1977–78 fiscal year, 65.6 per cent went to police services and 1.9 per cent to crown counsel services, for a total of 67.5 per cent. Only 1.6 per cent was allocated to legal aid. See also Chan and Ericson (1981).

16 This practice is discussed by Heumann (1978: especially 34, 182).

CHAPTER FIVE: Order out of Court II: The Position of the Accused and the Plea Decision

1 For further documentation, see chapters 3 and 6. In Arcuri's (1976: 182) study, almost two-thirds of the respondents judged the plea bargaining in their own case as 'fair' on the grounds that it apparently brought them a lighter sentence and/or a lesser number of convictions than they thought they would have had otherwise.

2 Other studies in Canada have documented a lower rate of guilty pleas. Friedland (1965: 89) presents a figure of 69 per cent for magistrates' courts in the city of Toronto in 1964; Hann (1973: 313) states that only 43.5 per cent of defendants in magistrates' courts in Toronto studied in 1970–71 pleaded guilty; and MacKaay (1976: 31) reports that in 1975, 62.3 per cent of defendants at the Montreal court house pleaded guilty, while at the

Montreal Municipal Hall court the figure was 51 per cent. The Sheffield, England, study by Bottoms and McClean (1976: 105, 108) reports a rate of 93 per cent guilty pleas in the lower (magistrates') courts and 65 per cent in the higher (county) courts. Most American jurisdictions report guilty plea rates near or over 90 per cent. See Heumann (1978) re Connecticut; Vera Institute (1977) re New York City; Law Enforcement Assistance Administration (1978) for US survey data.

3 Of course, as mentioned in chapter 2 and as analysed elsewhere (Ericson 1981, 1982), the police sometimes have other ends in mind apart from conviction when they decide to lay a charge. A charge can be used to obtain bail conditions and attendant controls over a suspect, to harass, to hold a suspect for investigation on other matters, to 'lever' the suspect to return stolen property, to cool out participants in a hostile interpersonal conflict, etc. From the police viewpoint, in cases with one of these elements the conviction outcome is of secondary or no importance.

4 In Canada there is authority that a plea of guilty should be considered as a mitigating factor with respect to sentencing: *R.* v *de Haan* (1967), 52 Cr App R 25; *R.* v *Johnston and Tremayne* (1970) 4 CCC 64 (Ont CA). Salhany (1978) states that the basis of this ruling is that pleading guilty is not only in the public interest but is also a sign of remorse on the part of the accused. However, the court has also ruled that a plea of not guilty should not be held against the accused: 'It is quite improper to use language which may convey that a man is being sentenced because he had pleaded not guilty, or because he has run his defence in a particular way. It is, however, of course proper to give a man a lesser sentence if he has shown genuine remorse amongst other things by pleading guilty'; *R.* v *Harper* (1967) 3 ALL ER 619 (CCA).

5 Our observational data on the police confirm that one of the four co-suspects in this case was not charged at all in an exchange for information and a written statement implicating the other three (see Ericson 1981: chapter 6).

6 Criminal Code sec 312, which deals with possession of stolen property, includes a requirement of guilty knowledge as part of the definition of the offence.

7 Cf Baldwin and McConville's recent research study (Royal Commission on Criminal Procedure, 1980b) in which they report that over 90 per cent of defendants who made written statements to the police in Birmingham, and 76 per cent in London, pleaded guilty at trial.

8 The law of confession in Canada makes any threat or promise regarding release as a means of inducing a confession grounds for ruling that statement of confession inadmissible in court (Kaufman, 1974).

9 See chapter 5, note 4. Several accused believed a not guilty plea resulting in a finding of guilt would lead to a more severe penalty than a guilty plea because the judge would see it as 'lying' and take it as another indication of the 'dishonest' character of the accused. In a separate question on the effect of plea on judges' sentencing decisions, several accused expressed this belief, even to the point of describing a not guilty plea as 'perjury.'

CHAPTER SIX: Order in Court

1 Evidence from a study of traffic courts suggests that the resolution on the initial case is highly influential on subsequent cases, i.e. when the initial case was a guilty plea it was more likely to be followed by guilty pleas, whereas, when the initial case was a not guilty plea it was more likely to be followed by not guilty pleas (Brickey and Miller, 1975).

2 Friedland (1968) describes magistrates' courts across Canada and indicates the consistency in their elements.

3 In the jurisdiction under study 'upstairs' was a metaphor for the next level of court, the county court. As documented in chapter 3, there was also confusion about the roles of duty counsel and legal aid lawyers.

4 In England and Wales a police inspector often prosecutes in magistrates' courts. In other cases, the police hire a solicitor to prosecute. Only very serious matters are handled by the director of public prosecutions. In this area at least, the English display less pretension than we do: they explicitly put prosecution in the hands of the police, rather than employing an intermediate agent who appears as a check on the police but in most cases cannot be (cf Ericson, 1981, 1982).

5 Balbus (1973: 17) provides a succinct summary of this: 'A system of justice based on the presumption of innocence of the accused and in which proof of guilt requires a combat between the prosecution and the defense before a neutral judge or jury has been replaced by a covert system of justice which revolves around the presumption of guilt of the accused and the plea bargain – involving the cooperation of the prosecution, the defense, and the judge – as the institutionalization of this presumption. Consistent with their long-run legitimacy interests, every effort has been made by court authorities to disguise this radical transformation by means of continued verbal and symbolic invocations of the norms and procedures of formal legal rationality.'

6 In *R.* v *Lee Kun* (1916) 9 KN 337 and 11 CAR 293 at p 300 it was stated: 'The presence of the accused means not merely that he must be physically in attendance, but also that he must be capable of understanding the nature of the proceedings. The prisoner may be unable, through insanity or deafness or dumbness, or the combination of both conditions, to understand the proceedings or to hear them, either directly or by reading a record of them, or to answer them either by speech or writing. In these cases a jury is sworn to ascertain whether the prisoner is "fit to plead" ... If you think there is no certain method of communicating the details of the trial to the prisoner so that he can clearly understand them and be able properly to make his defence to the charge you ought to find that he is not of sane mind. If the accused is not fit to plead, he is not tried, but is detained during his Majesty's pleasure.'

7 No information was obtained from three persons. When discussing their 'experience' with criminal courts, accused often made reference to media sources: 'Q: Did you understand the trial proceedings and who the various people were in court? A: Oh yes, I knew that for sure. Q: How did you know that? A: Oh, I have watched an awful lot of Perry Mason.' Relying upon knowledge from the media sometimes added to the confusion. For example, the lawyer of one accused decided that his client should plead not guilty to a rape charge before a judge and jury. The accused commented on why he thought the choice of a trial by jury was a bad one: 'A: I thought it was bad really. Q: Why? A: I figured – get the old people, the old women on the jury and old men. Q: What do you mean by old women and old men? A: You know. Q: Why do you think they were going to be old women and old men? A: When you see them on television most of them are old people.'

8 'Confusion and a state of anomie may arise when one interactant cannot fathom any meaning from the other's behaviour and thus is left in a state of diffuse anxiety. Such a state is likely to occur when the interactants employ entirely different and mutually exclusive impenetrable universes of discourse and gesture' (Lyman and Scott, 1970: 35).

9 There was no information on this question from five accused.

10 As Emerson (1969: 165) states, 'An attack on the police ... symbolically attacks the legal order which the court both represents and feels obligated to protect. An attack on the police represents a denial of the normative or moral order on which the court's activities are based.' As we learned in previous chapters, lawyers as well as accused people appreciate the implications of challenging the police, and thus usually refrain from doing so.

11 'The risks of denouncing, however, are greatly reduced where the denunciation can be presented as an occupational responsibility of an official or expert who has some pre-established right to concern himself with other people's misbehaviour ... Second, inherent in this legitimated capacity is the assumption that the occupant of the status is acting on behalf of important professional and public values, for this is the very meaning of

legitimate. His motives are then by definition not personally selfish. Consequently, the
licensed denouncer has to establish neither immediate motive for the denunciation (it is
assumed to derive from the objective nature of his duties and responsibilities) nor his own .
personal rectitude, for it is built into the very professional or official status as a representative of which he is assumed to be acting' (Emerson, 1969: 168).

12 In dealing with this problem, the Criminal Law Revision Committee in England states
that an accused when undefended should be allowed to address the court to offer anything
in mitigation of his sentence and when he is defended an address by the accused should
remain a matter for the judge's discretion; Criminal Law Revision Committee, Seventh
Report, *Felonies and Misdemeanours* (1965), amendment 2659 para 62, as reported in Thomas, 1979.

Bibliography

Alschuler, A. 1968 'The Prosecutor's Role in Plea Bargaining,' *University of Chicago Law Review*, 36: 50–112
- 1978 'Sentencing Reform and Prosecutorial Power: A Critique of Recent Proposals for "Fixed" and "Presumptive" Sentencing,' *University of Pennsylvania Law Review*, 126: 550–77
American Friends Service Committee 1971 *Struggle for Justice*. New York: Hill and Wang
Arcuri, A. 1976 'Lawyers, Judges and Plea Bargaining: Some New Data on Inmates' Views,' *International Journal of Criminology and Penology*, 4:177–91
Atkinson, J. and P. Drew 1979 *Order in Court: The Organization of Verbal Interaction in Judicial Settings*. London: Macmillan
Ayres, R. 1970 'Confessions and the Court,' in A. Niederhoffer and A. Blumberg ed *The Ambivalent Force*. Waltham, Mass.: Ginn
Babigian, H., E. Gardner, H. Miles, and J. Romano 1965 'Diagnostic Consistency and Change in a Follow-up Study of 1215 Patients,' *American Journal of Psychiatry*, 121: 895–901
Balbus, I. 1973 *The Dialectics of Legal Repression: Black Rebels before the American Criminal Courts*. New Brunswick, NJ: Transaction Books
Baldwin, J. and M. McConville 1977 *Negotiated Justice: Pressures on Defendants to Plead Guilty*. London: Martin Robertson
- 1978 'The Influence of the Sentencing Discount in Inducing Guilty Pleas,' in J. Baldwin and A. Bottomley (ed) *Criminal Justice: Selected Readings*. London: Martin Robertson
Beattie, J. 1977 *Attitudes towards Crime and Punishment in Upper Canada, 1830–1850: A Documentary Study*. Toronto: Centre of Criminology, University of Toronto
Becker, H. 1967 'Whose Side Are We On?,' *Social Problems*, 14: 239–47
Berger, P. and T. Luckmann 1966 *The Social Construction of Reality: A Treatise in the Sociology of Knowledge*. Harmondsworth: Penguin
Bittner, E. 1970 *The Functions of the Police in Modern Society*. Rockville, Md.: NIMH
Black, D. 1972 'The Boundaries of Legal Sociology,' *Yale Law Journal*, 81(6): 1086–1100

- 1976 *The Behavior of Law*. New York: Academic Press

Blomberg, T. 1977 'Diversion and Accelerated Social Control,' *Journal of Criminal Law and Criminology*, 68: 274–82

Blumberg, A. 1967 *Criminal Justice*. Chicago: Quadrangle

- 1970 'The Practice of Law as a Confidence Game: Organizational Cooptation of a Profession', in A. Niederhoffer and A. Blumberg ed *The Ambivalent Force*. Waltham, Mass.: Ginn

Blumer, H. 1969 *Symbolic Interactionism*. Englewood Cliffs, NJ: Prentice-Hall

Bohnstedt, M. 1978 'Answers to Three Questions about Juvenile Diversion,' *Journal of Research in Crime and Delinquency*, 15(1): 109–23

Bottomley, A. 1973 *Decisions in the Penal Process*. London: Martin Robertson

Bottomley, A. and C. Coleman 1980 *Understanding Crime Rates*. Farnborough: Saxon House Studies

Bottoms, A.E. and J.D. McClean 1976 *Defendants in the Criminal Process*. London: Routledge and Kegan Paul

Brickey, S. and D. Miller 1975 'Bureaucratic Due Process: An Ethnography of a Traffic Court,' *Social Problems*, 22: 688–97

British Journal of Criminology 1979 *Special Issue on Behaviour Modification*, vol. 19, no. 2

Brooks, N. 1978 'The Law Reform Commission of Canada's Evidence Code,' *Osgoode Hall Law Journal*, 16: 241–320

Burnett, D. 1977 'The Society's Computer,' *The Law Society of Upper Canada Gazette*, 11: 70–6

Carlen, P. 1974 'Remedial Routines for the Maintenance and Control of Magistrates' Courts,' *British Journal of Law and Society*, 1: 101–17

- 1976 *Magistrates' Justice*. London: Martin Robertson

- 1976a 'The Staging of Magistrates' Justice,' *British Journal of Criminology*, 16: 48–55

Casper, J. 1972 *American Criminal Justice: The Defendant's Perspective*. Englewood Cliffs, NJ: Prentice-Hall

- 1978 *Criminal Courts: The Defendant's Perspective*. Washington, DC: National Institute of Law Enforcement and Criminal Justice

Chambliss, W. and R. Seidman 1971 *Law, Order and Power*. Reading, Mass.: Addison-Wesley

Chan, J.B.L. and R.V. Ericson 1981 *Decarceration and the Economy of Penal Reform*. Toronto: Centre of Criminology, University of Toronto

Chatterton, M. 1976 'Police in Social Control,' in *Control without Custody*, Cropwood Papers, Institute of Criminology, University of Cambridge

Chevigny, P. 1969 *Police Power*. New York: Vintage

Christie, N. 1977 'Conflicts as Property,' *British Journal of Criminology*, 17: 1–15

Church, T. 1976 'Plea Bargains, Concessions and the Courts: An Analysis of a Quasi-experiment,' *Law and Society Review*, 10: 384–8

Cohen, S. 1979 'Guilt, Justice and Tolerance: Some Old concepts for a New Criminology,' in D. Downes and P. Rock ed *Deviant Interpretations*. Oxford: Martin Robertson

- 1979a 'The Punitive City: Notes on the Dispersal of Social Control,' *Contemporary Crises*, 3: 339–63

Cohen, S. and L. Taylor 1978 *Prison Secrets*. National Council for Civil Liberties –
Radical Alternatives to Prison

Coleman, J. 1973 'Loss of Power,' *American Sociological Review*, 38: 1–17

Conklin, J. 1972 *Robbery and the Criminal Justice System*. Philadelphia: Lippincott

Cousineau, D. and S. Verdun-Jones 1979 'Evaluating Research into Plea Bargaining
in Canada and the United States: Pitfalls Facing the Policy Makers,' *Canadian
Journal of Criminology*, 21: 293–309

– 1979a 'Cleansing the Augean Stables: A Critical Analysis of Recent Trends in the
Plea Bargaining Debate in Canada,' *Osgoode Hall Law Journal*, 17: 227–60

Dahrendorf, R. 1961 'On the Origin of Inequality,' in R. Dahrendorf *Essays in the
Theory of Society*. London: Routledge and Kegan Paul

Davis, K.C. 1969 *Discretionary Justice* Baton Rouge: Louisiana State University
Press

Degler, C.N. 1979 *At Odds: Women and the Family in America from the Revolution to
the Present*. Oxford: Oxford University Press

Dell, S. 1971 *Silence in Court*. London: Bell

Donzelot, J. 1979 *The Policing of Families*. New York: Pantheon

Doob, A. and J. Chan 1977 *The Exercise of Discretion with Juveniles*. Centre of
Criminology, University of Toronto

Drucker, P. 1973 'Managing the Public Service Institution,' *The Public Interest*, 33:
43–60

Eisenstein, J. and H. Jacob 1977 *Felony Justice: An Organizational Analysis of Criminal Courts*. Boston: Little, Brown

Emerson, R. 1969 *Judging Delinquents: Context and Process in Juvenile Court*. Chicago: Aldine

Ennis, B. and T. Litwack 1974 'Psychiatry and the Presumption of Expertise: Flip-
ping Coins in the Courtroom,' *California Law Review*, 62: 693–752

Erickson, P. 1980 'Cannabis Criminals: The Social Consequences of Punishing Drug
Users,' unpublished ms, Addiction Research Foundation of Ontario

Ericson, R.V. 1975 *Young Offenders and Their Social Work. Farnborough: Saxon
House*

– 1975a *Criminal Reactions: The Labelling Perspective*. Farnborough: Saxon House

– 1977 'From Social Theory to Penal Practice: The Liberal Demise of Criminological Causes,' *Canadian Journal of Criminology and Corrections*, 19: 170–91

– 1981 *Making Crime: A Study of Police Detective Work*. Toronto: Butterworths

– 1982 *Reproducing Order: A Study of Police Patrol Work*. Toronto: University of Toronto Press

Feeley, M. 1973 'Two Models of the Criminal Justice System: An Organizational
Perspective,' *Law and Society Review*, 7: 407–25

– 1979 *The Process Is the Punishment*. New York: Russell Sage Foundation

Feeley, M. and M. Lazerson 1980 'Prosecutors versus Cops: Organizational Cleav-
ages within the "System,"' unpublished paper, Department of Political Science,
University of Wisconsin, Madison

Feeley, M. and A.D. Sarat 1980 *The Policy Dilemma: Federal Crime Policy and the
L.E.A.A. 1968 – 1978*. Minneapolis: University of Minnesota Press

Feltman, S. 1981 'Law, Counter Law and Prisoners' Rights in Canadian Penitentiaries,' unpublished paper, Centre of Criminology, University of Toronto

Ferguson, G. 1972 'The Role of the Judge in Plea Bargaining,' *Criminal Law Quarterly*, 15: 26–51

Ferguson, G. and D. Roberts 1974 'Plea Bargaining: Directions for Canadian Reform,' *Canadian Bar Review*, 52: 498–576

Foucault, M. 1977 *Discipline and Punish: The Birth of the Prison*. New York: Pantheon Books

– 1979 'On the Concept of the "Dangerous" Individual in Nineteenth Century Legal Psychiatry,' in D. Weistub ed *Law and Psychiatry: A Symposium*. Toronto: Pergamon

– 1980 *Power/Knowedge*. New York: Pantheon

Fox, J. and T. Hartnagel 1979 'Changing Social Roles and Female Crime in Canada: A Time Series Analysis,' *Canadian Review of Sociology and Anthropology*, 16: 96–104

Frank, J. 1949 *Courts on Trial: Myth and Reality in American Justice*. London: Oxford University Press

Freedman, D. and P. Stenning 1977 *Private Security, Police and the Law in Canada*. Toronto: Centre of Criminology, University of Toronto

Friedenberg, E. 1975 *The Disposal of Liberty and Other Industrial Wastes*. New York: Doubleday

– 1980 'The Punishment Industry in Canada,' *Canadian Journal of Sociology*, 5: 273–83

– 1980a *Deference to Authority: The Case of Canada*. New York: Sharpe

Friedland, M. 1965 *Detention before Trial*. Toronto: University of Toronto Press

– 1968 'Magistrates' Courts: Functioning and Facilities,' *Criminal Law Quarterly*, 11: 52–75

– 1975 *Access to the Law*. Toronto: Carswell/Methuen

Friedmann, L. 1978 'A Historical Study of Criminal Justice,' paper presented at the Centre for Socio-Legal Studies, Oxford

Fromm, E. 1965 *Escape from Freedom*. New York: Avon Books

Galanter, M. 1974 'Why the "Haves" Come out Ahead: Speculations on the Limits of Legal Change,' *Law and Society Review*, 9: 95–160

Gaylin, W. 1978 'In the Beginning: Helpless and Dependent,' in W. Gaylin et al *Doing Good: The Limits of Benevolence*. New York: Pantheon

Gaylin, W. et al 1978 *Doing Good: The Limits of Benevolence*. New York: Pantheon

Gerson, E. 1976 'On the Quality of Life,' *American Sociological Review*, 41: 266–79

Glaser, B. and A. Strauss 1967 *The Discovery of Grounded Theory: Strategies for Qualitative Research*. Chicago: Aldine

Glaser, D. 1964 *The Effectiveness of a Prison and Parole System*. Indianopolis: Bobbs-Merrill

Goffman, E. 1956 'The Nature of Deference and Demeanor,' *American Anthropologist*, 58: 473–502

– 1961 *Asylums*. New York: Doubleday

– 1962 'On Cooling the Mark out,' in A. Rose ed *Human Behaviour and Social Processes*. London: Routledge

– 1968 *Stigma*. Middlesex: Pelican

– 1971 *Relations in Public*. New York: Harper and Row

Goldman, N. 1963 'The Differential Selection of Juvenile Offenders for Court Appearance,' National Research and Information Centre, National Council on Crime and Delinquency, Washington, DC

Greenawalt, K. 1974 'Perspectives on the Right to Silence,' in R. Hood ed *Crime, Criminology and Public Policy.* London: Heinemann

Greenberg, D. 1975 'Problems in Community Corrections,' *Issues in Criminology*, 10: 1–33

Greenberg, D.F. and D. Humphries 1980 'The Cooptation of Fixed Sentencing Reform,' *Crime and Delinquency*, 26(2): 206–25

Greenwood, P. et al 1975 *The Criminal Investigation Process: Volume III. Observations and Analysis.* Santa Monica: Rand Corporation

Griffiths, J. and R. Ayres 1967 'A Postscript to the Miranda Project: Interrogation of Draft Protesters,' *Yale Law Journal*, 77: 305–6

Grosman, B. 1969 *The Prosecutor.* Toronto: University of Toronto Press

Hagan, J. et al 1979 'Ceremonial Justice: Crime and Punishment in a Loosely Coupled System,' *Social Forces*, 58: 506–27

Hagan, J. and C. Albonetti 1980 'The Differential Sentencing of White Collar Offenders in Ten Federal District Courts,' *American Sociological Review*, 45 (forthcoming)

Hann, R. 1973 *Decision Making in the Canadian Criminal Court System: A Systems Analysis.* Centre of Criminology, University of Toronto

Hartnagel, T. and D. Wynne 1975 'Plea Negotiations in Canada,' *Canadian Journal of Criminology and Corrections*, 17: 45–56

Harvard Center for Criminal Justice 1972 'Judicial Intervention in Prison Discipline,' *Journal of Criminal Law and Criminology*, 63: 200–28

Hasson, R. 1980 'Tax Evasion and Social Security Abuse–Some Tentative Observations,' *Canadian Taxation*, vol. 2, no. 2

Hay, D. 1975 'Property, Authority and the Criminal Law,' in Hay, Linebaugh, Rule, Thompson, and Winslow, *Albion's Fatal Tree.* Harmondsworth: Penguin

Helder, H. 1979 'The Police, Case Negotiation, and the Para-Legal System,' MA dissertation, Centre of Criminology, University of Toronto

Heumann, M. 1978 *Plea Bargaining: The Experience of Prosecutors, Judges and Defence Attorneys.* Chicago: Chicago University Press

Heumann, M. and C. Loftin 1979 'Mandatory Sentencing and the Abolition of Plea Bargaining: the Michigan Felony Firearm Statute,' *Law and Society Review*, 13(2): 393–430

Heydebrand, W. 1977 'Organizational Contradictions in Public Bureaucracies: Toward a Marxian Theory of Organizations,' *The Sociological Quarterly*, 18: 83–107

Hogarth, J. 1971 *Sentencing as a Human Process.* Toronto: University of Toronto Press

Holzner, B. 1972 *Reality Construction in Society*, 2nd edn. Cambridge, Mass.: Schenkman

Hostika, C. 1979 'We Don't Care What Happened, We Only Care about What Is Going to Happen: Lawyer-Client Negotiations of Reality,' *Social Problems*, 26: 599–610

Hunt, G.M. and N.H. Azrin 1973 'A Community Reinforcement Approach to Alcoholism,' *Behavior Research and Therapy*, 11: 91–104

Ignatieff, M. 1978 *A Just Measure of Pain*. London: Macmillan

Illich, I. et al 1977 *Disabling Professions*. Don Mills: Burns and MacEachern

Inbau, F. and J. Reid 1967 *Criminal Interrogations and Confessions*. Baltimore: Williams and Wilkins

Irwin, J. 1970 *The Felon*. Englewood Cliffs, NJ: Prentice-Hall

Jackson, R. 1967 *Enforcing the Law*. London: Macmillan

Kadish, M. and S. Kadish 1973 *Discretion to Disobey: A Study of Lawful Departures from Legal Rules*. Stanford: Stanford University Press

Kaufman, F. 1974 *Admissibility of Confessions*. Toronto: Carswell

Kittrie, N. 1971 *The Right to Be Different: Deviance and Enforced Therapy*. Baltimore: Johns Hopkins University Press

Klein, J.F. 1974 'Official Morality and Offender Perceptions of the Bargaining Process,' PhD dissertation, Department of Sociology, University of Alberta

– 1976 *Let's Make a Deal*. Lexington, Mass.: Lexington Books

Klein, M. et al 1976 'The Explosion in Police Diversion Programs: Evaluating the Structural Dimensions of a Social Fad,' in M. Klein ed *The Juvenile Justice System*. Beverly Hills: Sage

Ku, R. and C. Blew 1977 *A University's Approach to Delinquency Prevention: The Adolescent Diversion Project*. Washington: LEAA

Lasch, C. 1980 'Life in the Therapeutic State,' *New York Review of Books*, 27 (10)

Law Enforcement Assistance Administration 1978 *Plea Bargaining in the United States*. Washington, DC: US Government Printing Office

Law Reform Commission of Canada 1973 *Evidence: Compellability of the Accused and the Admissability of His Statements*. study paper

– 1974 *Studies on Diversion*. Ottawa: Information Canada

– 1974–5 *Fourth Annual Report*. Ottawa: Information Canada

– 1975 *Diversion*. Ottawa: Information Canada

– 1975a *Criminal Procedure: Control of the Process*. Ottawa: Information Canada

– 1978–9 *Eighth Annual Report*. Ottawa: Information Canada

LeDain Commission of Inquiry into the Non-medical Use of Drugs *Final Report*. Ottawa: Information Canada

Lyman, S. and M. Scott 1970 *A Sociology of the Absurd*. New York: Appleton-Century-Crofts

Lynch, M. 1979 'Disclosure and Argument in "Plea Bargaining" Sessions,' in James L. Wilkins, 'The Prosecution and The Courts,' unpublished ms, Centre of Criminology, University of Toronto

McBarnet, D. 1976 'Pre-trial Procedures and the Construction of Conviction,' in Pat Carlen ed *The Sociology of Law*. Keele: Sociological Review Monograph 23

– 1977 'Review of *Defendants in the Criminal Process* by A.E. Bottoms and J.D. McClean (London: Routledge and Kegan Paul, 1976),' *British Journal of Law and Society* (Winter): 294–8

– 1979 'Arrest: The Legal Context of Policing,' in S. Holdaway ed *The British Police*. London: Edward Arnold

– 1981 *Conviction: Law, the State and the Construction of Justice*. London: Macmillan

McCabe S. and R. Purves 1972 *By-passing the Jury: A Study of Changes of Plea and Directed Acquittals in Higher Courts*. Oxford: Basil Blackwell

McDonald, L. 1976 *The Sociology of Law and Order.* London: Faber

Macfarlane, P.D. 1982 *Lawyering in the Criminal Courts: Making the Best of 'Bad' Cases* (forthcoming)

MacKaay, E. 1976 *The Path of Justice.* Groupe de Recherche en Jurimetrie, Faculté de Droit, Université de Montréal

Manning, P. 1980 *The Narcs Game.* Cambridge: MIT Press

March, J. and J. Olsen 1976 *Ambiguity and Choice in Organizations.* Oslo: Universitetsforlaget

Marcus, S. 1978 'Their Brother's Keeper: An Episode from English History,' in W. Gaylin et al ed *Doing Good: The Limits of Benevolence.* New York: Pantheon

Martin, J. and D. Webster 1971 *The Social Consequences of Conviction.* London: Heinemann

Matza, D. 1969 *Becoming Deviant.* New York: Prentice-Hall

Medalie R. et al 1968 'Custodial Police Interrogation in Our Nation's Capital: The Attempt to Implement Miranda,' *Michigan Law Review,* 66: 1347–1422

Meyer, J. and C. Rowan 1977 'Institutionalized Organizations: Formal Structure as Myth and Ceremony,' *American Journal of Sociology,* 83: 340–63

Morgan, D. 1975 'Autonomy and Negotiation in an Industrial Setting,' *Sociology of Work and Occupations,* 2: 203–26

Morris, N. 1974 *The Future of Imprisonment.* Chicago: University of Chicago Press

Morris, P. 1978 'Police Interrogation in England and Wales,' a critical review of the literature prepared for the English Royal Commission on Criminal Procedure

Morris, P., R. White, and P. Lewis 1973 *Social Needs and Legal Action.* London: Martin Robertson

Mueller, C. 1970 'Notes on the Repression of Communicative Behaviour,' in H.P. Dreitzel ed *Recent Sociology* (no. 2). New York: Macmillan

Nardulli, P. 1978 'Plea Bargaining: An Organizational Perspective,' *Journal of Criminal Justice,* 6: 217–31

Naylor, C.D. 1981 'Medical Aggression,' *Canadian Forum,* 60 (April): 5ff

Newman, D. 1956 'Pleading Guilty for Considerations: A Study of Bargain Justice,' *Journal of Criminal Law, Criminology and Police Science,* 46: 780–90

– 1966 *Conviction: The Determination of Guilt or Innocence without Trial.* Boston: Little, Brown

Nimmer, R. 1978 *The Nature of System Change: Reform Impact in the Criminal Courts.* Chicago: American Bar Foundation

Note 1973 'The Legitimation of Plea Bargaining: Remedies for Broken Promises,' *American Criminal Law Review,* 11: 771

Note 1976 'Revised Federal Rule 11: Tighter Guidelines for Pleas in Criminal Case,' *Fordham Law Review,* 44: 1010

Ontario Law Reform Commission 1973 'Report on Administration of Ontario Courts,' part II

Packer, H. 1968 *The Limits of the Criminal Sanction.* London: Oxford University Press

Polstein, R. 1962 'How to "Settle" a Criminal Case,' *The Practical Lawyer* 8(1): 35–44

Puglia, Judge 1979 'The California Uniform Sentencing Act,' paper to the Cambridge Conference on Research and Teaching in Criminology, July 1979

Ranson, S., B. Henings, and R. Greenwood 1980 'The Structuring of Organizational Structures,' *Administrative Science Quarterly*, 25: 1–17

Reiss, A. 1971 *The Police and the Public*. New Haven: Yale University Press

– 1974a 'Citizen Access to Criminal Justice,' *British Journal of Law and Society*, 1: 50–74

Reiss, A. and D. Black 1967 'Interrogation and the Criminal Process,' *Annals*, 374: 47–57

Rock, P. 1979 *The Making of Symbolic Interactionism*. London: Macmillan

Rosenhan, D.L. 1973 'On Being Sane in Insane Places,' *Science*, 179: 250–8

Ross, H. 1970 *Settled out of Court*. Chicago: Aldine

Ross, R. and P. Gendreau 1980 *Effective Correctional Treatment*. Toronto: Butterworths

Rothman, D. 1978 'The State as Parent: Social Policy in the Progressive Era,' in W. Gaylin et al *Doing Good: The Limits of Benevolence*. New York: Pantheon

– 1980 *Conscience and Convenience: The Asylum and Its Alternatives in Progressive America*. Boston: Little, Brown

Royal Commission on Criminal Procedure 1980 *Police Interrogation*. Research Studies 1 and 2 by B. Irving and L. Hilgendorf. London: HMSO

– 1980a *Police Interrogation*. Research Studies 3 and 4 by Pauline Morris and Paul Softley. London: HMSO

– 1980b *Confessions in Crown Court Trials*. Research Study 5 by J. Baldwin and M. McConville. London: HMSO

Ruby, C. 1976 *Sentencing*. Toronto: Butterworths

Ryan, L.J. ed 1964 *Tremeear's Annotated Criminal Code (Canada)*. 6th edn. Toronto: Carswell

Salhany, R.E. 1978 *Canadian Criminal Procedure*, 3rd ed. Agincourt, Ontario: Canada Law Book

Sanders, W. 1977 *Detective Work*. New York: Free Press

Schur, E. 1971 *Labelling Deviant Behavior*. New York: Harper and Row

– 1973 *Radical Non-intervention*. Englewood Cliffs, NJ: Prentice-Hall

Scott, M. and S. Lyman 1970 'Accounts, Deviance and Social Disorder,' in Jack Douglas ed *Deviance and Respectability: The Social Construction of Moral Meanings*. New York: Basic Books

Scull, A. 1977 *Decarceration*. Englewood Cliffs, NJ: Prentice-Hall

– 1981 'Progressive Dreams, Progressive Nightmares: Social Control in 20th Century America,' *Stanford Law Review*, 33: 301–16

Seeburger, R.H. and R.S. Wettick jr. 1967 'Miranda in Pittsburgh–A Statistical Study,' *University of Pittsburgh Law Review*, 29 1–26

Shapiro, M. 1975 'Courts,' in F. Greenstein and N. Polsby ed *Governmental Institutions and Processes: Handbook of Political Science*, vol. 5, pp 321–71. Reading, Mass.: Addison-Wesley

Silverman, D. 1970 *The Theory of Organizations*. London: Heinemann

Skolnick, J. 1966 *Justice without Trial*. New York: Wiley

Solicitor General of Canada 1979 *Selected Trends in Canadian Criminal Justice*. Ottawa: Communication Division, Ministry of the Solicitor General of Canada

– 1979a *National Inventory of Diversion Projects: An Update*. Ottawa: Communication Division, Ministry of the Solicitor General of Canada

Solomon, P. 1980 'Reforming Canadian Criminal Justice: The Policy Implications of Criminological Research,' unpublished working paper, Centre of Criminology, University of Toronto

Strauss, A. 1978 *Negotiations: Varieties, Contexts, Processes, and Social Order.* San Francisco: Jossey-Bass, Inc

Sudnow, D. 1965 'Normal Crimes: Sociological Features of the Penal Code in a Public Defender's Office,' *Social Problems*, 12: 255–72

Taylor, I., P. Walton, and J. Young 1973 *The New Criminology.* London: Routledge and Kegan Paul

– 1975 *Critical Criminology.* London: Routledge and Kegan Paul

Thomas, D. 1974 'The Control of Discretion in the Administration of Criminal Justice,' in R. Hood ed *Crime, Criminology and Public Policy.* London: Heinemann

– 1979 *The Principles of Sentencing.* 2nd edn. London: Heinemann

Utz, P. 1978 *Settling the Facts: Discretion and Negotiation in the Criminal Courts.* Lexington, Mass.: Lexington Books

Vera Institute 1977 *Felony Arrests: Their Prosecution and Disposition in New York City's Courts.* New York: Vera Institute

von Hirsh, A. 1976 *Doing Justice: The Choice of Punishments.* New York: Hill and Wang

Wald, M. et al 1967 'Interrogations in New Haven: The Impact of Miranda,' *Yale Law Journal*, 76: 1521–1648

Waller, I. 1974 *Men Released from Prison.* Toronto: University of Toronto Press

– 1979 'Making Corrections Work,' unpublished paper, Ministry of the Solicitor General of Canada (Research Division)

Whittingham, M. 1981 'Criminality and Correctional Reformism in Ontario, 1831 to 1954,' unpublished Ph D dissertation, York University, Toronto

Wilkins, J. 1976 'Discovery,' *Criminal Law Quarterly*, 18: 355–73

– 1982 *The Prosecution and the Courts* (forthcoming)

Wolin, S. 1980 'Reagan Country,' *The New York Review of Books*, 27(20): 9–12

Zander, M. 1969 'Unrepresented Defendants in the Criminal Courts,' *Criminal Law Review*, 632–45

– 1978 'The Right of Silence in the Police Station and the Caution,' in P. Glazebrook ed *Reshaping the Criminal Law.* London: Stevens

Zellick, G. 1980 'Prison Offences,' *British Journal of Criminology*, 20: 377–84.

Index